American Foreign Policy

American Foreign Policy

REALISTS AND IDEALISTS:

A CATHOLIC INTERPRETATION

★★★

By Sister Dorothy Jane Van Hoogstrate, S.L., Ph.D.

DEAN OF WEBSTER COLLEGE
WEBSTER GROVES, MISSOURI

B. HERDER BOOK CO.

15 & 17 South Broadway, St. Louis 2, Mo.

AND *33 Queen Square, London, W. C.*

TO MY MOTHER

Introduction

THE Great Debate in American foreign policy between the "Realists" and the "Idealists" is pursued with renewed intensity today, but the issue is as old as the United States itself. The controversialists raise questions like these: Is national self-interest to be sought irrespective of the welfare of other countries? Are nations bound by the moral law to meet the demands of justice and charity in the international community? Can one really understand more than the national good? Is material power the primary element in politics? May responsibilities in an international organization be assumed or shirked as a matter of arbitrary will? What does prudence dictate with regard to the desirable and the possible?

One perceives immediately that the answers to these queries will be governed by philosophical considerations of the nature of man, the effects of original sin, the dictates of natural law, the purpose and origin of the state, sovereignty and the international community, the components of peace, etc. Because Catholic philosophy and social doctrine are expressed systematically enough to be applied in such an investigation, it was thought worthwhile to state in parallel fashion the ideas from Catholic sources. The presentation does not challenge explicitly any writer or his thesis, but his degree of harmony or variance with Catholic thought will be self-evident.

All Realists and all Idealists do not begin with the same first principles, nor do they proceed to the same conclusions. This survey reveals the various shades of opinion. The Realist generally maintains that he faces life as it is, not as it should be. With this approach he justifies his skepticism about the ability of nations to transcend self-interest, or to curb the inevitable international conflict by appeals to principle or by resort to institutional devices. The Idealist pursues such goals as justice among nations, enduring peace, the spiritual and material advancement of mankind, respect for international law, and cooperation in a juridical organization.

Because the writers do not define the objective basis of moral law or man's method of arriving at knowledge of it, it remains doubtful in the debate whether they are on common ground. Often there is the tendency to identify sentiment and emotion with moral principles, and to equate a man's temperamental limitations with his ideals. When the authors appear to be criticizing principles, one wonders whether they are not disagreeing more about the timing or the feasibility of a procedure. Some of the Realists, viewing the misapplication of good principles by impractical Messiahs, and the smoke screen of slogans by irresponsible propagandists, seem to follow the logic: "To cure the headache, cut off the head." Both truth and error are expressed by proponents of either approach.

To illustrate how their values influence their estimate of events, summaries of American history by authors of both persuasions are incorporated.

In casting the spectrum of Catholic thought over the broad field—which touches upon topics like colonialism, democracy, foreign aid, socialism, Communism, war and armaments—one must sacrifice depth in any single aspect for the sake of bringing manifold ramifications to focus in a single overview. Future research should isolate the individual subjects for a thorough analysis.

Among the Catholic sources, reliable scholars were selected, but only the pronouncements of the popes carry the weight of the teaching authority of the Church. Considerable reliance might be placed upon the *Code of International Ethics,* however, by the fact that it represents a composite view of leading theologians, sociologists, and students of philosophy and law throughout the world.

The usefulness of this parallel of ideas is reflected in such a comment as this:

To some it will seem like beating the air to attempt to present a political theory from a Catholic standpoint when its fundamental postulate is rejected by the majority of contemporary authorities. Still unless we are willing to have our philosophy remain an affair of textbooks and classrooms, we must bring it out into the strife of systems to take its chance of being mishandled or ignored. And if it is objected that in so doing we are convincing no one except ourselves, yet is it not something if we do succeed in convincing ourselves? [1]

The endeavor might seem purposeful also in the light of this indictment:

Generally, Catholics tend either to forget the ideals which should motivate their conduct, or they tend to remain true to those ideals and withdraw contemptuously from the world of men. . . . They are called upon to judge the society of which they are a part, and they are incapable of diagnosing its disease. On the other hand, those who remain true to their ideals but withdraw from the world come not to know this world they are called upon to improve.[2]

For their great helpfulness in the course of my research, I wish to extend gratitude to my director, Reverend Martin F. Hasting, S.J., whose interest gave rise to this study, and to the other members of the Department of History at Saint Louis University; to the superiors and members of my religious community, the Sisters of Loretto at the Foot of the Cross, for providing me with

[1] John F. McCormick, S.J., "The Individual and the State," *Philosophy of State,* ed. Charles A. Hart (Baltimore: Watkins Printing Co., 1940), 13. Father McCormick was professor of Philosophy at Loyola University, Chicago, at the time.
[2] Thomas P. Neill, *Weapons for Peace* (Milwaukee: Bruce, 1945), 16. Dr. Neill is professor of history at St. Louis University and an author of wide repute.

the most favorable opportunities for study; to Sister Anne Roberta, S.L., and to Sister Elizabeth Mary, S.L., for their untold hours of typing; to Dr. E. Taylor Parks, Chief of the Historical Division Advisory and Review Branch of the State Department; to Mrs. Kieran Carroll of the National Archives; to Dr. Vance of the Manuscript Division, Library of Congress; to Mr. Herman Kahn, Director of the Franklin D. Roosevelt Library at Hyde Park; to Mr. Robert Jacoby, Archivist at Hyde Park; and to the staffs of the Saint Louis University Library, the Webster College Library, and the Saint Louis Public Library.

Contents

Introduction vii

I. *The Realists* 1
    Reinhold Niebuhr 4
    Charles A. Beard 8
    George F. Kennan 14
    Hans J. Morgenthau 19
    Paul S. Mowrer, Albert K. Weinberg, Nicholas Spykman . . 29
    Georg Schwarzenberger, Felix Morley, Charles O. Lerche . . 32
    Frederick L. Schuman 33
    Emery Reves 36
    Ernst B. Haas 38

II. *American History According to the Realists* 42
    Charles A. Beard 43
    George F. Kennan 56
    Hans J. Morgenthau 66

III. *The Idealists* 82
    Robert E. Osgood 84
    Walter Lippmann 88
    Dexter Perkins 91
    Vera Micheles Dean 94
    Charles Burton Marshall 97
    William Yandell Elliott 101

A. H. Feller, William T. R. Fox 104
Philip C. Jessup, Edgar A. Mowrer 107
Louis J. Halle 108
Frank Tannenbaum 112
F. S. C. Northrop 115
Thomas I. Cook, Malcolm Moos 117
Raymond L. Buell, Hamilton Fish Armstrong, Charles G.
 Fenwick 119
Samuel Flagg Bemis, Harold C. Hinton, Lawrence Sears . . . 121
Harry B. Price, Paul M. A. Linebarger 123
Harry W. Flannery, Dorothy Fosdick, Thomas E. Murray . . 125

IV. *American History Evaluated by the Idealists* 128
Dexter Perkins 128
Robert E. Osgood 144
Frank Tannenbaum 162

V. *Catholic Principles Relating to Man and to the State* . 170
Thomistic Approach to Truth and Reality 170
The Nature of Man 176
The Origin of the State 181
The Common Good 184
Church-State Relationship 188
Norms of Morality 190
Natural Law and Positive Law 192
The Role of the State 198
The Nation and Nationalism 204
The Concept of Power 209
The State Bound by Moral Law 211
The "Perfect Society" Qualified 213

VI. *International Society and Its Responsibilities* 214
International Society a Demand of Human Nature 215
State Sovereignty and International Society 219
The Rights of States 231
The Functions of a World Organization 238
Catholic Realism 241
International Law 245
The Validity of Treaties 249
An Evaluation of Democracy 252

VII. *Selected Applications of Catholic Social Doctrine* . . 258
    Colonialism 258
    Trade and the Use of the World's Resources 263
    Socialism 273
    How To Deal with Communism 275
    The Duty of Intervention 281
    The Morality of War and Its Practices 284
    Disarmament 290
    Neutrality 291
    The Realism of Peace 292

    Conclusion 303

    Bibliography 308
    Catholic Opinion 308
    Realist-Idealist Controversy 314

    Index 323

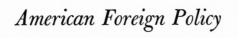

American Foreign Policy

* I *

The Realists

ALTHOUGH a wide latitude of opinion will be evident within the camp of the Realists, the survey will probably be more meaningful if some common denominators are first expressed, and if the position is summarized in the words of a few of the controversialists. The term Realism here has a connotation distinct from its use in metaphysics. In this political and moral theory, it denotes the disposition to take into account "all the factors in a social and political situation, which offer resistance to established norms . . . particularly the factors of self-interest and power." [1] Hans Morgenthau says the theory has earned the name because of its "concern with human nature as it actually is, and with the historic processes as they actually take place." [2] Those acquainted with the vogue in literature called Realism will find in this version of history and political science its counterpart; pessimism seems to be the proper response to the limited area of life which they designate as reality.

Robert E. Osgood gives the most comprehensive definition:

[1] Reinhold Niebuhr, *Christian Realism and Political Problems* (New York: Scribner's Sons, 1953), 119. Hereafter referred to as *Christian Realism*.

[2] Hans J. Morgenthau, *Politics Among Nations:* the Struggle for Power and Peace (2d ed.; New York: Knopf, 1954), 4. Hereafter referred to as *Politics*.

The Realist, because he is skeptical of the ability of nations to transcend their self-interest, sees the struggle for national power as the distinguishing characteristic of international relations. He tends to view international conflict as an inevitable state of affairs, issuing from man's tenacious, patriotic instincts and conditioned by relatively immutable influences, such as geography or some primordial urge, like the drive to dominate. Consequently, he is skeptical of attempts to mitigate international conflicts with appeals to sentiment and principle or with written pledges and institutional devices unless they register the relative power among nations. He believes that if power conflicts can be mitigated at all, they can be mitigated only by balancing power against power and by cultivating a circumspect diplomacy that knows the uses of force and the threat of force as indispensable instruments of national policy.[3]

Osgood further distinguishes the Realist position from that of the national egoist. The Realist believes that as a matter of fact nations are moved by self-interest; the egoist holds that nations ought to pursue only their own self-interest, though he might try to rationalize his actions in terms of "ideal principles or circumstances beyond control." Egoism is a manifestation of his self-love transferred to the national group.[4] Morgenthau elucidates the Realist conviction in this way:

. . . the world, imperfect as it is from the rational point of view, is the result of forces inherent in human nature. To improve the world one must work with those forces, not against them . . . moral principles can never be fully realized, but must at best be approximated through the ever temporary balancing of interests and the ever precarious settlement of conflicts. . . . It appeals to historic precedent rather than to abstract principles and aims at the realization of the lesser evil rather than of the absolute good. . . .[5]

[3] Robert E. Osgood, *Ideals and Self-Interest in America's Foreign Relations* (Chicago: University of Chicago Press, 1953), 9. (Copyright 1953 by the University of Chicago.) Hereafter referred to as *Ideals*.

[4] *Ibid.*, 8–9.

[5] This might be compared with Herbert Spencer's explanation of "Relative Ethics" in which the injunctions are "relatively right or least wrong."

A realist theory of international politics will guard against two popular fallacies: the concern with motives and the concern with ideological preferences. . . . Political realism does not require, nor does it condone, indifference to political ideals and moral principles, but it requires indeed a sharp distinction between the desirable and the possible, between what is desirable everywhere and at all times and what is possible under the concrete circumstances of time and place. . . . International politics cannot be reduced to legal rules and institutions.[6]

Perhaps the Realist position would be further clarified if one were to see briefly the observation made by a Realist about the "Legalist-Moralists" and the reciprocal judgment passed upon the Realists by one of the opposing school. Morgenthau summarizes the idealistic approach as one which:

. . . believes that a rational and moral political order, derived from universally valid abstract principles can be achieved here and now. It assumes the essential goodness and infinite malleability of human nature, and blames the failure of the social order to measure up to the rational standards on lack of knowledge and understanding, obsolescent social institutions, or the depravity of certain isolated individuals or groups. It trusts in education, reform, and the sporadic use of force to remedy these defects.[7]

An ardent attack upon the Realists is evidenced in the following:

This doctrine is confessedly, nay gleefully, amoral. It prides itself upon being realistic and takes Machiavelli as its great teacher. It is contemptuous of the simple beliefs of honest men, jeers at the sentimentalism of those who believe that men may strive for peace among nations, and looks upon democracy as a hindrance to skilled diplomacy. . . . Its

---

Spencer says, ". . . ideal conduct such as ethical theory is concerned with is not possible for the ideal man in the midst of men otherwise constituted. . . . There requires a certain congruity between the conduct of each member of a society and other's conduct. A mode of action entirely alien to the prevailing modes of action cannot be successfully persisted in—must eventuate in death of self, or posterity or both." Herbert Spencer, *The Data of Ethics* (New York: A. L. Burt, 1879), 324-25.

[6] Morgenthau, *Politics*, 4, 5, 7, 15.

[7] *Ibid.*, 3.

adherents believe that international wars, instead of being made by men and supported by institutions humanly contrived, have their origin in the nature of man himself and are inevitable. . . . Now the advocates of *realpolitik* would sweep away all of our old beliefs as foolish, sentimental and moralistic. They would have us build our future upon the concept of balance of power in international relations, throw all morality and law out of the window as a nuisance and hindrance to skilled diplomacy. . . .

The view of the advocates of power politics and balance of power seems to be that man is now and always has been in a sad state from which he cannot extricate himself. He has no one to help him. He has no law to live by, no morality to support him—he has nothing except the balance of power—and if he will not believe in that, then God help him—but in that view of the world, even that comfort is denied to man, for it could not abide any concept of a teleological universe.[8]

Reinhold Niebuhr

Alexander Hamilton is claimed by the Realists as their intellectual father, but Reinhold Niebuhr is reputed to be the precursor of this American school of "Political Realism." Writing in *Moral Man and Immoral Society* (1933), he stated his thesis that a sharp distinction must be drawn between the moral and social behavior of individuals and of groups:

. . . this distinction justifies and necessitates political policies which a purely individualistic ethic must always find embarrassing. . . . Individual men may be moral in the sense that they are able to consider interests other than their own in determining problems of conduct, and are capable, on occasion, of preferring the advantages of others to their own. They are endowed by nature with a measure of sympathy and consideration for their kind, the breadth of which may be extended by an astute social pedagogy. . . . But all these achievements are more difficult, if not impossible, for human societies and social groups. . . .

[8] Frank Tannenbaum, *The American Tradition in Foreign Policy* (Norman: University of Oklahoma Press, 1955), xi, xiii, 163. Hereafter referred to as *American Tradition*.

The inferiority of the morality of groups to that of individuals is due in part to the difficulty of establishing a rational social force which is powerful enough to cope with the natural impulses by which society achieves its cohesion; but in part it is merely the revelation of a collective egoism, compounded of the egoistic impulses of individuals. . . . those elements in man's collective behavior which belong to the order of nature and can never be brought completely under the domination of reason or conscience.[9]

Niebuhr charges that all the moralists, both religious and rational, in their failure to recognize the power of self-interest in intergroup relations, are unrealistic and confused in their political thought. He criticizes the romantic overestimate of human virtue which expresses the hope that a "new pedagogy or a revival of religion" would make future conflict unnecessary. He states that perpetual peace and brotherhood can be approximated but not realized in actual history.[10] Hypocrisy he deems the most significant and necessary "moral characteristic" of nations in their effort to claim the loyalty of their people. Although the use of force might be more "morally redemptive" in the hands of the community of nations, he is skeptical of its ability to be impartial. An individual might sacrifice his own selfish interests, but when he is responsible for the group, he may not sacrifice theirs. While no political Realism can absolve the individual of his obligation to check his own egoism, yet a social group, impervious to the influence of pure love, can be checked only by competing assertions of interest.[11]

Whenever religious idealism brings forth its purest fruits and places the strongest check upon selfish desire it results in policies which, from the political perspective, are quite impossible. . . . It would therefore seem better to accept a frank dualism in morals than to attempt a

[9] Niebuhr, *Moral Man and Immoral Society: a study in Ethics and Politics* (New York: Scribner's Sons, 1933), xi–xii. Hereafter referred to as *Moral Man*. Niebuhr is a Protestant theologian and the founder-editor of the biweekly, *Christianity and Crisis*. This year he is lecturing at the Institute for Advanced Study, Princeton University.

[10] *Ibid.*, xx–xxi, 22.

[11] *Ibid.*, 95, 110, 267, 272, 275.

harmony between the two methods which threatens the effectiveness of both.[12]

In what might seem a contradiction to the above, Niebuhr explains that religious Idealism is a desirable, practical tool. The redemption of human enterprise from corruption will be achieved most effectively by men who adopt the "illusion" that collective life can achieve perfect justice:

It is a very valuable illusion for the moment; for justice cannot be approximated if the hope of its realization does not generate a sublime madness in the soul. Nothing but such madness will do battle with such malignant power and "spiritual wickedness in high places." The illusion is dangerous because it encourages terrible fanaticisms. It must therefore be brought under the control of reason. One can only hope that reason will not destroy it before its work is done. . . .

If we contemplate the conflict between religious and political morality it may be well to recall that the religious ideal in its present form has nothing to do with the problem of social justice. . . . [Pure religious idealism] does not give itself to the illusion that material and mundane advantages can be gained by the refusal to assert your claims to them. It may believe, as Jesus did that self-realization is the inevitable consequence of self-abnegation. But this self-abnegation is not attained on the level of physical life or mundane advantages. . . .

[12] *Ibid.*, 270–71. A Catholic criticism of his position is to be found in James V. Schall, "The Political Theory of Reinhold Niebuhr," *Thought*, XXXIII (Spring, 1958), 62–80. His [Niebuhr's] insights always seem flavored by a mentality which opposes love to justice, reason to faith, sin to virtue, in such a way that the problems are not only overcome with difficulty, but are ultimately insoluble. . . . [For him] to accept the need for power is simultaneously to open the door for sin. . . . However true the notion that sin causes untold and unexpected friction in the process of government, it does not follow that sin is the only source of this difficulty. . . . A considerable number of problems arise from honest disagreements about the best means of political procedure. . . . But the fact is that society is not necessarily immoral when its responsible leaders must make choices that affect adversely some of the citizens. . . . If Niebuhr fails to see that finiteness, as well as sin, causes trouble to man, then all must be attributed to sin, even that which is not sinful. . . . The link between natural law and

The paradox of the moral life consists in this: that the highest mutuality is achieved where mutual advantages are not sought as the fruit of love. . . . That is how the madness of religious morality, with its trans-social ideal, becomes the wisdom which achieves wholesome social consequences.[13]

Interestingly enough, Niebuhr claims that St. Augustine was "by general consent, the first great 'realist' in western history." [14] His title rests upon his portrayal of social reality in his *Civitas Dei* in which the resolving of factions and tensions was depicted as no simple achievement. Augustine is said to trace evil on every level of community life to self-love or egocentricity, not to "some residual natural impulse which mind has not yet completely mastered." Unlike the modern Idealists, Augustine did not believe a world community could be easily actualized; he showed that linguistic and ethnic factors could be divisive. Mr. Niebuhr's own judgment on the fallacy of world government is that governments are not created by *fiat*, and that they have limited efficacy in integrating a community. He sees as the two major errors in world affairs the idea of man's perfectibility and the idea of progress.[15]

Again declaring his admiration for Augustine, he says:

If Augustine's realism is contained in his analysis of the *civitas terrene*, his refutation of the idea that realism must lead to cynicism or relativism is contained in his definition of the *civitas dei*, which he declares to be "commingled" with the "city of this world" and which has the "love of God" rather than the "love of self" as its guiding principle. . . . Augustine's doctrine of love as the final norm must be distinguished from modern sentimental versions of Christianity which regard love as a simple possibility and which think it significant to assert the obvious proposition that all conflicts in the community would be avoided if only people and nations would love one another. Augustine's

concrete political action is prudence. And without prudence, natural law is indeed the rigid formalism Niebuhr fears.

[13] *Ibid.*, 263, 265–66, 270–71, 277.
[14] *Id.*, *Christian Realism*, 126–27.
[15] *Ibid.*, 3, 17.

approach differs from modern forms of perfectionism in the fact that he takes account of the power and persistence of egotism, both individual and collective, and seeks to establish the most tolerable form of peace and justice under conditions set by human sin.[16]

Niebuhr, however, takes issue with the Realist who counsels that a nation consult only its own interests, since this will work against its broader interests which are tied up, for instance, with an alliance of free nations. "The loyalty of a leavening portion of a nation's citizens to a value transcending national interest will save a 'realistic' nation from defining its interests in such narrow and short range terms." [17] He concludes that Augustine is the most reliable guide among all the Realists since he avoided the mistakes of many of the moderns like the pragmatists, who, understanding the irrelevance of fixed and detailed norms, "do not understand that love must take the place as the final norm for these inadequate norms." [18]

Charles A. Beard

Charles A. Beard deserves the next priority of investigation because his exhaustive study of the use of the term "national interest" stimulated the later debate. In that work, he does not popularize the category "Realist," but the label fits:

There do not seem to exist any independent, objective criteria for determining the relationship between moral obligation and the national interest, either as currently conceived or as may be conceived under any known system of knowledge and thought. That is to say, objective criteria appear to be lacking both for the interpretation and testing of moral obligation, and for determining "the true national interest." [19]

[16] *Ibid.*, 129, 131.
[17] *Ibid.*, 136.
[18] *Ibid.*, 146.
[19] Beard, *Idea of National Interest*, 406. Beard is most noted in American historical scholarship for his economic determinism in the interpretation of history.

The contrast between the ideal that seems possible and the real that oppresses us is painfully evident to contemporary knowledge; and it is increasingly understood that science, which once supplanted theological assurance, can furnish no unequivocal prescriptions for national policy and action. . . . While the philosopher not called upon to act may enjoy luxury of utopianism—pacific or revolutionary—the statesman driven to action by his craft and profession must have some sense for the practical and must work with things that will be—in spite of his efforts—as well as with those that may yield to ideal purposes.[20]

He condones the fact that national interest has been conceived "primarily in materialistic and amoral terms, as springing from utilitarian purposes and concerned with power and practical ends." This he feels to be in keeping with politics where one seeks positive goals not controlled by "some abstract scheme of moral idealism." After observing that the statesman should avoid quixotism and refrain "from imperilling the practical affairs of his own country by adventures in the moral improvement of others," he retreats somewhat: "Yet the separation of economics, politics, and morals has never been absolute in theory or practice. It is a question of emphasis and usage." [21] He favors bringing ethics out of its obscure corner, but in his definition of ethics he links the latter with esthetics as "the knowledge of good and beautiful things and conduct," and distinguishes it from "morality (mores)." [22]

In distinguishing "national interest" from older formulas of international relations, Beard points out its positive relation to tangibles, especially economic operations. With the spread of secularism and commerce, it took on this worldly character as con-

[20] *Id., The Open Door at Home* (New York: Macmillan, 1935), 19, 178. Hereafter referred to as *Open Door*.

[21] *Id., Idea of National Interest*, 358.

[22] *Id., Open door*, 32. His approach to morals is reminiscent of John Dewey who said, "For practical purposes morals mean customs, folkways, established collective habits. . . . [The individual] can, if he will, intelligently adapt customs to conditions, and thereby remake them. Customs in any case constitute moral standards." John Dewey, *Human Nature and Conduct* (New York: Henry Holt, 1922), 75.

trasted with things of the spirit. He states that Christian teaching did not countenance national interest because of the religion's claim to universality.[23] The dichotomy was made final when political economy replaced theology as the central concern:

Political economy was transformed into economics, the science of private gain. Darwinism introduced a principle which was interpreted as implying an eternal struggle for existence on a material plane, as lending biological sanction to the primary significance of material interests. The Church was divorced from the state and the desiderata of politics became fundamentally secular.[24]

He assigns to "moral obligation" as it is employed in American foreign policy, a secular, utilitarian significance, effective for domestic purposes mainly, a position "part way between the requirements of sacrificial ethics and the frank exploitation of the province for the benefit of the metropolis." [25]

Defining "interest" as "motive or force of attention, affection and action" inherent in human beings, he says it cannot be isolated as material interest alone, since it is bound up with ideas also, and cannot be fully comprehended by the human mind. Although the nebulous fringes of national interest involve the whole interpretation of world history, he lists as fundamentals: territory, security, cohesiveness, cooperative capacity, economic resources, technical arts, productive economy, and cultural heritage.[26] In spite of the tendency to regard the national interest as an aggregation of particular interests, or to interpret it in terms of the most active group, there is a supreme national interest of American society which stands above these:

The supreme interest of the United States is the creation and maintenance of a high standard of life for all its people and ways of industry conducive to the promotion of individual and social virtues within the frame of national security. . . . In this statement, national security,

[23] *Id., Idea of National Interest*, 4–5, 22.
[24] *Ibid.*, 25; same thought in *Open Door*, 155.
[25] *Ibid.*, 388–89.
[26] *Id., Open Door*, 156–57, 177.

considered in terms of stable economy maintained at a high operating tempo and of appropriate defense, becomes the supreme and controlling consideration in national interest . . . there is little use in attempting to create and maintain a high standard of life . . . if security is ignored and military defense against predatory nations is neglected. National security, therefore, comes first.[27]

Beard's isolationism is evident in his reminders [28] that there should be the least possible dependence on foreign imports, that defense of the present geographical home is the only determining factor for the size of the army and navy, that conquest of foreign territories occupied by alien races is a betrayal of national interest, and that the armed forces are not to be huckstering agencies for profit-seekers in the name of trade. One way of avoiding outward thrusts of private interests to dispose of alleged surpluses, is more efficient distribution of wealth and ownership within the United States. If production of basic necessities would require a three or four hour workday, then it would be the duty of the state to increase production of "non-consumable intangibles, such as education, science, music and medicine, and non-consumable tangibles, such as parks, roads, and public services." For the attainment of these objectives he would create a Foreign Trade Authority under the State Department. A prime consideration would be "utmost insulation of internal price levels . . . from wars, dumping, revolutions and price-cutting conflicts."

He advises [29] withdrawing from the imperialist rivalries, tracing defense lines upon zones that can be defended, multiplying outlays for scientific research so as to decrease our reliance on world markets, setting an example of self-restraint "which is certainly easier than restraining fifty other nations in an international conference, or beating them in war," adopting a policy of fair commodity exchange with other nations, and refraining from giving them "any moral advice on any subject." He would collaborate with other

[27] *Ibid.*, 210.
[28] *Ibid.*, 213, 261, 224, 228, 232, 288–90.
[29] *Ibid.*, 273–74, 283.

like-minded nations and enter into agreements for curtailment of armaments.

Regarding immigration, he holds that the guiding principle must be the necessity of maintaining social cohesiveness; freedom of migration to the United States would enlarge the areas of low-standard living and human misery, and because of the fecundity of Orientals, would increase the population within fifty years to three or four hundred millions. He admits that the restrictive policy runs counter to the assumption that peoples of all races and colors are brothers worthy to be admitted to fellowship even at the cost of unlimited sacrifice, but he concludes:

American interest repudiates the philosophy and implications of universal ethics as applied to immigration and to the development of the American nationality. Existing race mixtures, language, traditions, and consensus of community feeling are not to be seriously altered. . . . This is the American nationality around which issues of interest in international relations will revolve.[30]

Beard describes his policy as neither traditional internationalism nor isolationism:

It is based upon the conviction that the conflicts and controversies of nations do not arise outside the respective nations, but spring from outward thrusts originating in domestic economies and forces. . . . It does not make world-wide claims and then withhold from its soldiers and sailors the power necessary to defend them in fact. It is cautious but not cowardly; pacific but not pacifist. . . . It does not rule out of consideration the League of Nations, but proposes the conditions on which the League can be brought into harmony with national interests. . . . It does not exclude any noble sentiments associated with historic internationalism.[31]

Since he wishes to explore the various concepts of national interest, Beard proceeds to evaluate the many approaches. He dismisses Adam Smith's laissez-faire system, in which the enrichment

[30] *Ibid.*, 206–09.
[31] *Ibid.*, 303–04.

of the whole is thought to follow automatically from the economic gain of the members seeking self-interest, by saying that it actually admitted security and defense as the primordial considerations in policy, ahead of individual opulence.[32] He refutes the argument of industrial statecraft which promotes foreign outlets for surplus goods and capital, by saying that the American people have not the full access to all the goods to which their labor and intelligence entitle them. The solution is to try to eliminate backwardness from the American nation before assuming the role of salvation in some other benighted area. The consequence of the industrialist program is an increase of manufacturing over agriculture, and the transformation of more men into members of the urban proletariat, trained in narrow specialties, and subject to being displaced by new inventions. Meanwhile wealth accumulates in the hands of the few whose qualities of courage and leadership are undermined by the standards and artificialities they assume.[33]

Throughout these analyses, Beard places the economic motive as fundamental in individual activities and in those of the state. He explains the Marxian concept of national interest without editorial comment.[34] His answer to the argument of agrarian statecraft is that historical experience does not verify the assumption that outlets will be found for surpluses if trade barriers are eliminated; the proposition "rests upon nothing more than maxims devised for a pretechnological or handicraft era when the differentiation of national economies . . . was sharply marked and presumed to be permanent." [35] He does not seem to have much regard for the concept of national interest which "makes the State sheer power, grounded in emotions. . . . common national feeling, patriotism, love of power, joy in battle, predilection for physical courage, and national honor." [36]

[32] *Ibid.*, 160–64.
[33] *Ibid.*, 48–49, 55, 69.
[34] *Ibid.*, 165–68.
[35] *Ibid.*, 89.
[36] *Ibid.*, 170–72.

Beard criticizes as heresies in foreign policy four doctrines proclaimed by political leaders since the opening of the twentieth century; these have created "moral and intellectual disorder and hostility toward the United States among the nations of the earth." [37] The first is the jubilant cry that the United States, now a world power, must assume obligations and exert influence over the affairs of other countries; this course weakens it own efficiency. He warns of the wrecks of over-extended empires, and counsels prudent calculation for the sake of survival midst the struggles of power politics. The second danger is the doctrine that the President has a constitutional and moral right to proclaim noble sentiments of politics, economics, and peace, committing the United States by his speeches and signatures. He points to the following examples as proof of the futility of this practice: the Open Door, the Fourteen Points, the Kellogg Pact, the Four Freedoms, and the Atlantic Charter. Though often intended for domestic propaganda, they are accepted by foreigners as meaningful and enforceable; disappointed hopes or ingratitude for the favors are the end results.

The third mistake is to announce proudly that the United States has the duty to maintain the moral leadership of the world; this provokes discord rather than comity among nations. The fourth error is that international commerce promotes peace; it will lead to the spending of tax money, and bring on collisions with controlled economies in other countries. He sees grave peril in the powerful private agencies which in the name of peace promote presidential omnipotence in foreign affairs. They subsidize professors and students of international relations with the consequence that American education on all levels is permeated by the theory of presidential supremacy in this field.

George F. Kennan

George F. Kennan merits the next position of prominence because he popularized the term "Legalist-Moralist" to stigmatize the

[37] *Id., President Roosevelt and the Coming of the War* (New York: Yale University Press, 1948), 592–97.

proponents of political Idealism. We shall introduce him with his own words:

The process of government, after all, is a practical exercise and not a moral one. It is primarily a sorry chore consisting of the application of restraint by man over man, a chore devolving upon civilized society, most unfortunately, as a result of man's irrational nature, his selfishness, his obstinacy, his tendency to violence. The performance of this regrettable and almost embarrassing chore is not an undertaking in which such things as altruism and sacrifice can find any pure expression.

Moral principles have their place in the heart of the individual and in the shaping of his own conduct, whether as a citizen or as a government official. In this capacity they are essential to the successful functioning of any political society that rests on popular consent. . . . But when the individual's behavior passes through the machinery of political organization and merges with that of millions of other individuals to find its expression in the actions of a government, then it undergoes a general transmutation, and the same moral concepts are no longer relevant to it. A government is an agent, not a principal; and no more than any other agent may it attempt to be the conscience of its principal.

Morality as the foundation of civic virtue and accordingly as a condition precedent to successful democracy—yes. . . . But morality as a general criterion for the determination of the behavior of states and above all as criterion for measuring and comparing the behavior of different states—no. . . . Of course this does not preclude efforts on the part of individual citizens or groups to project private altruism and generosity across national frontiers.[38]

He sees as the most serious fault of our policy formulation in the past fifty years, the "legalistic-moralistic" approach to international problems.[39] It consists in the belief that the chaotic aspira-

[38] George F. Kennan, *Realities of American Foreign Policy* (Princeton: Princeton University Press, 1954), 48–49. Hereafter referred to as *Realities*. Kennan set up and directed the Policy Planning Committee of the Department of State, 1947–49. He was formerly Ambassador to Russia, and is currently a member of the Institute for Advanced Study at Princeton University.

[39] *Id., American Diplomacy, 1900–1950* (Chicago: University of Chicago

tions of governments can be suppressed by a system of legal rules. It is an effort to make applicable to governments as to individuals the Anglo-Saxon concept of an institutional and juridical framework. People are unable to understand why the experience of the thirteen colonies could not be extended to the world. Instead of dealing with the awkward conflicts of national interest to bring about the least unsettling effects, these adherents would adopt some formal criteria to define permissible behavior. He observes that Americans find it incredible that other peoples might regard certain aspirations to be more legitimate than peacefulness and orderliness in international life.

Kennan notes in America a national sociability, a certain embarrassment at being a big and great nation, and an urge to show itself friendly to newer and smaller nations and almost to share their status. The United States has taken for granted the enlightenment of these countries, "uncontaminated with the curse of bigness or the sinfulness of maturity . . . people yearning only for peace and economic development." He comments:

Smallness and newness in nations might not be indicative of wisdom and moderation. We should not attempt to involve in complicated international problems large numbers of countries whose interests are but remotely affected by them. . . . And we have frequently given the impression that even a purely declamatory resolution, so long as it commanded the adherence of an international majority, was more important to us than action on our own part that might actually have affected the course of events. In this way there has grown in some American circles a cast of thought which holds the form in higher esteem than the substance, and views international affairs simply as a long series of voting contests, in which the decisive thing is not whatever practical effect the vote might have, but the position in which you are found to be, the company in which you are discovered, at the moment of voting.[40]

Press, 1951), 95–96. (Copyright 1951 by the University of Chicago.) Hereafter referred to as *American Diplomacy*.

[40] *Id., Realities*, 40–41.

He traces this stress upon verbal undertakings to the American belief in the power of public opinion to overrule governments, and the thought that international society could and should operate on the basis of contractual obligation. It has resulted in public misunderstanding of realities, in the impression that a community of outlook exists among nations. He judges that American statesmen assumed that whatever was urged in the name of moral or legal principle involved no specific responsibility on our part. If others failed to heed our warnings, it would bring world opinion to bear against them; if they followed our leadership, they risked handling the resulting problems alone.[41]

Mr. Kennan summarizes the weaknesses in the Legalist-Moralist position as follows.[42] In subordinating states to a juridical regime which limits their possibilities for aggression, we assume that like ourselves they are content with their international borders and status. Secondly, it confers an absolute value upon national sovereignty making all equal in status, and it inhibits the process of change. Thirdly, it makes no provision against ideological attack, intimidation, penetration, etc., the devices used on puppet states. It assumes that a nation will always be able to form a government qualified to speak for it in the world arena. Fourthly, it is impractical with regard to sanctions, and it overestimates the effectiveness of a wide military coalition.

The final and greatest deficiency is the asumption that state behavior is a fit subject for moral judgment. When one affirms a law and feels a moral superiority toward the law-breaker, the indignation leads to a contest for unconditional surrender. Although rooted in a desire to eliminate war and violence, the legalist approach has made the latter even more destructive of political stability; it is closely identified with total war and total victory. Kennan observes that when the objective is an effort to change the attitudes and traditions of an entire people, military means alone and a short space of time are inadequate for the task. His conclu-

[41] *Id.*, *American Diplomacy*, 46–47.
[42] *Ibid.*, 97–103.

sion is that we need not abandon our respect for international law as a civilizer, nor follow "appeasement," but merely admit that our own national interest is all we really understand, and if we pursue it without arrogance or hostility toward other peoples, it will be "conducive to a better world."

Kennan agrees with advocates of world government in only one respect, that is, in their readiness to merge the country's life with that of other peoples. While they would reach out and embrace the entire world community at once, he would begin by building relationships with the peoples closest to us. He advocates that the United States learn to take as well as to give things on the "economic, demographic, cultural, and intellectual" levels. At this point of the nation's development, economic protectionism is a form of "infantile escapism." One reason why he advises a liberal immigration policy is that the "old American virtues" lauded by the restrictionists "are dependent for their survival on the degree to which they can commend themselves to great masses of people who had no share in their origin." [43]

Regarding foreign aid, he quotes Hamilton to support his contention that pure acts of charity do not emanate from nations, nor should gratitude or obligation be expected from the recipients. We should use our resources where they can do the most good for our national purpose; in the success of these undertakings lies the reward. The aid should be relative to their effort to help themselves, and in lines which are to their own interest also. To help others who are threatened by Russia is a duty of enlightened responsibility as a world power.[44]

The introduction to Mr. Kennan in this paper found him refusing to talk about morality; in these concluding remarks he does not use the term, morality, but that genus is present:

To the extent that we are able to develop a social purpose in our own society, our life and our experiences will become meaningful to peoples

[43] *Id., Realities,* 105–08.
[44] *Id.,* "Foreign Aid in the Framework of National Policy," *Proceedings of Academy of Political and Social Science,* XXIII (January, 1950), 105–11.

in other parts of the world. We must remember that we are practically the only country that has been able to afford for any length of time the experimentation with the uninhibited flow of self-interest. Almost everywhere else, men are convinced that the answers to their problems are to be found in the acceptance of a high degree of collective responsibility and discipline. To many of them, the sight of an America in which there is visible no higher social goal than the self-enrichment of the individual, and where that self-enrichment takes place primarily in material goods and gadgets that are of doubtful utility in the achievement of the deeper satisfactions of life—this sight fails to inspire either confidence or enthusiasm.[45]

Hans J. Morgenthau

The Realist whose works require priority of attention as the most forceful and comprehensive presentation is Hans J. Morgenthau. To his remarks, quoted in the preliminary survey of Realism, these few may be added. He requests that the test by which his theory is judged be "not a priori and abstract but empirical and pragmatic." Explanation of his approach to man is a necessary preliminary:

Intellectually, the political realist maintains the autonomy of the political sphere, as the economist, the lawyer, the moralist maintain theirs. . . . The moralist asks: "Is this policy in accord with moral principles?" And the political realist asks: "How does this policy affect the power of the nation?" . . . Real man is a composite of "economic man," "political man," "moral man," "religious man," etc. A man who was nothing but "political man" would be a beast, for he would be completely lacking in moral restraints. A man who was nothing but "moral man" would be a fool, for he would be completely lacking in prudence.[46]

To the religious sphere, Morgenthau says the Realist applies the standards of thought appropriate to it; he seems to abstract each

[45] *Id., Realities*, 115.

[46] Morgenthau, *Politics*, 10–12. Morgenthau, who came to the United States from Germany in 1937, is the director of the Center for the Study of American Foreign Policy at the University of Chicago.

of the above from the other aspects of human nature and deal with it as though it were the only one. Morgenthau deplores the "erection of private virtues as the sole standard by which the qualifications of both private and public action . . . are to be judged." Because this destroys the tension between man *per se* and man as a citizen, it makes meaningless Aristotle's question of whether the virtue of a good man is identical with the virtue of a good citizen. Noting that excellent men have done more harm to the nation than some less worthy predecessors, he states that society will have to learn that "it needs protection also from the good men who are too good even to take note of the rules of the political game." [47] He jests about the most vociferous critics of statesmen, the politicians, who themselves make deals, and who would not act in their own constituencies as they expect framers of foreign policy to act. They wish to convert foreign policy into a sort of fairyland where virtue triumphs, and knights come to the rescue of ravished nations, taking the life of the villain without thought of personal safety.[48]

With Morgenthau's discussion of the Will to Power in individuals and in nations, we come to the very core of his political philosophy, and this factor seems to justify the use of extensive direct quotes in order to follow accurately his reasoning:

When we speak of power, we mean man's control over the minds and actions of other men. . . . Political power, however, must be distinguished from force in the sense of the actual exercise of physical violence. . . .[49]

Politics is a struggle for power over men, and whatever its ultimate aim may be, power is its immediate goal and the modes of acquiring, maintaining, and demonstrating it determine the technique of political action. . . . To the degree in which the essence and aim of politics is

[47] *Id.*, "The Decline of American Government," *New Republic*, CXXXVII (December 16, 1957), 7–9.
[48] *Id.*, *In Defense of the National Interest* (New York: Knopf, 1952), 224. Hereafter referred to as *In Defense*.
[49] *Id.*, *Politics*, 26–27.

power over man, politics is evil, for it is to this degree that it degrades man to a means for other men. . . .[50]

Foreign policy, like all politics, is in its essence a struggle for power, waged by sovereign nations for national advantage. . . . By its very nature this struggle is never ended for the lust for power, and the fear of it, is never stilled. . . . The best a nation longing for tranquility and peace can expect is to be passed for a time by the stream of events; but it must ever be ready to man the ramparts for defense or attack.[51]

Man is a political animal by nature. . . . Man is born to seek power, yet his actual condition makes him a slave to the power of others. Man is born a slave, but everywhere he wants to be a master. . . .[52]

The state as the receptacle of the highest secular loyalty and power devaluates and actually delimits the manifestations of the individual desire for power. The individual, power hungry for his own sake, is held in low public esteem; and the mores and laws of society endeavor to strengthen through positive sanctions the moral condemnation of individual aspirations for power, to limit their modes and sphere of action, and to suppress them altogether. While, however, the state is ideologically and physically incomparably more powerful than its citizens, it is free from all effective restraint from above. The state's collective desire for power is limited, aside from self-chosen limitations, only by the ruins of an old, and the rudiments of a new, normative order, both too feeble to offer more than a mere intimation of actual restraint. Above it, there is no centralized authority beyond the mechanics of the balance of power, which could impose actual limits upon the manifestations of its collective desire for domination. The state has become indeed a 'mortal God' and for an age that believes no longer in an immortal God, the state becomes the only God there is. . . .

[50] *Id., Scientific Man and Power Politics* (Chicago: University of Chicago Press, 1946), 195. (Copyright 1946 by the University of Chicago.) Hereafter referred to as *Scientific Man*. In private correspondence with Professor Morgenthau, I asked whether he disagreed with Aristotle's statement that politics is the noblest of the arts. He answered that he fully subscribed to the philosopher's view, for in it there was room for the struggle for power. (Morgenthau to the author, December 6, 1957).

[51] *Id., In Defense*, 92.

[52] *Id., Scientific Man*, 168.

By transferring his egotism and power impulses to the nation, the individual gives his inhibited aspirations not only a vicarious satisfaction. The process of transference transforms also the ethical significance of the satisfaction. What was egotism—and hence ignoble and immoral— there becomes patriotism and therefore noble and altruistic here. While society puts liabilities upon aspirations for individual power, it places contributions to the collective power of the state at the top of the hierarchy of values. . . .[53]

For in a world where power counts, no nation pursuing a rational policy has a choice between renouncing and wanting power; and if it could, the lust for power for the individual's sake would still confront us with its less spectacular yet no less pressing moral defects. This sham battle against power politics, however, gives our civilization at least the satisfaction of having paid tribute to its ethical standards and of being able to continue to live as though these standards did not exist. . . .

There is no escape from the evil of power, regardless of what one does. Whenever we act with reference to our fellow men, we must sin, and we must still sin when we refuse to act; for the refusal to be involved in the evil of action carries with it the breach of the obligation to do one's duty. . . . Political ethics is indeed the ethics of doing evil.[54]

Neither science nor ethics nor politics can resolve the conflict between politics and ethics into harmony. We have no choice between power and the common good. To act successfully, that is, according to the rules of the political art, is political wisdom. . . . To choose among several expedient actions the least evil one is moral judgment.[55]

[53] *Ibid.*, 197–98.
[54] *Ibid.*, 200–01.
[55] *Ibid.*, 203. This entire interpretation of Will to Power might be compared with Nietzsche's analysis: To refrain mutually from injury, from violence, from exploitation, and put one's will on a par with that of others: this may result in a certain rough sense in good conduct among individuals. . . . As soon, however, as one wished to take this principle more generally, and if possible, even as the fundamental principle of society, it would immediately disclose what it really is—namely, a Will to the *denial* of life, a principle of dissolution and decay. . . . Life itself is *essentially* appropriation, injury, conquest of the strange and weak, suppression, severity, obtrusion of familiar forms, incorporation, and at least, putting it mildest,

Morgenthau posits the balance of power as an inevitable and essential stabilizing factor in a society of sovereign nations; [56] the temporary instability in the society is a result of particular conditions, not of the invalidity of the principle. He uses the term without qualification, and defines it as "an actual state of affairs in which power is distributed among several nations with approximate equality." He names as the two factors at the basis of international society, the multiplicity and the antagonism of its elements. Since no nation can be sure that its calculation of the distribution of power is correct, it must provide against error by aiming at superiority of power. To offset a large miscalculation it must ultimately seek maximum power; still not secure after it has gained an apparent edge over the competitors, it must use its advantage to change the distribution of power permanently in its favor.[57]

The possibility of limited sovereignty he declares to be illogical since sovereignty means "supreme authority." "There can be no half-way house between national sovereignty and supranational sovereignty. . . . In federal states, ideological satisfaction is given by developing constitutional flatteries upon the once sovereign members." [58] Collective security is also discounted as impossible of achievement:

---

exploitation. . . . [A group] will endeavor to grow, to gain ground, attract to itself and acquire ascendancy—not owing to any morality or immorality, but because it *lives*, and because life *is* precisely Will to Power. . . . "Exploitation" does not belong to a depraved, or imperfect and primitive society: it belongs to the *nature* of the living being as a primary organic function; it is a consequence of the intrinsic Will to Power, which is precisely the Will to Life. Friedrich W. Nietzsche, *Beyond Good and Evil*, Vol. XII of *Complete Works of F. Nietzsche*, ed. Oscar Levy, trans. Helen Zimmern (Edinburgh: T. N. Foulis, 1911), 225–26.

[56] *Id., Politics*, 155.

[57] *Id., In Defense*, 189–90. When questioned in private correspondence as to whether this type of equilibrium is a natural need of international society, which could not be replaced in a well-ordered juridical institution, he replied in the affirmative (Morgenthau to the author, December 6, 1957).

[58] The above-mentioned correspondence, and *Politics*, 303.

Collective security, then, can succeed only on the further assumption
that all or virtually all nations will come to the defense of the status quo,
threatened in the security of a particular nation, even at the risk of war,
regardless of whether they could justify such a policy in view of their
own individual interests. . . . There is no law-enforcing agency above
the individual nations and there are no overwhelming moral and social
pressures to which they can be subjected. Conflicts between national
interests and morality are inevitable. . . . Those nations cannot help
resolving such a conflict in favor of their own individual interests and
thus paralyzing the operations of the collective security. . . . Under
the assumption of collective security, any war anywhere in the world,
then, is potentially a world war. Thus a device intent upon making war
impossible ends by making war universal.[59]

Whereas he affirms that a lasting and just peace cannot be attained in a society of sovereign nations, he discredits the possibility
of a world state:

No society exists coextensive with the presumed range of a world state.
. . . There does not exist a supranational society that comprises all
individual members of all nations and, hence, is identical with humanity
politically organized. . . . The nation is, as we have seen, the recipient
of man's highest earthly loyalties. Beyond it there are other nations,
but no community for which man would be willing to act regardless of
what he understands the interests of his own nation to be . . . . they
are not prepared to perform that revaluation of all values, that unprecedented moral and political revolution which would force the
nation from its throne and put the political organization of humanity
on it. They are willing and able to sacrifice and die so that national
governments may be kept standing. . . .

There is no shirking the conclusion that international peace cannot be
established under the present moral, social, and political conditions of
the world. . . . The community of the American people ante-dated
the American state, as a world community must ante-date a world
state.[60]

[59] *Id., Politics*, 391–92.
[60] *Ibid.*, 479, 481, 485.

Mr. Morgenthau denies the equation of "political moralizing with morality," and of "political realism with immorality." The choice is between moral principles divorced from, or moral principles derived from, political reality. In the absence of social institutions which safeguard moral principles, "it would be both foolish and morally wrong to ask a nation to forego its national interests not for the good of a society with a superior moral claim but for a chimera." [61]

He makes an interesting commentary on justice:

There is a profound and neglected truth hidden in Hobbes' extreme dictum that the state creates morality as well as law and that there is neither morality nor law outside the state. . . .[62] What justice means in the United States can within wide limits be ascertained; for interests

[61] *Id., In Defense,* 33, 36. When asked whether he accepted the notion that states as moral persons are bound to obey the moral law as are individuals, he replied that "the moral restraints to which nations are subject are, by virtue of the near anarchy in which they live with each other, less stringent and effective." (Morgenthau to author, December 6, 1957).

[62] Hobbes stated: And in this law of nature [that men perform the covenants made] consisteth the fountain and original of justice. For where not covenant hath preceded, there hath no right been transferred, and every man has right to every thing, and consequently, no action can be unjust. But when a covenant is made, then to break it is unjust: and the definition of injustice, is no other than the not performance of covenant. And whatever is not unjust, is just. . . .

"Before the names of just, and unjust can have place, there must be some coercive power, to compel men equally to the performance of their covenants, by the terror of some punishment, greater than the benefit they expect by the breach of their covenant . . . . such power there is none before the erection of a commonwealth. And this is also to be gathered out of the ordinary definition of justice in the Schools: for they say, *that justice is the constant will of giving to every man his own.* And therefore where there is no *own,* that is no propriety, there is no injustice; and where is no coercive power erected, that is where there is no commonwealth, there nothing is unjust. So that the nature of justice, consisteth in keeping of valid covenants: but the validity of covenants begins not but with the constitution of a civil power, sufficient to compel men to keep them: and then it is also that propriety begins." Thomas Hobbes, *Hobbes Selections: Leviathan, Modern Student's Library,* ed. Frederick J. E. Woodbridge (New York: Scribner's Sons, 1930), 295–96.

and convictions, experiences of life and institutionalized traditions have in large measure created a consensus concerning what justice means under the conditions of American society. No such consensus exists in the relations between nations. For above the national societies there exists no international society so integrated as to be able to define for them the concrete meaning of justice or equality, as national societies do for their individual members. In consequence, the appeal to moral principles by the representative of a nation vis-a-vis another nation signifies something fundamentally different. . . . The appeal to moral principles in the international sphere has no concrete universal meaning.[63]

Before drawing the distinction between liberal and nonliberal aims in international life, Morgenthau states that both are ideological because men will support only those which they are persuaded are "justified before reason and morality." The nonliberal aims fulfill temporary concrete political functions and then disappear; hence they are relatively immune from the danger of being at variance with reality. Some of these concepts are: living space, encirclement, new order, etc. The liberal ideologies, because of their abstractness and their claim for absolute validity, must be kept alive as though "realities" were not dependent upon time and space. Among the second category of aims are collective security, universal democracy, permanent and just peace. He concludes that though these latter ideal goals may "inspire the actions of men and supply standards for the judgment of philosophy and ethics," they are not capable "of immediate and complete realization through political action." A permanent gap exists between them and political reality.[64]

[63] Morgenthau, *In Defense*, 33.
[64] *Id., Scientific Man*, 72–73. When asked whether he was suggesting that a change of heart could not be wrought by *political action alone*, or whether he was criticizing their stress on the *here* and *now*, he replied that his objection went farther: "Both liberalism and Marxism believe that the evils to which the flesh is heir can be remedied here and now by man's unaided efforts. In other words, liberalism and Marxism are really secular religions which believe that salvation can be attained in this world through, say, social

While the individual may sacrifice himself in defense of a moral principle, a State has no right "to let its moral disapprobation of the infringement of liberty get in the way of successful political action, itself inspired by the moral principles of national survival." [65] Political ethics, based upon prudence, judges by political consequences. Nations tend to identify their own moral aspirations with the moral laws that govern the universe, and this eventuates in a holy mission to save the world and remake it. An age of political moralizing is apt to issue in a series of religious world wars.

To know that nations are subject to the moral law is one thing, while to pretend to know with certainty what is good and evil in the relations among nations is quite another. There is a world of difference between the belief that all nations stand under the judgment of God, inscrutable to the human mind, and the blasphemous conviction that God is always on one's side and that what one wills oneself cannot fail to be willed by God also. [66]

In politics the nation and not humanity is the ultimate fact. . . . When a nation invokes "world public opinion" or "the conscience of mankind" in order to assure itself as well as other nations, that its foreign policies conform to the standards of men everywhere, it appeals to nothing real. . . . What is real are national public opinions fashioned in the image of the political philosophies, ethics, and aspirations of the respective nations. [67]

He concludes that a "world society" and a "universal morality" by which to judge actions on the international scene do not exist. [68]

reform, economic and technological development, or political revolution." (Morgenthau to author, December 6, 1957).

[65] *Id., Politics*, 9.

[66] *Ibid.*, 10.

[67] *Ibid.*, 244.

[68] This notion that public opinion is the norm of morality might spring from Adam Smith's equation of morality with propriety whose basis is "sympathy." Adam Smith, *The Theory of Moral Sentiment*, ed. Dugald Stewart (London: W. Strahan, J. F. Rivington, W. Johnston, T. Longmans, 1774), 121. Perhaps the term "morality" here reflects the positivist explanation given in *Encyclopaedia of the Social Sciences:* The pluralization of morality into morals follows upon the recognition that morality

Morgenthau laments the deterioration of international morality in recent years; dissolution of the ethical system which imposed its restraints upon day-to-day operations of foreign policy, is due to two factors: "the substitution of democratic for aristocratic responsibility in foreign affairs and the substitution of nationalistic standards of action for universal ones." [69] Gentlemen of the seventeenth and eighteenth centuries played a game of diplomacy whose rules were common to all. With the growth of democratic nation states in the nineteenth century, government by clearly identifiable men accountable for their acts, was replaced by a fiction of international law which dealt with nations as though they were persons; no moral obligation corresponds to this legal concept. Nationalism destroyed international society itself within which the morality had operated.

For the past century and a half the ethics of nationalism, not that of the Sermon on the Mount, had been in the ascendancy. National unification and democratic liberation made the masses of the peoples active participants in wars; they now had the "cohesion and emotional impetus" necessary for policies of conquest; the interests of the people seemed to be at stake and thus the sovereignty of the state was intensified. The particularism of democratic nationalism was an obstacle to the realization of free trade, international law, and international organization. [70]

The national interest of the United States consists, according to Morgenthau, in three concrete goals: the predominant position in the western hemisphere, a European balance of power, and an Asiatic balance of power. [71] From concern for our precarious situa-

---

also consists in manifold, changeful and contingent techniques of conduct. Considered thus morals so largely overlap manners, folkways, mores, laws, ethics and public opinion that only convention or fiat decides where these others leave off and morals begin. "Morals," *Encyclopaedia of the Social Sciences*, Vol. X, ed. Edward R. A. Seligman (New York: Macmillan, 1933), 643.

[69] Morgenthau, *Politics*, 220–29.

[70] *Id., Scientific Man*, 67.

[71] *Id.,* "What Is the National Interest of the United States?" *Annals of the*

tion surrounded by outposts of the great powers, our attention passed to the guaranteeing of American predominance. That status could not be challenged from within the hemisphere without the accompanying support of an outside power, so it was imperative to isolate the western hemisphere and safeguard its territories against foreign acquisition. Hence the Monroe Doctrine is a permanent national interest.[72]

If a European nation's predominance were unchallenged within Europe, so that it could attempt conquest in America without fear of attack in the homeland, then America would be subject to intervention. For this reason, Morgenthau asserts, America has consistently pursued policies aiming at balance of power in Europe, with the sole exception of the War of 1812. In both World Wars the United States has joined the "weaker" coalition, and has paralleled Britain's role of balancer. Because the Asiatic balance of power has concerned the United States only since the opening of the twentieth century, it has never been so unequivocal a part of national interest. In this quarter, the policies have been more subject to moralistic influence, but they have consistently reflected opposition to the domination of China by another nation, lest it threaten the security of the United States.[73]

Mowrer, Weinberg, Spykman

Paul Scott Mowrer seems to have anticipated the great debate as early as 1924 when he spoke for policies based upon enlightened self-interest, not upon the spirit of illusion or of crusade.[74] Those concrete interests were: first, preservation of world peace, and secondly, extension of foreign trade and investment; these founda-

---

American Academy of Political and Social Science, CCLXXXII (July, 1952), 1-7.

[72] *Id., In Defense*, 5.

[73] *Ibid.*, 5-6.

[74] Paul Scott Mowrer, *Our Foreign Affairs: A Study in National Interest and the New Diplomacy* (New York: E. P. Dutton, 1924), 4, 49. Mowrer, a former foreign correspondent, is currently engaged as an author.

tions were sunk in firm rock. Policies based on a sense of moral superiority and reform were built upon quicksand. Of greater danger to the world than that nations should act reasonably in accordance with their own interests, was that they should act at the dictation of a "megalomaniac dream."

His thought parallels Morgenthau's in the mention of the tendency of nations to believe in their own moral superiority, and as a result, to arrive at opposite interpretations of right and justice. He deems himself a staunch advocate of the development and extension of international law, but since most disputes are still held to be nonjusticiable, he feels it would be better to adopt another course:

For all practical purposes, it will be found best to take diplomatic controversies off the moral plane altogether, and to place them on a plane, if not of potential force, then of fact and of common interest. Let us continue to believe in our own problematic moral superiority; above all let us try to obtain and to maintain real moral superiority, and to act accordingly; but let us not obtrude our self-complacency upon others.[75]

. . . the formula or institution will never be devised which can yoke the nations and make them pull together, when their interests do not lie in the same direction. Internationalism is going to develop and hold what it gains, to just the extent that the nations, viewing the world in the loftiest way, find that they have interests in common. . . . The true internationalist is he who is ever making analyses in terms of national interest, and who searches to discover those points, ever more numerous in our modern world, at which the diverse peoples converge.[76]

Albert K. Weinberg in 1935 pointed up the two theories about international morality, reducing them either to altruism or to egoism. The former holds that for nations as for individuals, Christ's law of love must apply; the egoist, old as Machiavelli, posits a dual morality and idealizes self-aggrandizement. Weinberg's purpose is

[75] *Ibid.*, 34–35.
[76] *Ibid.*, 54–55.

to explain the nationalist philosophy of "Manifest Destiny," which he defines as "the doctrine that one nation has a preeminent social worth, a distinctively lofty mission, and consequently, unique rights in the application of moral principles." [77]

Nicholas Spykman, entering the fray in 1942, was more extreme in his "realism." Beginning with the premise that in a world where there is no international government, only power can achieve the objective of foreign policy, he says:

The statesman who conducts foreign policy can concern himself with values of justice, fairness, and tolerance only to the extent that they contribute to or do not interfere with the power objective. They can be used instrumentally as moral justification for the power quest, but they must be discarded the moment their application brings weakness. The search for power is not made for the achievement of moral values; moral values are used to facilitate the attainment of power.[78]

He poses the imperative of maintaining the nation's faith in its "just cause" for the sake of morale, since man responds better as a fighter in the service of abstract values, than he does with the promise of material gain. Whereas men divide regarding interest, they unite for defense of the moral order, and hence the struggles become crusades against sin and the devil, fought successfully only in the atmosphere of "unreality and make-believe." Mr. Spykman warns that the United States should not fall victim to the psychological attack which stresses the fact that the nation has committed all the crimes of which it accuses its opponent, and therefore, that it should not pass judgment on another. His conviction is stated thus:

The nation which suffers from a feeling of guilt about its use of force in the past is at a great disadvantage compared to the nation which not

[77] Albert K. Weinberg, *Manifest Destiny:* a study of nationalist expansion in American history (Baltimore: Johns Hopkins Press, 1935), 5–8. Weinberg is a lecturer in political science at Johns Hopkins University.

[78] Nicholas J. Spykman, *American Strategy in World Politics:* the United States and the Balance of Power (New York: Harcourt, Brace, 1942), 18. Spykman, a native of Holland, was teaching at Yale University at the time of his death, 1943.

only accepts the reality of force but affirms its creative value with no sense of shame or sin.[79]

Schwarzenberger, Morley, Lerche

Georg Schwarzenberger reiterates the point that, as actually applied among states, the primary task of international morality is to reinforce state policy; the gestures are directed primarily to public opinion at home and abroad. "Thus within a system of power politics, the chief function of international morality does not consist in controlling one's own behavior, but in the use of morality as a powerful weapon against potential or actual enemies." [80]

Felix Morley explains in this way why moral considerations are of secondary importance in determining relations among governments:

In dealing with other sovereignties . . . political rulers have never been and are not now much influenced by ethical considerations as such. Rulers raise no taxes from those outside the area of their control and therefore have no politically compelling reason to treat the subjects of other sovereignties with respect. It is not that the ruler is less humanitarian in his instincts or more immoral in his behavior than any other individual. But having the responsibility of the state on his shoulders, the tendency is to put what seems to be its immediate interest above all other considerations, including those of an ethical nature.[81]

Charles O. Lerche maintains that in its orientation, national interest is "supremely egoistic," springing from indigenous sources, incorporating a value system with no allowance for the "existence or objectives of other states." [82] It arises out of the interaction of

[79] *Ibid.*, 37–38.

[80] Georg Schwarzenberger, *Power Politics* (2d ed.; New York: Frederick A. Praeger, 1951), 225–27.

[81] Felix Morley, *Foreign Policy of the United States* (New York: Knopf, 1952), 42. Morley is the president of Haverford College, Haverford, Pennsylvania.

[82] Charles O. Lerche, *Principles of International Politics* (New York: Oxford University Press, 1956), 34–35.

geographic and strategic position, the level of political, economic, and social development, the national history and culture, and the over-all *Weltanschauung* of the people. The individual's hopes and objectives are thus sublimated, and this pattern is divorced from the interests of a particular group. He notes that today state morality is independent of private morality, and the requirements of citizenship have pretty well accustomed people to the disparity. It is questionable to think in terms of international society as having any meaning when applied to sovereign states; immersed in their own interests, they have no room for a sense of obligation to the whole group. Rather than being amoral, the state "serves as creator of a morality of its own." [83] The theoretical premises upon which international politics are built resemble the anarchy described by Hobbes. Lerche makes a final alarming conclusion:

. . . in international politics there are virtually no absolute values except the existence of the state and the satisfaction of its interests. . . . The only concepts of "good" and "bad" which have any reference to the international conduct of the state are relative to its success or failure in attaining its objectives. . . . It has proved particularly difficult for Americans to grasp this idea, because it runs directly counter to our native political philosophy, the doctrine of natural rights.[84]

Frederick L. Schuman

Frederick L. Schuman agrees that the first and last test of a foreign policy is its success in achieving its purpose; one based upon tangible self-interest is more likely to meet this requirement than one couched in the "evanescent fictions and fantasies of messianic

[83] *Ibid.*, 35, 105, 115.

[84] *Ibid.*, 114–15. There might be something of Jeremy Bentham's utilitarianism here: "If they [motives] are good or bad, it is only on account of their effects: good, on account of their tendency to produce pleasure, or avert pain: bad, on account of their tendency to produce pain, or avert pleasure." Jeremy Bentham, *An Introduction to the Principles of Morals and Legislation* (New York: Hafner, 1948), 102.

universalism." Repeated failures in pursuit of objectives like "The War to End Wars," "The Atlantic Charter," and the "Four Freedoms" may beget a reorientation toward *Realpolitik,* which might have good consequences in promoting "acquiescence in the inevitable diversity of the world, and foster toleration of many varieties of pagans and infidels, however obnoxious they may be, so long as they do not threaten the security of America and its allies." [85]

He places a low estimate on international law, depicting it as a set of rules which sovereigns observe only out of convenience and expediency. Lacking effective government and enforceable law, this is a society of anarchy in which force is the ultimate determinant. "It is therefore the obligation of every statesman to pursue power rather than virtue. Under anarchy the virtuous who lack power succumb, while the powerful who lack virtue often survive. For states no less than for individuals, survival is the first law of life." [86] He censures statesmen who assume the role of Don Quixote, since in a system of sovereignties when there is conflict, interest invariably prevails over ethical ideals. When countries wage war in the name of peace, principles have no operational function "save as devices to rationalize the quest for aggrandizement." He states his agreement with Kennan and Morgenthau that prudent concern with national interest, "reasonably defined," is less likely to lead to global catastrophe; it is probable that ethical standards will become the tools of "symbol manipulators" in order to rally public support for "Gargantuan adventures in mutual murder and destruction." [87]

While competing sovereignties exist, he contends, it is not within the capacity of men to make right rather than might the test of statecraft.

[85] Frederick L. Schuman, "Doctrine of Self-Interest," *American Scholar,* XIX (Winter, 1944–45), 100. Schuman is the Woodrow Wilson professor of government at Williams College.

[86] *Id.,* "International Ideals and the National Interest," *Annals of American Academy of Political and Social Science,* CCLXXX (March, 1952), 29–32.

[87] *Ibid.,* 32–36.

The immorality or amorality of high politics and diplomacy has little to do with the virtues or vices of particular politicians, diplomats, peoples, social systems, ideologies, or religious faiths. It arises from the fact that in the rivalry among sovereignties the immediate criteria of success or failure, and the ultimate determinants of political survival or extinction, have no demonstrable relation to the ethical or unethical qualities of behavior.[88]

As long as politics among nations is shaped by the rules of anarchy, indignation against the ways of Machiavelli is futile. The quest for peace must be grounded upon the facts of man's nature in society. Apostles for the brotherhood of man are expressing a faith which fails to touch men's daily lives; it resembles the concern of monks and mystics. Conditions remaining the same, "the way of love, of voluntary cooperation, of a kindly and conscious broadening of men's sympathies, loyalties, and interests to embrace everwider areas of the human community . . . is a way that never approaches the goal, despite the wishful thinking of poets and priests, historians and prophets." [89]

Beyond all this pessimism, Schuman sees hope; the picture of black despair has been a conditioner for presentation of the panacea, the abolition of national sovereignties and the creation of a world government.[90] Under this method, human beings are capable of acting together in the service of their needs; the means to attainment of this end, he leaves open to experimentation.

Only on this condition [of world government] can moral precepts have instrumental meaning in international affairs. For the condition presupposes that some minimal code of ethics and law for the entire world community will be accepted by, and can therefore be enforced upon, all mankind—not through the coercion of states by states, which always means war, but through the effective application of the rules of law to individuals, which sometimes means peace, order, and justice.

[88] *Id., The Commonwealth of Man:* an Inquiry Into Power Politics and World Government (New York: Knopf, 1952), 38.
[89] *Ibid.,* 107, 485.
[90] *Ibid.,* 489–92.

In the absence of such a revolution in attitudes, policies, and institutional arrangements, all national action in world affairs indicated by "morals" rather than by "interest" threatens the betrayal of the interests which are thus ignored and the destruction of the morals which are thus sought to be vindicated.[91]

Emery Reves

Because of his skepticism that a nation can transcend its own self-interest or harmonize it with that of others, Emery Reves also advocates the abolition of national sovereignties. The only other alternative would be to reduce contact between them to a minimum for the sake of a somewhat longer period without war; but really violent conflicts are inevitable "until sovereign institutions are integrated into higher institutions expressing directly the sovereignty of the community." [92] "Delegates of fifty sovereign nations meeting in a council and defending their own national interests, will never arrive at a satisfactory solution and settlement of any problem concerning the interrelations of the sovereign national units." He describes the nation-states as modern feudal lords desperately trying to preserve their "accumulated and abused privileges and power to the detriment of the peoples they oppress."

Reves declares Christianity to be a failure as a civilizing force in society; "two thousand years is time enough to judge the efficacy of a method, no matter how valuable the doctrine." [93] It has succeeded in creating only a thin veneer of ethical conduct which the social eruptions of the twentieth century have blasted away. The "age-old superstitions and venerable symbols" which were used to propagate ideals centuries ago have been destroyed by modern science. "Just as prayer, sermons, and ritual are inadequate to

[91] *Id.,* "International Ideals and the National Interest," 36.

[92] Emery Reves, *The Anatomy of Peace* (New York: Harper & Bros., 1945), 213–14, 222. Reves, a naturalized Englishman, the president of Co-operation Press Service, has a doctorate in political economy from Zurich University.

[93] *Ibid.,* 77–79.

impose upon mankind a social conduct based on principles, so pledges, declarations, and promises are inadequate to achieve the same purpose. . . . Man can become a conscious and constructive social being only if society imposes upon him certain principles in the form of a legal order." He charges that all churches have abandoned universalism by adapting to nationalism; their principles are now valid only within segregated groups of people.[94] His conclusion about the nature of man would indicate that human beings will be difficult to curb even in a world state since they are "exceptionally perverted and ferocious creatures, capable of murdering, torturing, persecuting, and exploiting each other more ruthlessly than any other species in this world." [95]

In his analysis he shows that internationalism has been an erroneous notion from its inception since it means "between nationalisms"; it tries to alleviate the symptoms of a sick world without treating the disease. He characterizes nationalism as "a collective inferiority complex, that gives comforting reactions to individual fear, loneliness, weakness, inability, insecurity, helplessness, seeking refuge in exaggerated consciousness and pride of belonging to a certain group of people." [96] Since the League of Nations with its "Wilsonism" was based upon the assumption that peace could prevail among nations, it was bound to fail regardless of its procedures or the attitudes adopted by the members. Because democracy means sovereignty of the people, it cannot exist in a world where the sovereignty of each group tends to cancel out the sovereignty of the others.[97] In fact, the nation-states are refusing people their most elementary freedom of movement, since they chain them to the soil of their homeland. Industrialism inevitably conflicts with nationalism, since it embraces the whole globe in its needs for raw materials and for markets.[98] Peace treaties and alliances merely

[94] *Ibid.*, 80–81.
[95] *Ibid.*, 129.
[96] *Ibid.*, 186.
[97] *Ibid.*, 162.
[98] *Ibid.*, 133–34.

divide the world arbitrarily into a number of sovereign social units, and try to prevent any change in the status quo "except by unanimous consent, which makes no sense, or by force, which makes war." [99]

The inclusion of Emery Reves among the Realists might be challenged because his solutions are at such variance with those of other members of the school. Perhaps this illustrates the diverse possibilities to which the original premise, that a nation cannot transcend its own selfish interest, can lead. Irving L. Horowitz comments upon Reves' political fanaticism as an attempt "to banish the real and objective conditions men find themselves in. . . . Any attempt forcefully to impose international association on a nation or a people or a race will result in failure because peace like a social system cannot be exported." [100]

Ernst B. Haas

Ernst B. Haas, the last Realist to be treated in this survey, really represents a bridge between that school and the Idealists. In an analysis of various collective security methods, he recommends that the United Nations become the balancer in which regional systems would negotiate and compromise.[101] While not discrediting the traditional approach, he shows that pre-existing conditions make impossible the operation of some of the concepts today; as a solution, he proposes a theory, not predicated on selflessness, but still capable of achieving collective security and of promoting the national interest.

In the past experience with collective security, two ideological concepts have been present: the notion of universal moral obliga-

[99] *Ibid.*, 209.

[100] Irving L. Horowitz, *The Idea of War and Peace in Contemporary Philosophy* (New York: Paine-Whitman, 1957), 148–50.

[101] Ernst B. Haas, "Types of Collective Security," *American Political Science Review*, XLIX (March, 1955), 40–62. Haas teaches at the University of California, Berkeley.

tion in the League Covenant, and the concert of big powers explicit in the United Nations Charter. He shows that both failed to result in the peace expected, because the institutions were based upon assumptions which erred in not coinciding with the actual values and conduct of the member states, who merely paid lip-service. The League called for voluntary national association and collective judgment as the key, presuming that all nations were convinced that peace and stability were preferable to war and anarchy. The United Nations was less demanding, since collective action was to follow the unanimous will of the five great powers supported by two smaller states. This supposed an identity of policy aims among the great powers or the conviction that they would settle their differences privately.

Under the current impasse, Haas suggests two alternative schemes, permissive enforcement and the concept of balancing, though he really advocates only the latter. These are derived from the operations of the United Nations, and as such reflect the ends and conflicts of national policy, and the manner in which they are being reconciled. They more or less ignore the convictions of en-thusiastic internationalists, but they imply values in maintaining a precarious coexistence of the two major power blocs within a uni-versal collective security organization.

Permissive enforcement,[102] evidenced in the Korea action and in the Uniting for Peace Resolution, gives the Assembly permission to recommend, not order, collective action in which participation by the various nations is optional. Rather than involve the organiza-tion directly, this allows for delegated power to the members who are willing to use their armed forces. This type of arrangement, initiated by the United States, has had little support from other countries since 1950; it seems to require a sense of emergency and global identification with anti-Communist aims of the United States. Fear of nuclear weapons makes its future less promising.

The concept of balancing, on the other hand, would use the United Nations forum as an agency of conciliation and mediation

[102] *Ibid.*, 47–54.

in ameliorating the Cold War.[103] It recognizes the *de facto* polarization of nations into American and Soviet blocs, so it minimizes use of the Security Council, and proposes that the uncommitted blocs (as Arab-Asian) provide the initiative in bringing the antagonists together for compromise. The super-powers are likely to take seriously the balancing efforts, not because of good will, but out of reluctance to alienate allies or offend important neutrals. Allowing for Russia's resistance to a "roll back" of the Iron Curtain, and for her continuance of ideological subversion, he forecasts that Russia would wish to avoid a major war and to prevent further U.N. alliance against Communism by remaining in the organization where she can "unmask imperialist designs." NATO allies of the United States might also be a balancer in watering down American aspirations. This method would depend on the "built-in restraint" among the super powers who would not wish to forego the advantages of having their national policies approved by the General Assembly. The Arab-Asian states seem to favor this idea since they oppose permissive enforcement, but they are strong advocates of East-West rapprochement.

Mr. Haas epitomizes the choice as one between a rump organization dedicated to the West's victory over Communism, and a universal organization seeking to avoid war between the two camps through multilateral diplomacy within the Charter framework, as was used in the settlement of the Korean War.[104] He points out that the balancing concept transcends the "age-old and unproductive conflict between 'realism' and 'idealism' in world organization." While it is true that in taking the "is" for granted, the "ought" of normative principles is pushed into the background, still it imposes restraint upon the potential belligerents through their respect for the Charter. Although these Charter provisions be invoked only for the sake of rhetoric, still the powers will use moderation so long as their acts might result in undesirable propaganda.

[103] *Ibid.*, 54–56.
[104] *Ibid.*, 60–61.

"Balancing" remains within the procedural framework of United Nations, but it resembles traditional diplomacy more than Wilsonian devices. It would depend upon regional military strength, closed conciliation efforts rather than Security Council or Assembly inquiries, neutral truce supervision, and plebiscite activities.[105] The success of these operations might tilt the scales in favor of such multilateral compromise in preference to unilateralism. The United Nations would thus be the "balancer" in the Cold War.

[105] *Ibid.*, 61–62.

* II *

American History According to the Realists

THE Realist historians accentuate the pursuit of self-interest where it is to be found in America's record, and deplore the situations in which it did not find primacy. Sometimes they probe beneath what they claim are altruistic disguises, and elevate self-interested motives to the position of dominance which they believe they actually held. Because of their insistence that practical men accommodate the definition of justice and charity to suit the nation's immediate advantage, they tend to discredit as gullible and visionary statesmen who conformed their actions to the demands of their ideals. Apologizing for what they are sure was naïveté, they attribute these mistakes to political immaturity in America's "age of innocence." Since this leading world power can no longer pass for an infant or even an adolescent, they prescribe the course which hard-headed Realism indicates for the nation's present and future behavior.

The three writers selected for this survey are Charles A. Beard, George F. Kennan, and Hans J. Morgenthau. Their summaries of American history will be pursued in the above-mentioned order because the periods of their concentration fall chronologically into that scheme.

Charles A. Beard

Charles A. Beard's interest in the debate centers upon three dominant strains: the importance of commerce, the various types of territorial expansion, and criticism of internationalism. National interest will be discussed largely in terms of economics; his view of reality presupposes man's subservience to the processes of production, distribution, and consumption of wealth.

In *The Federalist* papers, he sees a clear-cut philosophy of *Machtpolitik*, a secular view of the motives prompting governments in their international relations.[1] As evidence of this he cites John Jay's statement in the fourth paper:

It is too true, however disgraceful it may be to human nature, that nations will make war whenever they have a prospect of getting anything by it; nay that absolute monarchs will often make war when their nations are to get nothing by it, but for purposes and objects merely personal, such as a thirst for military glory, revenge for personal affronts, ambition, or private compacts to aggrandize or support their particular families, or partisans.

He attributes to Jay insight into the fact that conflicts of economics, such as those over fisheries, China trade, and navigation of the Mississippi and St. Lawrence rivers, were the root of international rivalries; only a strong government could deter countries from resorting to war for gain.

Although America's leaders in the early period understood the role of force in serving national interest, the occasions for application were shunted aside because of the preoccupation of people and of capital with westward expansion and continental development.[2] For almost a hundred years the nation did not

. . . employ the engines of diplomacy and force for the purpose of doing good to other peoples by interfering with their domestic and

[1] Beard, *Idea of National Interest,* 34–35, 116.
[2] *Ibid.,* 154–55.

international quarrels, by imposing upon them American systems of economy, politics, and morals, and by withholding recognition from *de facto* governments whose theories and principles were not pleasing to the administration in Washington. The idea was foreign to the conceptions of the Fathers who founded the Republic.[3]

Without passing judgment on the virtue of governments thrown up by revolutions and war, the United States gave them recognition, though it sometimes acted with greater speed toward a new republic. Although the Monroe Doctrine suggested some element of Idealism, the attitude toward other countries in the western hemisphere was more negative than positive, and the Doctrine's real purpose was the United States' interest in self-preservation. Beard finds no transcendent philosophy of national interest for determining the relationship of lesser and particular interests to that of the whole; as revealed by the state papers, the concept of national interest is an "aggregation of particularities assembled like eggs in a basket." [4] He judges that all the early political parties agreed upon the importance of commerce for different reasons.

As distinct from the Jeffersonians, the "Federalist-Whig-Republican" succession afforded protection to manufacturing, lent aid to shipping, promoted an effective navy, acquired naval bases and outlying points for trade, and gave frank endorsement to what later became known as "dollar diplomacy." Alexander Hamilton's encouragement of manufacturing in the interest of all parts of the Union, as well as his desire for peace as a necessary condition for strengthening the internal economy, is well known.

The Jeffersonians, as agrarians, were interested in commerce to the extent of securing markets for their agricultural products and of buying manufactured products at the lowest cost. However, they were strongly averse to aids for shipping, banking affiliations, tariffs, a powerful navy, and overseas territories for the support of trade. Jefferson thought that only farmers truly repre-

[3] *Ibid.*, 358–59.
[4] *Ibid.*, 167.

sented American sentiments. Beard sums up Jefferson's attitude in this way:

Traders, investors, and manufacturers . . . were not attached to the soil by bonds of interest and affection but were mobile and connected with similar groups in foreign countries; for this reason they were often prepared to sacrifice the country to their particular advantage—momentary gain. . . . Agriculture moreover gave the nation a high degree of self-sufficiency and independence and made it possible for its government to avoid the intrigues, entanglements, and collisions common to European powers.[5]

Although Jefferson considered great urban centers as "sores on the body politic" and thought trade would be accompanied by practices detrimental to morals, Beard felt that he changed his attitude in the course of the Napoleonic wars which disrupted American commerce and ruined many agriculturists.[6] He admitted then that manufacturing was as necessary to independence as it was to comfort.

James Madison encouraged a provident policy of developing industries necessary for defense and primary wants; here exception was to be made to the general rule of "consulting cheapness alone." When memories of the twenty-three year period of French-centered war had faded away, and again American agricultural products were carried overseas, the Democrats abandoned the later thinking of Jefferson and Madison. They were led by the cotton planters who regarded protection only as a scheme of vested and private interests.[7]

Territorial expansion as a concept of national interest prevailed for more than a hundred years, whether under the slogan "manifest destiny" or "moral obligation to benighted peoples." The Jeffersonian approach favored the acquisition of unoccupied, contiguous regions to be exploited by free American farmers or by

[5] *Ibid.*, 53–54.
[6] *Ibid.*, 317.
[7] *Ibid.*, 320.

planters with slave labor; it opposed the annexation of far-flung regions inhabited by races which could not be assimilated easily and which would require naval protection and involvement in European imperial wars.[8] However, Jefferson did not seem averse to expansion north and south on the American continents so long as the area, such as Cuba, could be defended without a navy.[9]

The Hamiltonian concept of national interest opposed westward continental expansion, lest the new area occupied by farmers overbalance the eastern commercial interests. In contrast, it supported the acquisition of distant naval bases and markets, even if these territories were inhabited by races which could not easily be assimilated. This policy would be carried forward even more under the second Republican party.[10] The cleavage between agrarian and commercial interests was evident in regard to the Louisiana Purchase and the annexation of Florida, of Texas, and of the Mexican Cession territory to the Pacific. Until the Civil War the agrarian Democratic interests won out, but afterward the commercial type of territorial expansion held dominance. It was foreshadowed in the designs relating to the Orient in the 1850's, accomplished in the purchase of Alaska, and attempted in Grant's overtures to acquire Santo Domingo. Grant used the language of commerce almost exclusively in advocating acquisition of the latter, when he addressed his message to Congress December 5, 1870, but he also intimated that the Islands could be used for emigration of American Negroes who would find "a genial home where their civil rights would not be disputed." [11]

The first expedition of interference in the affairs of other peoples for the sake of improving their manners and morals came in the action on Samoa. Beard observes that President Cleveland found this inconsistent "with the mission and traditions of the United States," and that Secretary of State Gresham had stated that restraint of such

[8] *Ibid.*, 549.
[9] *Ibid.*, 54.
[10] *Ibid.*, 550–51.
[11] *Ibid.*, 64.

a propensity was the part of wisdom as well as duty in order to show "the strength, the moderation, and the beneficence of popular government." [12]

Beard points to the documentary evidence which makes highly probable the hypothesis that Cuba would have obtained its independence by pressure on Spain, had President McKinley's administration chosen that course. But this method would not have given the United States a naval base at Guantanamo which commands the Windward passage, nor an occasion for annexing Puerto Rico which commands the Mona passage, nor an opportunity to acquire the Philippines as a naval base and stepping stone to commerce in the Orient.[13] There was confusion in the minds of officialdom and the public; the war sentiment voiced only sympathy for the heroic Cubans whose struggle for their independence recalled America's experience a hundred years before, but the outcome of conformity "to the pattern of commercial and naval expansion could not have been neater, had it been deliberately planned." In the matter of Hawaii's annexation, he finds two motives predominant, "the strategic value of the Islands and the close relation of their economic structure to America's interests." [14]

To substantiate his judgment of the Spanish-American War, Beard cites letters of Assistant Secretary of Navy Theodore Roosevelt written six months before the war, indicating action to be taken in the Pacific "if things looked menacing about Spain." [15] A month after the opening of the war Senator Henry Cabot Lodge had replied to Roosevelt in confidence, that the administration was at last grasping his whole policy and that the United States meant to have Puerto Rico. Beard notes that only after the war did McKinley specifically renounce national interest (consisting of investments, commerce, and national defense), in favor of moral obligation. After quoting another historian's judgment that McKinley was

[12] *Ibid.*, 364–65.
[13] *Ibid.*, 68.
[14] *Ibid.*, 71.
[15] *Ibid.*, 80–81.

moved by the apostolic injunction, "now we that are strong ought to bear the infirmities of the weak and not to please ourselves," Beard cites evidence to support his case that Theodore Roosevelt approved war as a good in itself for regenerating the fibre of a people growing soft.[16] According to private correspondence with German Ambassador Sternberg, reported in December, 1899, Roosevelt was supposed to have declared that he had worked to bring about a war, and for more than ten years it had been his ambition to take part in one.

Beard does credit Roosevelt with motives greater than narrow self-interest, nevertheless. He quotes liberally from the President's annual message of 1906 in which he denies that it is a sign of hypocrisy when a nation advances ethical reasons for its actions.

It is neither wise nor right for a nation to disregard its own needs, and it is foolish—and maybe wicked—to think that other nations will disregard theirs. But it is wicked for a nation to regard only its own interest, and foolish to believe that such is the sole motive that actuates any other nation.[17]

Beard approves the fact that in the former Spanish colonies, peace, justice, and liberty were advanced, education was fostered, self-government was enlarged, "religious fanatics" were put down, the living standard was raised, public works were constructed, industry and investment were enlarged, and material advantages were gained by Americans.

Of the proponents of dollar diplomacy, Beard says:

Like Hamilton, its sponsors rejected sentimentality and generosity in diplomacy and permitted the exercise of beneficence only where the exercise coincided with American interest. But unlike Hamilton they did not make the rule universal, for they spoke of the "traditional friendship of the English-speaking peoples"—a sentiment which could be indulged in safely only where there was no evident conflict of interests and inexorable competition in commerce.[18]

[16] *Ibid.*, 370–72.
[17] *Ibid.*, 374.
[18] *Ibid.*, 111.

He sees the Republican industrial leadership as handicapped in pursuit of *Machtpolitik* almost from its very inception, since it inherited an agrarian wing at the Compromise of 1860 in Chicago when "free homesteads were exchanged for a protective tariff." [19] It could take naval bases if they were few in number and if the action were encased with sentiments of moral obligation. It could interfere in China, but yet not participate in the unashamed division and spoliation practiced by the other powers. He points out that after World War I, the Washington and London conferences seemed to make *Machtpolitik* too dangerous for any of the subscribing powers.

Beard quotes President Taft's plea for national unity in foreign affairs on the part of the intellectual, financial, industrial, labor and farm elements in the population. Then he gives a cynical evaluation:

President Taft's call for national solidarity in the enforcement of national interest and a similar appeal by President Coolidge in later years were demands for support for their particular interpretations of that interest, and had no higher or greater claim upon the nation than President Wilson's insistence on his League of Nations program. A claim to higher validity is an assertion, not an axiom.[20]

In Woodrow Wilson, Beard finds a complete repudiation of the Federalist-Whig-Republican tradition, both in domestic and international policies. On the home front, for the first time since the Civil War, the tariff was reduced considerably, corporate and individual incomes were taxed heavily, agriculture was favored by the Farm Loan Act, industrial combinations were attacked under the Clayton Anti-Trust Law, opportunities to push trade and investment in China were thwarted with the result that Japan used the occasion to disregard the open door policy and impose the twenty-one demands.[21] On the international scene Wilson's

[19] *Ibid.*, 143–44.
[20] *Ibid.*, 120.
[21] *Ibid.*, 121–22.

reversals included removal of trade barriers ardent championing of freedom of the seas, renunciation of annexations, replacement of imperialist exploitation by the establishment of a mandate system, the promise of independence to the Philippines by the Jones Act of 1916, a reduction of armaments, renunciation of war "as an instrument of commerce and expansion," and formation of a League of Nations to reorganize the world community "and to stabilize the existing political distribution of the earth's backward places and peoples." [22]

Wilson wished to spread democratic theories rather than to use government to advance economic interests; he trusted that commerce would flow naturally as a consequence of peace and stability. He was courageous enough to point out the selfishness of Americans when their own interests were at stake, a contradiction to their sympathy for freedom and equity everywhere. Beard quotes Wilson's statement to illustrate better why the Senate forces marshalled themselves against him with such determination:

We have shown ourselves kin to all the world, when it came to pushing an advantage. . . . Our action against Spain in the Floridas, and against Mexico on the coasts of the Pacific, and then with the French, with regard to the control of the Mississippi; the unpitying force with which we thrust the Indians to the wall, wherever they have stood in the way, have suited our professions of peacefulness and justice no more than the aggressions of other nations that were strong and not to be gainsaid.[23]

Beard proposes that the opposition of Wilson's foreign policy to the Federalist-Whig-Republican tradition is conclusively demonstrated by Senator Lodge's management of the Senate rejection:

Since these measures and policies broke in upon the course of commercial and territorial expansion pursued under Federalist-Whig-Republican auspices, it was natural that leadership in defeating President Wilson's program should be taken by Senator Lodge, early formulator

[22] *Ibid.*, 122.
[23] *Ibid.*, 124, quoting from Ray Stannard Baker, *Woodrow Wilson: Life and Letters* (New York: Doubleday, Doran, 1931), IV, 423-24.

of the imperial program finally adopted by President McKinley, opponent of Philippine independence, high tariff advocate, and confidant of Admiral Mahan, the author of *Machtpolitik* on the high seas. Nor was it an accident that a large part of the money which financed the campaign to defeat the League of Nations was furnished by two great Republican industrialists—Henry C. Frick and Andrew D. Mellon— the latter on the solicitation of Senator Knox, the exponent of dollar diplomacy. Something more than the abstractions of peace were at stake in the formulas of the League of Nations Covenant.[24]

Of Warren G. Harding, Beard observes that while he objected to Wilson's "moral internationalism," as a Senator he gave orations on America's role in the Philippines to contribute to the weal of humanity and "to go on with the same thought that impelled Him who brought a plan of salvation to the earth." [25] For reinstating dollar diplomacy and isolation as national interest, he finds that the Republicans through the 1920's paid a heavy price. For Japan's apparent relinquishment of supremacy in China, the United States agreed to naval restrictions at the Washington and London conferences which made Japan supreme in its own waters, and this country bound itself not to construct great fortifications in the Philippines. The United States further surrendered sea power by accepting an equality with Great Britain, and in subsequently failing to build up to the established ratio because of agrarian opposition in Congress. The government tied its hands in commercial expansion by renunciation of war as an instrument of policy, with confidence that others like Japan would observe their pledges.[26]

With the appearance of Franklin D. Roosevelt, Beard sees a completely different attitude toward the place of foreign trade in national interest. Looking back with historical perspective, he finds dominant from the time of the Constitution to the end of President Hoover's administration, a heavy reliance upon foreign mar-

---

[24] *Ibid.*, 126.
[25] *Ibid.*, 380–81, quoting from W. F. Johnson, *The Life of Warren G. Harding*, 172–78.
[26] *Ibid.*, 151–52.

kets, on the assumption that this was "*necessary* to prevent gluts of surpluses at home" and that a continuous dilation was possible of attainment. Even the Jeffersonians had supported some of this theory as a means of marketing agricultural products and of securing cheap manufactures; it conformed to the Manchester school of political economy, especially to the idea of Cobden and Bright. But with the collapse of the economic structure in 1929, a new approach was adopted, "a conception that a high standard of national well-being is possible with a minimum reliance on foreign trade and is desirable besides."[27] The central idea of Franklin D. Roosevelt was to be, "by domestic planning and control the American economic machine may be kept running at a high tempo supplying the intranational market, without relying primarily upon foreign outlets for 'surpluses' of goods and capital."[28]

At this point of Beard's historical writing, his approval of the Roosevelt policies ceases, since the administration abandoned the above in short order and involved itself in internationalism of which he strongly disapproved. The thesis which he takes under consideration in *American Foreign Policy in the Making 1932–40* is this:

. . . the President was convinced that collaborative intervention in the conflict of Europe and Asia was the right policy but the American people, with contemptible stubbornness, clung to an opposite doctrine —non-intervention and neutrality despite the wars raging in Europe and Asia.[29]

The implication in the above is that public opinion in hampering the President, was really responsible for the catastrophe at Pearl Harbor.

Beard questions in precisely what public documents the President and Secretary of State tried to educate public opinion. In his investigation of Roosevelt's early years as President, he finds him

[27] *Ibid.*, 545–46.
[28] *Ibid.*, 552.
[29] *Id., American Foreign Policy in the Making 1932–40: a Study in Responsibilities* (New Haven: Yale University Press, 1946), 27.

anything but an internationalist. He cites Roosevelt's address to the New York State Grange on February 2, 1932, two days after William Randolph Hearst's invitation to him to repudiate the League of Nations:

But the League of Nations today is not the League conceived by Woodrow Wilson. It might have been, had the United States joined. Too often through these years, its major function has been not the broad overwhelming purpose of peace, but rather a mere meeting place for the political discussion of strictly European political national difficulties. In these the United States should have no part. . . . Because of these facts, therefore, I do not favor American participation.[30]

In addition to this "self-indictment," he notes that Joseph Tumulty, former secretary of Wilson, charged Roosevelt with expediency in trying to win the nomination for the presidency in 1932 by opposing the League. Raymond Moley told of Roosevelt's decision to sidetrack in the campaign the idea of a speech on foreign relations. The President's references to Wilson as a great leader did not manifest sympathy for internationalism as such. In regard to the World Economic Conference, he showed open hostility since he did not believe the depression could be conquered by international measures.[31] The Recovery Act of 1933 demonstrated his predisposition to protective tariff; on his own motion or on the application of any labor, industrial or trade organization, the President could direct inquiry into whether a foreign import was cutting into maintenance of hour-wage-price codes: he could then prescribe limitation of the import if necessary.[32] He paid little heed to Cordell Hull's urging that tariff cuts would result in a general rise of standard of living throughout the world and an advance in the cause of peace. In Roosevelt's message of March 2, 1934,

[30] *Ibid.*, 76, quoting from *Public Papers of Franklin D. Roosevelt, Forty-Eighth Governor of the State of New York, Second Term 1932* (New York: State Government of New York, 1939), 551.

[31] *Ibid.*, 76, 102–03, 130. He cites Raymond Moley, *After Seven Years*, 47 ff., 62, 196–296.

[32] *Ibid.*, 150.

which eventuated in the Reciprocal Tariff Act, he outlined only a program of promoting American agriculture and industry by "cautious bargaining with commercial rivals abroad." [33]

Beard finds in the President's nonrecognition of Japan and Manchukuo no sign that he contemplated further action alone or with others. In according recognition to Russia in 1933, he departed from Wilson's policy of outlawing governments whose political and economic institutions were contrary to American standards of morality and propriety. Beard uncovers the explanation for this recognition in the fact that the depression-ridden economy needed every avenue of commerce available, and in the fact that the recovery of Russia as a check upon Japan was in accord with his notions of the Stimson Doctrine in the Far East.[34]

Of Roosevelt's urging that the embargo on munitions be repealed, Beard points out the President's promise to the people that such an act would enable the United States to remain at peace longer than if the embargo stood. Though both political parties in 1940 pledged aid to peace-loving peoples in their fight against aggressors, the Republicans provided that this should not be in violation of international law. The Democrats promised aid "consistent with law" and this, according to Beard, "left the way open for the Government of the United States to make its own law—if need be, in defiance of international law—and supply one or more of the belligerents with munitions, money, food, or anything else at public expense—a form of action directly contrary to international law." [35]

Mr. Beard finds many discrepancies between "official representations and official realities" in foreign affairs of 1941. He summarizes thus the way such inconsistencies are supposed to be justified:

The great end which President Roosevelt discerned and chose justified the means which he employed. As a far-sighted statesman he early discovered that unless the United States entered the war raging in

[33] *Ibid.*, 159.
[34] *Ibid.*, 144–46.
[35] *Ibid.*, 236, 294–95.

Europe, Hitler would be victorious, and the United States, facing alone this monstrous totalitarian power, would become a victim of its merciless ideology and its despotic militarism. According to this interpretation, it was a question of democracy, the Four Freedoms, the noble principles of the Atlantic Charter, and world security on the one side; of totalitarianism, consummate despotism, and military subjugation on the other side. Since the American people were so smug in their conceit, so ignorant of foreign affairs, and so isolationist in sentiment that they could not themselves see the reality of this terrible threat to their own safety and a necessity to meet it by resort to war, President Roosevelt had to dissemble to be reelected in 1940 as against Wendell Willkie, then the anti-war candidate of the Republicans on an anti-war platform.[36]

In answer to this defense of the President's "clairvoyance" and the maintenance of a noninvolvement appearance because of vigorous congressional opposition to war, Beard states:

With regard to consequences in foreign affairs, the noble principles of the Four Freedoms and the Atlantic Charter were, for practical purposes discarded in the settlements which accompanied the progress, and followed the conclusion of the war. To the validity of this statement the treatment of peoples in Estonia, Lithuania, Poland, Rumania, Yugoslavia, China, Indo-China, Indonesia, Italy, Germany and other places of the earth bear witness. . . . Since as a consequence of the war called "necessary" to overthrow Hitler's despotism, another despotism was raised to a higher pitch of power, how can it be argued conclusively with reference to inescapable facts that the "end" justified the means employed to involve the United States in that war? [37]

Domestically, Beard sees ill consequences also in that it actually transformed the United States into an armed camp with a permanent conscript army, a huge national debt, grinding taxes, and vast outlays for armaments.[38] This permanently barred the reforms at home from which Roosevelt had to turn his attention. Two years

[36] *Id., President Roosevelt and the Coming of the War* (New Haven: Yale University Press, 1948), 574.
[37] *Ibid.*, 576.
[38] *Ibid.*, 579–80.

after the "nominal close" of the war, Beard found it almost academic to discuss domestic affairs at all, since everything was subordinate to foreign commitments. He criticizes President Truman's actions in 1947 whereby the United States "set out on an unlimited program of underwriting, by money and military 'advice,' poverty-stricken, feeble, and instable governments around the edges of the gigantic and aggressive Slavic Empire." His doleful conclusion is that the domestic affairs have become mere appendages dependent upon the needs of an indefinite number of governments for an indefinite measure of time.

George F. Kennan

Reviewing national interest historically, George Kennan discovers only two functions in the original intention of American society: assurance of the national security and promotion of private American activity abroad.[39] America was concerned with the foreign environment only inasmuch as it be favorable to her working out her own domestic convictions. There were no messianic tendencies, no proposing "ideological answers to everybody else's problems." But since the nation followed the latter pattern with the approach of the twentieth century, he turns his full attention to diplomatic history from the Spanish-American War to the present.

Admitting that records are indefinite as to what communication passed between the administration and Dewey prior to the battle of Manila, he still estimates that there was intrigue "which received absolution, forgiveness, and a sort of public blessing by virtue of war hysteria." [40] Had a thrilling victory not been won, he surmises the main figures might have been involved in an unpleasant congressional investigation. Kennan finds the argument that if the United States had not taken the territories, someone else would have, substantial only in regard to the Philippines, not to Puerto

[39] Kennan, *Realities*, 12–13.
[40] *Id., American Diplomacy*, 14.

Rico and Hawaii. Of all the explanations given by the expansionists of 1898, he suspects none was the real one—namely, that the American people of that day "simply liked the smell of empire and felt an urge to range themselves among the colonial powers of the time, to see our flag flying on distant tropical isles, to feel the thrill of foreign adventure and authority, to bask in the sunshine of recognition as one of the great imperial powers of the world." Yet simultaneously he recognizes the sincerity and logic of the anti-imperialists who contended that "a country which traces its political philosophy to the concept of the social compact has no business taking responsibility for people who have no place in that concept and who are supposed to appear on the scene in the role of subjects and not of citizens." [41]

The decision to rule Hawaii turned out well because Americans were able to dominate the situation, "because the native way of life was engulfed and reduced, as was the case with our American Indians, to the helpless ignominy of tourist entertainment." [42] But in the Philippines, on the contrary, the most ardent protagonist of the venture, Theodore Roosevelt, was in a few years wishing to be rid of them. Kennan sees the decision to set free the Philippines in any but an altruistic light. Instead of feeling the obligation to give them freedom for which they were prepared, the powerful private interests urged ridding the nation of this inconvenience of economic intimacy attendant upon their position under the American flag. He concludes that America was not prepared to endure even the "rudimentary sacrifices implied in 'the white man's burden.' " If the lesson to be learned from this episode is that the American system can be applied to only one kind of people who have the same kind of spirit and institutions as its citizens, then the United States should beware of accepting any "paternalistic responsibility" even in the form of military occupation for any period longer than is absolutely necessary.[43]

[41] *Ibid.*, 17.
[42] *Ibid.*, 18.
[43] *Ibid.*, 19.

Writing of the Open Door formula, Kennan is convinced John Hay did not understand its practical significance. One of his assistants had "bought it sight unseen" from an Englishman; it was erroneously believed to represent the current British policy, though it was actually an antiquated approach with no future.[44] Nor were Americans concerned enough about it to accept any particular responsibility. The device had an idealistic ring and it was hard to see what harm would come from trying it; besides it would improve the popularity of the administration's foreign policy at the coming election. Neither its obvious lack of practical results nor the subsequent departure from the policy served to shake the myth thus established that the Open Door notes had struck a tremendous blow for the triumph of American principles in international society. For forty years the Open Door and preservation of territorial integrity in China would be advanced by American diplomats for public adherence; the replies would be relayed to the citizens as acknowledgments of the justice of their view and as pledges to reform.

In no instance would we admit that this sort of intervention in the affairs of the other powers in China carried with it any specific responsibility for us or placed us under obligation to anybody or anything but our own consciences. In no instance would we be prepared to use force to compel compliance with these principles or to protect individual powers if they complied with them and others failed to do so. . . . these terms were not clear and precise ones which could usefully be made the basis of foreign policy.[45]

Without predicting that Pearl Harbor might have been avoided had the United States been more circumspect through the decades in considering Japan's requirements with the expanding population, etc., Mr. Kennan does think the course of events might have been altered somewhat by American "recognition of power realities in the Orient as a factor worthy of our serious respect," and by

[44] *Ibid.*, 35–36.
[45] *Ibid.*, 38, 45.

paying attention to stability and quietness there as much as to "legal and moral tidiness." [46] In its approach to the Orient, America showed none of the inhibitions which affected her relations with Europe; the eastern affairs were not dismissed as of no moment:

On the other hand, we find no greater readiness so far, to admit the validity and legitimacy of power realities and aspirations, to accept them without feeling the obligation of moral judgment, to take them as existing and unalterable human forces, neither good nor bad, and to seek their point of maximum equilibrium rather than their reform or their repression. . . . But it would seem that a nation which admits that its own capacity for assimilation is limited once you get beyond the peoples of Caucasian origin should observe a special reserve in its dealings with other peoples and in its hopes for intimacy of association with them . . . if . . . instead of making ourselves slaves of the concepts of international law and morality, we could confine these concepts to the unobtrusive, almost feminine function of the gentle civilizer of national self-interest in which they find their true value—if we were able to do these things in our dealings with the peoples of the East, then, I think posterity might look back upon our efforts with fewer and less troubled questions.[47]

Kennan traces to Woodrow Wilson's notion that there was something not quite right about being a great nation, much of his belief in self-determination, and his ideas about the Balkanization of eastern Europe with the breakup of the Austro-Hungarian empire.[48] His judgments about America's entrance into the war and its decisions in the peace are quite pitiless. He would grant that saving the British from final defeat would be a valid ground for intervention, but if this was the real motive it should have been frankly expressed so that the country could refrain from the attitude of a crusade with its moralistic slogans, could have negotiated with the enemy and not have broken up empires and overthrown political systems, could have avoided commitments to extreme allied war

[46] *Ibid.*, 50–51.
[47] *Ibid.*, 53–54.
[48] *Id., Realities*, 40.

aims, and could have used its bargaining power to end hostilities "with a minimum prejudice to the future stability of the Continent." [49]

Truly, this was a peace which had the tragedies of the future written into it as by the devil's own hand. . . . And this was the sort of peace you got when you allowed war hysteria and impractical idealism to lie down together in your mind, like the lion and the lamb; when you indulged yourself in the collosal conceit of thinking that you could suddenly make international life over into what you believed to be your own image; when you dismissed the past with contempt, rejected the relevance of the past to the future, and refused to occupy yourself with the real problems that a study of the past would suggest. [50]

To those who charge that he fails in his professed Realism when he suggests that from the standpoint of public opinion in 1913 it would have been possible to get the American people to vote money for armaments and to enter a war "as a cold calculation about the balance of power elsewhere," he replies that political leaders might have made greater efforts to inform the people of the true facts, and the people might even have understood them. If it is true that Americans must clothe "their military efforts in the language of idealism" and persuade themselves that the necessity of fighting on foreign soil can only be justified if it ends with a settlement of these affairs once and for all, he answers:

A nation which excuses its own failures by the sacred untouchableness of its own habits can excuse itself into complete disaster. . . . If it was the workings of our democracy that were inadequate in the past, let us say so. [51]

In the twentieth century, Kennan finds a tendency among many Americans to use the arbitral principle beyond its capabilities. Of the ninety-seven international agreements by the United States dealing with arbitration and conciliation from 1900 to the 1930's,

[49] *Id., American Diplomacy,* 71–72.
[50] *Ibid.,* 69.
[51] *Ibid.,* 73.

only two were invoked; every one of them negotiated by Secretaries Bryan, Kellogg, and Stimson remained barren. Of the Kellogg Pact he says, "competing groups of well-meaning peace enthusiasts in our country succeeded in needling two harried Foreign Ministers, M. Briand and Mr. Kellogg, into an embarrassing involvement from which the latter could see no graceful exit." [52] Because of these utopian distractions, attention had been diverted earlier from the real problems like the Russo-Japanese War, the Balkan situation, and the tension between England and Germany.

America's decision not to enter the Second World War until an overt action occasioned it, he likens to the behavior before the First World War when the declaration of unrestricted submarine warfare became the *causa belli*. He remarks the change in emotional attitude once the country is formally involved.

Theoretically, if the issues involved in the European struggle were really as vital to us as we persuaded ourselves they were in the years 1942–45, they were surely no less important from 1939 to 1941. Actually in that earlier period, before the German attack on Russia, the cause of the British and French could really be called the cause of freedom and democracy, for very little else was involved on the western side.[53]

With due allowance for the opinion-forming process, he sees in the emotional fervor stirred up, when participation alongside the Soviet really made the cause ambiguous, an illustration less of objective understanding of the issues and more of irritation at being provoked to take up arms. He mentions this punitive note in democratic war effort as indicative of the difficulty of employing force for "rational and restricted purposes rather than for purposes which are emotional and to which it is hard to find a rational limit." [54]

As a realistic approach to the necessary alliances formed in the the Second World War, Kennan posits the fact that only Japan

[52] *Id., Realities*, 21.
[53] *Id., American Diplomacy*, 83.
[54] *Ibid.*, 84.

could have been defeated by the democracies without the aid of one of the totalitarian powers. The help of Russia was the only means available for victory over Germany, and for that assistance a heavy price would have to be paid in the peace. "It was plain that a war between the Nazis and the Russian Communists could take place only over the prostrate bodies of the small states of eastern Europe." [55]

Kennan is not adversely critical of the concessions made by the western democracies in the conferences at Moscow, Teheran, and Yalta. He shows that the establishment of the Soviet in eastern Europe and in Manchuria was not the result of these talks, but rather of military operations late in the war.

There was nothing the Western democracies could have done to prevent the Russians from entering these areas except to get there first, and this they were not in a position to do. The implication that Soviet forces would not have gone into Manchuria if Roosevelt had not arrived at the Yalta understanding with Stalin is nonsense. Nothing could have stopped the Russians from participating in the final phases of the Pacific war, in order to be in at the kill and to profit by an opportunity to gain objectives they had been seeking for half a century.[56]

He denies that the Yalta agreement was a betrayal of Nationalist China. The terms stated that the United States would make recommendations to the Chinese. This was consonant with the latter's request before Yalta that the United States assist them in arranging their affairs with the Soviet. The Chinese were not averse to the recommendations at the time; in their independent negotiations with Russia subsequently, they made greater concessions on their own responsibility. Kennan sees value in the conferences as demonstrations of American patience and good will in resolving difficulties, and of honest effort to cooperate with the Soviet. More reprehensible, he feels, was the continuance of lend-lease after midsum-

[55] *Ibid.*, 76.
[56] *Ibid.*, 85.

mer of 1944 when Russian territory had been liberated and a successful second front had been launched.[57]

Among the mistakes of the Second World War he lists the failure to remember that the West was the weaker party, which as such, could achieve only a portion of its aims, and that at a price. A deeper misunderstanding was failure to appreciate the limitations of war in general for accomplishing democratic purposes. Defeat of an enemy is only a necessary preliminary.

But the actual prospering occurs only when something happens in a man's mind that increases his enlightenment and the consciousness of his real relation to other people—something that makes him aware that, whenever the dignity of another man is offended, his own dignity, as a man among men, is thereby reduced. And this is why the destructive process of war must always be accompanied by, or made subsidiary to, a different sort of undertaking aimed at widening the horizons and changing the motives of men and should never be thought of in itself as a proper vehicle for hopes and enthusiasms and dreams of world improvement. Force, like peace, is not an abstraction; it cannot be understood or dealt with as a concept outside of the given framework of purpose and method.[58]

Having forgotten in 1942 the problems which alliance with Russia might constitute in the future, Americans were shocked that this "earnest and upright partner" was a monster "setting aside the resources of half the world and the prostrate peoples of eastern Europe and China." [59] The danger of this combination of physical resources and manpower from Russia and China with technical skills and tools from Germany and eastern Europe in the hands of a hostile power suddenly occurred to Americans. Had they realized the real elements involved in World War II, they would have been better prepared for events after 1945, "less inclined to mistake

[57] *Ibid.*, 86.
[58] *Ibid.*, 88.
[59] *Id., Realities*, 26–27; *American Diplomacy*, 90.

them for the product of somebody else's stupidity or bad faith," more calm and united in facing the crisis.

Kennan proposes as the best policy toward the Soviet, a firm but vigilant containment of their expansive tendencies.[60] He characterizes this policy as having nothing to do with "outward histrionics; with threats or blustering or superfluous gestures of outward 'toughness' "; since threatening gestures make a nation unable to yield without losing face, the United States does not wish to preclude on Russia's part a compliance too detrimental to her prestige. Soviet pressure against free institutions would be contained by adroit application of counterforce following the shifts in Russian policy.

He explains thus the effectiveness of containment in bringing about results with Russia. Internal political security and the building of heavy industry have left the Russian population physically and spiritually tired, deprived of consumer goods, housing, and transportation, and aged prematurely by excessive labor. If disunity were to weaken the Party despotism, chaos would change this overnight into one of the weakest national societies. Meanwhile America could inspire world confidence by coping successfully with problems of internal life and by showing spiritual vitality as a World Power. By forcing greater moderation on the Kremlin, the United States might promote a breakup or mellowing of Soviet power, since no messianic movement like that of Communism can face frustration indefinitely without adjusting one way or the other to the state of affairs.[61]

The problem of containment is basically a problem of the reactions of people within the non-Communist world. . . . Whatever we do that serves to bring hope and encouragement and self-confidence to peoples outside the Soviet orbit has a similar effect on the peoples inside, and

[60] *Id.*, *American Diplomacy*, 90.

[61] *Ibid.*, 88. Mr. Kennan's expression of containment in the above-mentioned books is less explicit than his initial presentation of it under the famous signature "X" in "The Sources of Soviet Conduct," *Foreign Affairs*, XXV (July, 1947), 566–82.

constitutes the most potent argument for prudence and reasonableness on the part of the Soviet leaders . . . . containment and liberation are only two sides of the same coin and both part of a greater problem . . . commanding by behavior, the respect, hope, and confidence of all on whichever side of the Iron Curtain they may be.[62]

Kennan suggests that Communism can be dealt with effectively only by proceeding with positive undertakings in spite of it, by not letting it become the absorbing preoccupation.[63] This would work better results in the uncommitted countries which wish suggestions about a peaceful future and cooperation without political strings attached; they are less interested in being taught to combat Communism.

[62] *Id., Realities*, 87–88. Theodore H. White, commenting on the double tradition of the crusade and of the deal in American history, would seem to support containment also. Since a crusade would mean war with Russia, he would recommend the deal, which is shameful only if "approached naively, or in the spirit of friendship to be pledged with the enemy." He continues:

"If it is sought, however, on the only terms that the adversary might consider—as an interim solution in a long-range struggle until a new relation of force-dominance gives one or the other of us permanent advantage— it can be both shrewd and advantageous. . . . Their philosophy cannot be penetrated by our ideas and faith except by prolonged contact and the education of negotiation. The deal—made of the myriad little deals—is the easiest way of exposing them to the seepage of questions and perplexing alternatives which ultimately, we hope, will erode their system of politics, at home and abroad, into impotence.

"Starting off from these assumptions, each adversary believing he will outwit the other, we can make slow adjustments, wisely, carefully, successfully, provided we do so under certain conditions of thinking and practice. The first should be the realization that at no given date will it be ever possible to arrive at any one settlement of all the issues between ourselves and Communism in Russia. . . . The second condition is a program that does not jerk from impotent slackness to intolerable economic burden imposed by emergencies. . . . No maneuver of the enemy in the long period of negotiations that may now be likely could hurt America in the outside world as much as political squalor or economic chaos in the homeland." Theodore H. White, *Fire in the Ashes:* Europe in Mid-century (New York: William Sloane Associates, 1953), 394–398. Mr. White is a noted American foreign correspondent and author of books on Europe and Asia.

[63] *Ibid.*, 101–02.

His estimate of United Nations is that it is a "tremendously important symbol of the equal dignity of all nations and the ultimate community of responsibility that unites men everywhere," but that it cannot bring about the growth of interdependence and mutual responsibility, nor can it abolish or restrain the sources of international tension.[64]

Hans J. Morgenthau

Professor Morgenthau is the most articulate of the Realists in expressing his criticism of moralizing and his conviction that self-interest must be the real motivation in foreign policy. He judges that America has acted on the international scene "as all nations must, in power-political terms," yet it has viewed its own behavior in moralistic terms.[65] He traces this aversion to facing reality on the international scene to three peculiarities in the American experience: the uniqueness of America's democratic experiment, the remoteness of this nation from the centers of world conflict during the nineteenth century, and the humanitarian pacifism and anti-imperialism of the American ideology.

American democratic thought was particularly eloquent of two basic propositions which dominated the general philosophy of the western world in the ninteenth century: 1) that the struggle for power on the international scene is an accident destined to disappear with the triumph of democracy throughout the world, 2) that struggles between democratic and nondemocratic nations must not be conceived of as a contest for advantage in terms of power, but as a struggle between good and evil in which good would triumph, and the struggle for power disappear with autocratic government.[66] Because power politics was the vogue in 1796, the withdrawal from European politics was interpreted as a retreat

[64] *Ibid.*, 45.
[65] Morgenthau, *In Defense*, 7.
[66] *Id.*, "The Mainsprings of American Foreign Policy: The National Interest Versus Moral Abstraction," *American Political Science Review*, XLIV (December, 1950), 839. Hereafter referred to as "The Mainsprings."

from power politics itself on the part of Washington. The settling of the North American continent by a process of civilizing rather than of conquering was different from the imperialistic ventures of other nations, but he traces the uniqueness to the contiguous area of sparsely settled land and to the political, military, and numerical inferiority of the Indians, rather than to any moral superiority.[67] He concludes that the impression of a selfless humanitarian mission was further emphasized by the general lack of interest shown by the United States in "particular advantages definable in terms of power or territorial gain" outside the western hemisphere.

Morgenthau divides American foreign policy into three types and three periods according to the dominance of these opposing conceptions: 1) that international politics is an unending struggle for power in which the interests of individual nations must necessarily be defined in terms of power, or 2) that a nation may be guided by moral principles rather than by considerations of power.[68] The realistic policy, characterized by thinking and acting in terms of power, represented best by Alexander Hamilton, covered the first decade of independence. The ideological policy, marked by thinking in terms of moral principle but acting in terms of power, represented by Thomas Jefferson, covered the nineteenth century up to the Spanish-American War. The moralistic policy, effected by thinking and acting in terms of moral principle as in the case of Woodrow Wilson, extended through this half of the twentieth century.

Instead of using the general indictment that American foreign policy is in need of maturing, Morgenthau would say that this generation should shed the illusions of their fathers and grandfathers and relearn the principles which guided the Federalists in the first decade of the country's existence, and which continued to serve, though in moralistic disguise, during the entire first century.[69] He finds that political wisdom did not grow through accumulation of experiences, but rather that the full flowering of

[67] *Id., In Defense,* 8.
[68] *Ibid.,* 13.
[69] *Id.,* "The Mainsprings," 833.

wisdom was coincident with the nation's birth, and was responsible for its early survival. After the passing of this generation of statesmen in America's "classical age," improvisation or invocation of abstract moral principles was the pattern, and they were successful only because the margin of Allied and American power "generally exceeded the degree to which American improvidence fell short of the demands of the hour."

The Hamiltonian Federalists saw the interest of the United States as separate from that of Europe, to be pursued by means of isolation from the continental conflicts. They realized that this isolation was possible only if there was a balance of power in Europe which prohibited a dominant power from turning its attention across the Atlantic. Morgenthau distinguishes this early isolation from the twentieth century brand; the Federalists viewed it only as a means to accomplish the American experiment, to be replaced by other means when circumstances should require this; the later-day isolationists viewed intervention in non-American conflicts as a thing bad in itself.[70]

The special occasion calling forth the realistic foreign policy was Washington's proclamation of neutrality with regard to the War of the First Coalition against France, April 22, 1793. Hamilton in the "Pacificus" papers answered the arguments against the proclamation—faithfulness to treaty obligations, gratitude to France for assistance in independence, and affinity of republican institutions.[71] With reference to the benefit which France would realize from fulfillment of the stipulation, there was no just proportion to the peril which would follow for the United States; the latter had the duty to look to its own self-preservation first. Hamilton could find no basis of gratitude—that is, a benefit one has no right to claim. If the act produces reciprocal advantages for the party performing the service and is performed for its own immediate interest, the

[70] *Id.*, "What Is the National Interest of the United States?" *Annals of American Academy of Political and Social Science*, CCLXXXII (July, 1952), 1–2.

[71] *Id.*, *In Defense*, 14–18.

reward has already been enjoyed. The absolute limits of generosity for a nation prescribe that there be no detriment to the affairs of the benefactors. Opponents maintained that since America originated the principles which were the germs of the French Revolution, liberty here would be the next target. Hamilton wanted no equating of this cause with the war in France. He concluded that if the United States were to range itself with France against all of Europe, it would run grave risks with little expectation of good for itself or its ally.

Of the ideological period following the end of Federalist domination, Morgenthau would make this judgment:

> What was said of Gladstone could also have been said of Jefferson, John Quincy Adams, Grover Cleveland, Theodore Roosevelt, the war policies of Wilson and of Franklin D. Roosevelt: what the moral law demanded was by a felicitous coincidence always identical with what the national interest seemed to require.[72]

Tracing political opportunism in Thomas Jefferson, Morgenthau observes that in 1806 he favored English ascendancy on the sea as safer than that of France. Yet in 1807 he was compelled to wish for Bonaparte's success as a means of easing British tyranny. In 1812, with Napoleon at his peak, he hoped for a restoration of the balance. Only after the danger had passed in 1815 could Jefferson allow himself again "to indulge in the cultivation of moral principles divorced from political exigencies." [73]

Of John Quincy Adams he comments, ". . . the moral principles were nothing but the political interests formulated in moral terms, and vice versa. They fit the interests as a glove fits the hand. Adams's great contributions to the tradition of American foreign policy— freedom of the seas, the Monroe Doctrine, and Manifest Destiny —are witness to this achievement." [74] As with Grotius, freedom of the seas was a weapon to safeguard the independence of an in-

---

[72] *Ibid.*, 19.
[73] *Ibid.*, 20–22.
[74] *Ibid.*, 22.

ferior naval power. The Monroe Doctrine's anti-imperialism and mutual nonintervention were conditions for securing American isolation and continued predominance of the United States in the western hemisphere. Manifest Destiny was both a moral justification and a moral incentive for westward expansion.

Morgenthau finds that the moralistic or utopian period of foreign policy from the Spanish-American War forward, makes no distinction between the interests of the United States and those of the rest of the world. It identifies the national interest of the United States with human welfare and universal morality; it presumes that a natural harmony exists between national interests and those values. He feels that this philosophy culminates in "unconditional surrender and in the conception of wars as crusades fought for unlimited goals and waged with unlimited means." The moralistic arguments run as follows:

It is something base, something immoral, for a nation to put its own interests above the interests of other nations or above the interests of humanity . . . it is in favor of collective security as a matter of principle, and hence feels constrained to intervene whenever the security of any nation, regardless of its relation to the concrete interests of the United States is endangered.[75]

Of McKinley's entrance into the Spanish-American War, he would say that the President led the country, "ignorant of the bearing of this step upon the national interest, and guided by moral principles completely divorced from the national interest." [76] This policy in which moral principles replace national interest will find its fulfillment in Woodrow Wilson.

What passed for foreign policy was either improvisation or—especially in our country—the invocation of some abstract moral principle in whose image the world was to be made over. . . . The invocation of moral principles was hardly more than an innocuous pastime; embracing everything, it came to grips with nothing. In part, however, it was

[75] *Id.*, "What Is the National Interest of the United States?" 2–3.
[76] *Id.*, *In Defense*, 23.

a magnificent instrument for marshalling public opinion in support of war and warlike policies—and for losing the peace. The intoxication with moral abstractions, which as a mass phenomenon started with the Spanish-American War and which in our time has become the prevailing substitute for political thought is indeed one of the great sources of weakness and failure in American foreign policy.[77]

To make his point that Wilson actually opposed national interest on moral grounds, Morgenthau cites the Mobile Address of October 27, 1913 in which the President said that it is a perilous thing to determine a nation's foreign policy in terms of material interest.[78] He reinforces his case with quotes from the Fourth Liberty Loan Speech of September 27, 1918 in which Wilson said that "no special or separate interest of any single nation or any group of nations can be made the basis of any part of the settlement which is not consistent with the common interest of all."

Wilson adopted the heritage of liberal thought stretching back to Rousseau and Kant, the conviction that the universality of democratic or republican governments was a prerequisite to permanent peace.[79] The attitude of the League of Nations and of the United Nations toward membership of autocratic governments among their ranks, is traceable to this same philosophy. The Wilsonian liberal thought that to end oppression and war all that was needed was a change in the form of government; public opinion would then influence the replacement of secret diplomacy by democratic control of foreign policy. Of the inaccuracy of this approach, Morgenthau states:

The fundamental foreign policies of the Great Powers have survived all changes in the form of government and in domestic policies; France, Great Britain, and Russia during the last two hundred years are cases in point. Continuity in foreign affairs is not a matter of choice but a necessity, for it derives from geography, national character, tradition, and the actual distribution of power, factors which no government is

[77] *Ibid.*, 4.
[78] *Ibid.*, 23.
[79] *Id.*, *Scientific Man*, 62.

able to control but which it can neglect only at the risk of failure. . . .
Nations are "peace-loving" under certain historic conditions and are
warlike under others, and it is not the form of government or domestic
policies which make them so.[80]

Morgenthau points out three basic errors in Wilson's insistence
that democratic elections take place everywhere in the world.[81]
The first error is that the establishment of democracy is synonymous with peace. The second error is the assumption that democracy will be successful despite the qualifications and preferences of
the inhabitants. The third error is the failure to comprehend that
free elections can be used for anti-democratic ends. "In the last
analysis it is the democratic ethos of a people, their philosophy
of government and politics, their conception of what is right
and wrong, desirable and undesirable, feasible and unfeasible,
that determine the function free elections fulfill in a given
society."

Morgenthau discovers an inner affinity between isolationism and
Wilsonianism: both neglect the concrete issues upon which national interest must be based, both are unaware of precise interests
outside the western hemisphere, both use abstract moral principles.[82] Because of this relationship, he thinks that the debate
between internationalism and isolationism in the twenties and thirties was carried on primarily in moral terms. Evidences of the latter
are such questions: Was there a moral obligation for the United
States to contribute to world peace through the League of Nations
and the World Court? Did America have a mission to oppose
Fascism in Europe or uphold international law in Asia? The question of the balance of power in Europe and Asia was seldom faced.
The fact that the moral postulates of Franklin D. Roosevelt's administration coincided with real national interest was "due to the
impact of a national emergency upon innate common sense, and to

[80] *Ibid.*, 65–66.
[81] *Id., In Defense*, 215.
[82] *Ibid.*, 30.

the strength of the national tradition that holds in its spell the actions of even those who deny its validity in words." [83]

He finds inconsistency in the American attitude toward totalitarianism:

We were against Italy because of its aggression against Ethiopia, but we were against Franco because of his Fascism. We seemed to like Mussolini because he made trains run on time, but when he made an alliance with Hitler we did not like him any more. We did not like Stalin either; but when he was attacked by Germany and was defeating the German armies, we thought he was a somewhat uncouth democrat, essentially not so different from ourselves; and finally we turned around full circle, and regard him now as the incarnation of all evil.[84]

He infers that these extremes and "emotional preferences" indicate lack of recognition of the national interest as the only moral and intellectual standard for judgment and action available to a great nation. After the Second World War when the Axis was defeated, they were deceived in thinking that with the passing of that constellation of hostile powers, political evil would disappear. They had made the war an end in itself to be won "speedily, cheaply, and totally." That the war could be won politically with view to the creation of a new balance of power seemed to occur only to Winston Churchill and to Joseph Stalin.[85]

The greater part of the volume *In Defense of the National Interest* is devoted to an examination of four faults which he attributes to current foreign policy: utopianism, legalism, sentimentalism, and neo-isolationism. Under the classification "utopianism" is the United States' definition of its foreign policy as selfless and moral, with the implication that evil nations alone would dare oppose this "policeman" seeking world peace and order.[86]

Only against the background of a conspiratorial interpretation

[83] *Ibid.*, 30–31.
[84] *Id.*, "What Is the National Interest of the United States?" 6–7.
[85] *Id.*, *In Defense*, 32.
[86] *Ibid.*, 93.

of politics, in which all opposition can be traced to the other center of power, does he find any plausibility in the political policies of Wilson, Roosevelt, and Truman during the two world wars.[87] Only if the other side represents a worldwide conspiracy could it be a sane directive to crush the enemy with unconditional surrender, re-educate the people along democratic, peace-loving lines, and then prepare for the enjoyment of the millennium. He criticizes as unrealistic the course adopted both in 1918 and in 1945—that is, bring the soldiers home, sell the military surplus, and feel that with victory the source of all trouble is erased. In the memoirs of participants in the Teheran and Yalta conferences he detects lack of awareness

. . . that the downfall of one ambitious nation calls forth the ambitions of another, and that the business of war does not end with military victory but only with the establishment of a viable distribution of power, the groundwork for which must be laid while the war is still in progress. Least of all did it occur to the framers of American policy that the Soviet Union might be destined to succeed Germany and Japan as a threat to the balance of power in Europe and Asia, and hence to the security of the United States.[88]

The weakness called "legalism," Morgenthau attributes to the assumption that international politics is an undertaking by peace-loving nations, not greedy for power, but dedicated to making the world safe.[89] The United States has considered the United Nations as a substitute for power politics, balance of power, alliances, etc., while Britain and the Soviet have regarded it as an instrument of national policies, not a substitute for them. In his opinion, the United Nations has become the forum where the nations of the world fight their battles for power through the legalistic manipulation of voting procedures and the like.

Morgenthau notes that in the currently transformed United

[87] *Ibid.*, 94.
[88] *Ibid.*, 96–97.
[89] *Ibid.*, 101.

Nations, which finds its major political and military purpose in opposition to the Soviet bloc, the nations are grouped around the United States as the supplier of strength and central direction necessary to make it succeed.[90] The General Assembly operates by a two-thirds majority from which the Soviet bloc is excluded. The United States must appeal to the common interests of this group, and the common denominator is bound to be "below the maximum desired by the originator of the national policy." He shows that the relative material power of the nation seeking support, and of the nations being solicited will determine the extent of the compromise. He would place future hope for the United Nations in the opportunity which it provides for the unobtrusive resumption of traditional diplomacy techniques between the two blocs coexisting in the same international organization.

As another evidence of reliance upon "legalism," he would offer the Yalta agreement in which the abstract principles of cooperation and universal democracy were invoked against the fact of Russian military domination.[91] The damage to the interests of the West was really sustained in the decisions favoring military efficiency, such as in the Second Front through western Europe instead of the Balkans, without adequate consideration of the political consequences which would follow upon the distribution of military power at the end of the war. The Yalta conference did not create the "political abnegation"; it merely placed upon it the seal of legal ratification. Whether or not one considers that the surrender of eastern Europe was the result of inescapable military necessity, at Yalta it "was not possible either to force or to persuade the Red Army to retreat." He finds the American insistence upon compliance with the stipulations of free elections and democratic governments, and their indignation at the violations, both misplaced and psychologically revealing. Here was the evidence of the fact that in the face of superior power, moral right and legal title

[90] *Id., Politics*, 459–64.
[91] *Id., In Defense*, 109.

are impotent. The United States could use the violation of the Yalta agreement as justification for rearming, an act which otherwise would have appeared unnecessary.[92]

The third weakness in foreign policy which Morgenthau points out is "sentimentalism," derived from invoking moral principles and values as the ultimate objectives and motivations of political action. Among concrete examples of these values he would enumerate "gratitude, common dedication to liberty, manifest destiny, the Christian duty to civilize our Philippine brothers, support of democracy, good neighborliness, generosity." [93] He would not suggest that these were used exclusively to deceive people at home or abroad. "They have taken them seriously, . . . and in not a few instances have been ready to shed their blood, to spend their treasure, to jeopardize the very existence of the country, in order to make these moral principles prevail on the international scene." He estimates that this bending of political action to fit moral abstractions has resulted in the sacrifice of political success without any sizeable advance in universal morality; hence the sentimental approach should be abandoned, despite its "intrinsic nobility" and its "emotional attraction." As examples of how coldly realistic policies can be distorted with sentimentalism, he offers the Truman Doctrine, the Marshall Plan, and Point Four.

Since the interest of the United States in the balance of European power was always synonymous with that of Britain, it was only logical that after 1947 this country should succeed a weakened England as the main protector of independence for nations such as Greece and Turkey. These circumstances thus made it necessary for President Truman to appeal to Congress March 12, 1947. He shows that the President justified the aid, not in terms of "traditional American interest," but in moral terms of the struggle between totalitarianism and democracy, proclaiming the defense of free, democratic nations everywhere against direct and indirect aggression. "Upon what in its immediate import was a limited re-

[92] *Ibid.*, 111–12.
[93] *Ibid.*, 113.

quest for a limited purpose, the Truman Doctrine erected a message of salvation to all the world, unlimited in purpose, unlimited in commitments, and limited in its scope only by the needs of those who would benefit." [94]

In consequence of this inability to distinguish between what is desirable and what is essential, the policy has had to be halfhearted and contradictory in operation. A successful foreign policy must be commensurate with the available strength to carry it out. If one nation presumes to protect and promote democracy everywhere in the world, then the number of commitments will ensure only failure.[95] Because the defense of democracy in Europe is a vital part of defense against Russian imperialism, the requirements of the Truman Doctrine there coincide with American national interest, but in Asia where the situation is different, the Doctrine has bred much confusion.

Morgenthau feels that Dean Acheson in his speech before the National Press Club on January 12, 1950, really reformulated the administration's policy in Asia when he stated that to say the United States' real interest was to stop the spread of Communism, was to put the cart before the horse. The thing to oppose is Russian imperialism, of which Communism is but "the most subtle instrument." [96]

Accusing the Truman administration of being caught "in the pitfalls of its own sentimental philosophy," Morgenthau describes its conscious distortion of the Doctrine's nature and purpose as a preliminary to win popular support and Congressional appropriation. But he warns that the creating of synthetic scares and spurious promises automatically involves an administration in stronger doses of deception, "and the people inevitably react with even deeper doubt, bewilderment, and cynicism." [97] He compares the modest occasion and the grandiose declaration of the Truman Doctrine

[94] *Ibid.*, 116.
[95] *Ibid.*, 117–19.
[96] *Ibid.*, 121.
[97] *Ibid.*, 237.

with the similar techniques used in the Monroe Doctrine and the war messages of 1917 and 1941, and he concludes that the motivation was "primarily, if not exclusively, a matter of domestic politics."

Morgenthau finds nothing extraordinary in the fact that the United States as the strongest member of a coalition should give economic and military assistance to weaker members in western Europe so that they may withstand internal subversion and external aggression, and thus actuate a viable balance of power. But when the Marshall Plan and NATO were represented as selfless generosity, and "a mandate from America's humanitarian past," it was natural that opposition was voiced "in terms of the unworthiness of the recipients and of the sacrifices it imposed upon the giver." [98]

Morgenthau would recommend that American foreign policy not lay emphasis upon the ideological division between East and West on the basis of Communism and democracy. The great opportunity might lie, not in stopping Communist revolution all over the world, but in demonstrating that "a national leader can be a good Communist ideologically and still be opposed to Russia as a great power." [99] On this line of reasoning, he would support Yugoslavia.

On the basis of the thesis that he who controls Germany controls all of Europe and thus may proceed to control the world, he muses upon the wisdom of America's having fought Germany twice in a generation as a "moral outcast," and having approached that country "as a virtuous nation approaches a vicious yet reformable one." The turn of events has now caused the United States to think of it in terms of power rather than of moral abstractions.

Morgenthau posits as the motivation for Point Four technical assistance to underdeveloped countries, the national interest of restoring balance of power in Asia "through the limiting of Russian power and the political and economic stabilization of the new na-

[98] *Ibid.*, 122.
[99] *Ibid.*, 124.

tions of southeast Asia." [100] He criticizes the tendency to conceive of Point Four as generosity rather than as national defense, and to identify this program with those of social and economic improvement carried on by United Nations agencies. If one fosters the Point Four program as a gigantic TVA, then it can be attacked by opponents of the "welfare state," who do not even recognize the obligation of the government to aid this country's backward citizens.[101]

The fourth weakness in American foreign policy, he traces to neo-isolationism which expresses itself in an air of omnipotence: "We shall deal with the world, but only on our terms." [102] If a nation sets for itself a moral mission ordained by the moral purposes of the universe, it must be endowed with enormous power. Following from its assumption that the country is good enough and strong enough to do as it pleases, it equates negotiation with surrender and compromise with appeasement. Neo-isolationism results in three consequences: "the underestimation of the enemy, the overrating of one's strength, and the inability to preserve peace." This miscalculation produces a Maginot Line psychology in which security is imagined to exist permanently in an ocean barrier, an atom bomb, a Marshall Plan, or a NATO.

The only way to explain failures and defeats when we assume ourselves to be omnipotent is to look for some devilish machinations depriving us of the successes and victories that are rightfully ours. So it becomes plausible that we are unable to stop the revolutions in Asia by

[100] *Ibid.*, 127.

[101] *Ibid.*, 127. In private correspondence with Professor Morgenthau, I put this question to him regarding foreign aid in the form of excess agricultural products and loans for self-development: "Would you say that, aside from the purpose of helping countries to resist Russian aggression and internal Communist subversion, the United States has an obligation in justice and charity to share somewhat with the less fortunate peoples of the world?" He replied: "I would agree with this proposition as a general principle only for cases of distress caused by natural catastrophes. Nations have first of all a duty to themselves, for if they do not take care of their own interests nobody else will" (Morgenthau to the author, December 6, 1957).

[102] *Ibid.*, 129.

military means, not because they cannot be stopped that way, but because the State Department is full of Communists.[103]

Mr. Morgenthau deals at length with the current dilemma posed by Russia. He would subordinate the prevailing opinion that the conflict is a struggle between two systems of political morality. Conjuring up a condition contrary to fact—that Lenin and Trotsky died in obscurity and that the Czars held sway today in southeast Europe and threatened to engulf all Asia—he questions whether it would make such a difference for the United States "if Russian imperialism marched forward as it did in the eighteenth and nineteenth centuries, under the ideological banner and with the support of Christianity rather than of Bolshevism?" [104]

The confusion between the issues of Russian imperialism and Communism he traces to four sources. One is the public's tendency to reduce politics to a contrast of black and white in which one's own group represents good, and the other group evil. Russian propaganda is the second source, since it rationalizes imperialism in terms of Marxism. Thirdly, Americans forget that Communism has triumphed outside the Soviet only as a "by-product of conquest by the Red Army," not by a revolution in the realm of thought. Finally, the widespread fear of change has made some Americans imagine the specter of Communist revolution whenever social reform has been attempted. He feels that the United States' China policy is a prime example of the confusion of issues. If the safeguarding of national interest is replaced by an emotional crusade against Communism, he warns that America might inadvertently "raise the banner of universal counterrevolution abroad and of conformity in thought and action at home." [105]

After speaking of Woodrow Wilson's misguided notion that democracy was a panacea for the political woes of every nation, Morgenthau makes a comparison between this and the recent attempts to penetrate the Iron Curtain with "the" truth. In the sphere

[103] *Ibid.*, 131.
[104] *Ibid.*, 77.
[105] *Ibid.*, 88.

of political action, he judges that "there is no such thing as one and and the same truth for everybody." [106]

Because he is convinced that only those settlements last which express the complementary interests of the contracting parties, and because all the great peace settlements in the past have set up spheres of influence, Morgenthau would recommend a provisional partition of the world into a Russian and an American sphere by joint agreement.[107] Such proposals have been made by the Soviet since the breakdown of the Yalta terms. Since the satellite nations have already lost their freedom, and since the Red Army would not retreat without a *quid pro quo* negotiation, he would recommend this provisional partition as a means of building the two spheres together. He agrees with Mr. Churchill's words of June 5, 1946: "It is better to have a world united than a world divided; but it is also better to have a world divided, than a world destroyed." [108]

Of the Eisenhower administration's diplomacy, Morgenthau has little commendation. He applies the following indictment to the situation as late as December, 1957:

When we heard spokesmen for the government propound the legal and moral platitudes which had passed for foreign policy in the interwar period, we thought that this was the way in which the government —as all governments must—tried to make the stark facts of foreign policy palatable to the people. They were—so it seemed to us—the tinsel in the show window making the merchandise on the counter attractive to the customer. We were mistaken. Those platitudes *are* the foreign policy of the United States. The counter is bare; that tinsel is all the store has to sell. Hence the alarm, the sadness, and the sorrow.[109]

[106] *Ibid.*, 216.
[107] *Ibid.*, 150–56.
[108] *Ibid.*, 153, 156–57.
[109] *Id.*, "The Decline of American Power," *New Republic*, CXXXVII (December 9, 1957), 11.
Since the completion of this study, Hans J. Morgenthau has published a new volume of essays, *Dilemmas of Politics* (Chicago: University of Chicago Press, 1958).

* III *

The Idealists

IDEALISM, when used with regard to statesmen and to political theory in international relations, denotes the concern for moral values which transcend a nation's selfish interests. The Idealists who express all the implications of Christian western civilization approach man as a creature made in the image and likeness of God. Man is deprived of certain gifts as a result of original sin, yet capable of moral responsibility in pursuing a lawfully ordered world community in which he can realize his possibilities for good. All Idealists believe that in affairs of state, conscience and reason must place ethical restraints upon egoism so that truthfulness, freedom, fidelity to obligations, justice, and charity may prevail for the benefit of all mankind. While admitting that perfection cannot be attained on this earth, they strive to resolve human conflicts by appeal to morality and law through agreements and institutional devices, rather than by resorting to unilateral coercion or violence.

They recognize that realization of a state of peace requires some subordination of individual to group interests; in this process, politics becomes the art of accommodation rather than the unmitigated struggle for power. They endorse the pursuit of national interest which is consistent with the objective moral order of the universe, but at the same time they acknowledge that national power entails responsibility for a wider commitment. Ethical appeal and shared purpose are singled out as sources of power which the Realists have not reckoned with. Although the Idealists deprecate "balance of power" as the ultimate objective in international relations, they favor the use of power for law enforcement. Since the label "Legalist-Moralist" was applied to this school as a polite term of derision, the name will be discarded here as a handicap.

The authors of a current textbook note that while the devotees of *Realpolitik* do well in pointing up utopian tendencies in American foreign relations, still they do a "great disservice by underestimating the strong and healthy influence of idealism," which has been a major force in America's dealings with other nations.[1] They note that many of the faults in our twentieth century diplomacy were traceable to international environment rather than to the failure of statesmanship.

Within the classification of Idealists there are various degrees of faith in the efficacy of international institutions, in the probability of a nation's enduring self-sacrifice, in the feasibility of its abiding by the same moral code as that of the individual. In the survey there will be no attempt to apply a litmus test to the sincerity of their protestations, nor to ferret out pragmatism, utilitarianism, positivism, and liberalism, nor to isolate contractual theories of state and international relations, nor to arrange ideals according to a hierarchy of spiritual values. Because of the wide range of subjects discussed by each, the decisions regarding arrangement were based on an effort to achieve somewhat of coherence and continuity.

In the study of contemporary scholars, we shall consider first those who seem to absorb the crosscurrents of both Idealism and Realism; their moral premises will place them among the Idealists, but their interpretation of facts will sometimes resemble that of the Realists; in the interest of moderation, some of them criticize excesses in both schools. After this group, we shall proceed to the

---

[1] Norman D. Palmer and Howard C. Perkins, *International Relations* (Boston: Houghton Mifflin, 1953), 958, 963. Professors Palmer and Perkins teach at the University of Pennsylvania.

writers who give conscious rebuttal to the opinions of the Realists, and then to those who simply state the case for international Idealism.

Robert E. Osgood

Upon the following bases, Robert E. Osgood [2] is classified with the Idealists. He admits there is a place for sacrifice and altruism among nations, that there are some ideals for which a nation might transcend self-interest, though experience shows that unselfish behavior does not endure when self-interest and ideals do not coincide. He recommends that ideals be maintained as guides; he condemns national aggrandizement; he does not reject the possibility of collective security, but he feels that circumstances make it impractical if not based upon existing configurations of power.

At the outset of his work, he voices acceptance of the Christian-liberal-humanitarian ideals, but with a very illuminating qualification: "recognizing, at the same time, that there is no fundamental justification for these ideals beyond the ideals themselves; they are matters of faith, not empirical propositions; they are either self-evident or not evident at all." [3] Because of the complexity of the

[2] Robert E. Osgood, author of *Ideals and Self-Interest in America's Foreign Relations*, was a student of Hans J. Morgenthau and is currently a professor at the Center for the Study of American Foreign Policy, University of Chicago.

[3] Osgood, *Ideals and Self-Interest*, 20. This explanation of his stand is culled from personal correspondence with Mr. Osgood. He answered my query as to whether these ideals, founded on natural law, are not knowable by reason:

"I believe that for virtually all practical purposes which call upon one to make a moral judgment with respect to specific circumstances these moral values are knowable by reason. But for philosophical purposes—which, of course, are not irrelevant to practical judgments—one must find some grounds for accepting or not accepting the ultimate premises. . . . As for these ultimate premises, I am not sure what they are, and I am not sure upon what grounds they can legitimately be called right or wrong; but if I could satisfy myself that I had precisely identified them, I would be incapable of proving their validity to a rational person who disagreed with

human environment, he judges that the best means to an end will seldom conform perfectly with ideal standards. He advises that the American people keep their eyes upon the ultimate ideals "without losing their footing on the solid ground of reality." One of the greatest sources of "international sin" he attributes to man's unwillingness to believe that moral contradictions exist or that they are not easily reconcilable. But immediately he assures the reader that this does not imply a relativistic or nihilistic view of human conduct, for without the ideal standard, how can man judge the moral imperfection of his actions, and realize the "humility and critical self-appraisal which is the lifeblood of true idealism and the only antidote to national self-righteousness?" In international relations there must be continual "compromises with selfishness and sin." [4]

While he asserts that it is utopian to expect nations to conform to moral standards as do individuals, he would not lower his sights to what is practically attainable lest progress be sacrificed.[5] The following analysis illustrates a certain ambiguity in his delineation of this point:

Because of the crucial importance of national security, national egoism enjoys a rational and moral justification which renders the primacy of

---

me, in the sense that I might theoretically prove a scientific proposition about physical phenomena by reference to empirical observation. Since I cannot even theoretically envisage proving the validity of an ultimate value, which I nevertheless believe in, I am forced to justify my set of values, ultimately by belief itself, though I derive subordinate values from first premises by the processes of reason. Therefore, in one sense, I can agree with those who would say that the ideals I refer to in my book are founded on natural law, but I still cannot produce a rational argument for the validity of the natural laws" (Osgood to the author, December 6, 1957).

[4] *Ibid.*, 20–22.

[5] *Ibid.*, 444. In the same correspondence with Mr. Osgood, he approved my interpretation of this point—that nations are bound by the same moral law as are individuals, but since history reveals few of them acting in strict accord with it, statesmen must use caution. But, he added, "The concrete application of moral law in international relations is even more ambiguous than in personal relations" (Osgood to the author, December 6, 1957).

self-interest among national ends an indisputable and unavoidable reality of international politics. In practice, this means that the exercise of independent national power . . . is the important means of achieving national ends. . . . This competition for power may be mitigated by a variety of restraints upon rampant egoism—by ideals, sentiment, international law, collective power, mutual self-interest, etc.—but it will never be abolished or even transformed into orderly procedures enforced impartially by reference to custom or law until men undergo a psychological revolution that will permit them to owe their primary allegiance to some community greater than their nation-state; and this revolution does not seem likely to occur in the foreseeable future. . . . because of the relative weakness of supranational mores, laws, and ideals, the chief measure of national power is, ultimately the ability to deprive other nations of their self-interest, including their very survival as a last resort. Therefore coercion or the threat of coercion is an indispensable instrument of national policy.[6]

The fact that Idealism seldom overrules national self-interest he traces to the intensity of nationalism, which in the guise of patriotism, brings about the coalescence of altruism and egoism.

As a directive he states:

America's task is to be realistic in its view of the actual conditions of international politics without sacrificing its allegiance to universal ideals as an ultimate standard of conduct. . . . Certainly there is a vast area of international relations in which the universal ideals of peaceful settlement, humanitarianism, individual liberty, and the extension of material progress coincide with America's selfish advantage . . . . it is not a question of choosing between idealism or self-interest but of combining the two.[7]

He depicts rational self-interest divorced from ideal principles to be as weak and erratic a guide as undisciplined Idealism. Since men are motivated by faith and morals as well as by fear and self-preservation, ideals are as much an instrument of national power as weapons of war. Idealism is the dynamic element which will

[6] *Ibid.*, 13.
[7] *Ibid.*, 441–42, 446, 449.

move Americans to adopt bold measures necessary in the current crisis. However, he admits that the reconciliation takes place more readily on a verbal level than in actual conduct.

His reason for insistence upon this combination is one of the most explicit statements of Mr. Osgood's Idealism:

If one believes that enrichment of the individual's life, and not the aggrandizement of the state, is the ultimate goal of politics, if one believes that the object of survival is not mere breathing but the fulfilment of the liberal and humane values of western civilization, then the preservation and the promotion of American power and interests cannot be an end in itself . . . unless American security is measured by ideal standards transcending the national interest, it may take forms that undermine the moral basis of all social relations.

If the Christian, humanitarian, and democratic values, which are the basis of America's social and political institutions, are valid at all, they are as valid outside American borders as within. Consequently, if they cease to compel respect in America's foreign relations, they will, ultimately become ineffective in her domestic affairs. The resulting destruction of America's moral fiber through the loss of national integrity and the disintegration of ethical standards would be as great a blow to the nation as an armed attack upon her territory. . . .

If in the eyes of millions of people living in underdeveloped areas of the world the United States ceases to stand for a positive and constructive program of social and material progress, if American ideals no longer mean anything beyond smug generalities and hypocritical rationalizations of selfish national advantage, then all the wealth and military power the United States can muster will not render these people an asset to the free world. . . .

If national self-interest were the sole standard of conduct common to nations, an improvement in the power position of one nation would set off a wave of distrust among the rest; and eventually, the pressure of international conflict would loosen what moral and ethical restraints man has succeeded in placing on his collective behavior; international society would disintegrate into a Hobbesian state of anarchy.[8]

8 *Ibid.*, 442–43, 449–50.

In his specific enumeration of items of national interest he names territorial integrity, political independence, fundamental governmental institutions, national security (absence of fear), self-sufficiency (since desire for untrammeled national will is at the heart of national distinctness), prestige, and national honor.[9]

Walter Lippmann

Walter Lippmann in his recent *Essays in the Public Philosophy* deals primarily with domestic politics, but his highly moral tone here with reference to public conduct, qualifies him as an Idealist. However, his approach to foreign policy elsewhere is akin to that of the Realists. He defines the public philosophy as natural law "imposed on mankind by common human nature, that is, by reason in response to human needs and instincts." [10] The public interest is "what men would choose if they saw clearly, thought rationally, acted disinterestedly and benevolently." [11] The rational man, acting in a "real world," strikes a balance between what he desires and what he can do.

While he deplores the abandonment of the public philosophy, he explains how it fell out of fashion.[12] Lest power corrupt it, the government was denied proprietorship over this realm of the mind and spirit. From this provision was derived the notion that principles are private, with only subjective relevance, and that what man *should* do is not a subject of public accountableness. In answer to how the alienation can be overcome, Lippmann suggests that modern man will have to be convinced that the traditions of civility

[9] *Ibid.*, 5–16.
[10] Walter Lippmann, *Essays in Public Philosophy* (New York: Atlantic Monthly Press, 1955), 101, 107. He uses the definition in F. de Juleta, "The Science of Law," *The Legacy of Rome*, Cyril Bailey (ed.), (Oxford: Clarendon Press, 1928), 202. Mr. Lippmann writes primarily on politics and diplomatic history.
[11] *Ibid.*, 42–43.
[12] *Ibid.*, 99–106.

were not abandoned because they became antiquated, the public philosophy having preceded the advance of modern science and the industrial revolution. He cites the solidity over a two thousand year span in European thought, of the conviction that "the rational faculties of men can produce a common conception of law and order which possesses a universal validity."

His summary of the modern dilemma touches upon the premises of the Realists:

The modern trouble is in a low capacity to believe in precepts which restrict and restrain private interests and desire. . . . In the prevailing popular culture all philosophies are the instruments of some man's purpose, all truths are self-centered and self-regarding, and all principles are the rationalizations of some special interest. There is no public criterion of the true and the false, of the right and the wrong, beyond that which the preponderant mass of voters, consumers, readers and listeners happen at the moment to be supposed to want.[13]

His conclusion is that salvation lies in re-establishment of the ideas of Natural Law in the "minds of men of light and leading."

A major influence in the formulation of Wilson's Fourteen Points is attributed to Lippmann when he served as secretary of the House Inquiry in 1917.[14] As an editor of the *New Republic*, he did not, however, urge American participation in World War I on the basis of the President's lofty purposes. Although he recognizes that the occasion for United States entry was unrestricted submarine warfare (against merchant shipping), he posits the compelling reason to be the cutting of Atlantic communication leading to the conquest of western Europe by imperial Germany.[15] He denies that the war was engaged in to overthrow the Kaiser and to make Germany democratic; if our Atlantic defenses had not been threatened, "private citizens would still have made faces at the Kaiser, but the

---

[13] *Ibid.*, 114.

[14] Osgood, *Ideals and Self-Interest*, 275; Seymour (ed.), *Intimate Papers*, III, 171.

[15] Lippmann, *U.S. Foreign Policy: Shield of the Republic* (Boston: Little, Brown, 1943), 33–37.

nation would not have made war upon him." He attributes Wilson's failure to win support for the League to the fact that he refused to give the people the compelling reason for entering the war, and he represented League responsibilities as philanthropy rather than as a method of finding allies to support American commitments from the Western Hemisphere to the China coast. Regarding charters and declarations, he notes that they do not create associations; they merely regulate and ratify the pre-existing will of groups of men.

Lippmann sees the Wilsonian concept of aggression as "armed rebellion against the universal and eternal principles of the world society" in the Truman Doctrine, the Marshall Plan, NATO, intervention in Korea, and the Mutual Security Act. While he agrees that this approach has made it easier to push through Congress measures for use of American troops and money abroad, he holds this Wilsonian ideology to be an "impossible foundation for the foreign policy of a nation, placed as we are and carrying the burden of our responsibilities." [16] As a nation too bellicose in time of war and too pacifist in time of peace, America has not been able to prevent war, has not been prepared to fight, and has not known how to settle the peace afterward. Prior to this time, America has been able to stand apart or to support existing coalitions after measuring them by ideological standards. Today, because there is no rich and powerful nation sharing our ideals, on whom we can rely to redress the balance in our favor, the policies must be more cautious.

Lippmann criticizes the abandonment of the Atlantic Community partnership in 1945 in favor of unmitigated universalism in United Nations.[17] Had the United States made it clear before the end of the war that negotiations and treaties to establish United Nations would be entered upon by the Atlantic Community rather than by separate states, its position would not have been weakened. With the setting up of the Marshall Plan and NATO, the nation

[16] *Id.*, *Isolation and Alliances* (Boston: Little, Brown, 1952), 23–26.
[17] *Ibid.*, 39–41.

after a costly detour, had to begin working its way back to the right road.

Dexter Perkins

Dexter Perkins singles out the criticism of three men who are profoundly depressed with the state of American diplomacy: [18] George Kennan, Hans Morgenthau, and Walter Lippmann. While conceding that some of their observations are salutary, he is disturbed by their latent distrust of popular government itself. Perkins, disavowing elitism, says that the best wisdom is to be found in the collectivity, not because a single member is superior, but because

. . . the reconciliation of the wills, the aspirations, and the interests of all, even the prejudice of all, provides a more solid and enduring basis of action than the will, the aspiration, and the interest of any individual or of any class. . . . To assume that there is any form of governmental organization that will exorcise sentiment and install pure and abstract reason on the throne would be to take a view of human nature that has little warrant in experience.[19]

His second criticism of the Realists is that many of their charges depend upon hypothetical history and a certain omniscience.

In his defense of democratic nations' conduct of diplomacy, he grants [20] that they are loath to resort to violence and that they underestimate the role of force, since the genius of democracy lies in reconciliation of conflicting views. America has an unwarranted optimism about human nature. There is the tendency in democratic governments to talk too much, to make conflicting public pronouncements, to give out too much information on national defense

[18] Dexter Perkins, *Popular Government and Foreign Policy* (Pasadena: Ford Foundation Fund for Adult Education, April, 1956), 6–7. This volume contains three lectures: "The First Great Testings 1914–29," "Meeting the Totalitarian Challenge 1930–55," "The Road to Success." Hereafter referred to as *Popular Government*. Professor Perkins of Cornell University is a diplomatic historian.

[19] *Ibid.*, 6–8.

[20] *Ibid.*, 58–62.

in order to secure the assent of Congress. There is the tendency to sentimentalize issues and to be rigid in vesting every question with an aura of principle. While a democratic government will not barter away liberties of others as diplomats have sometimes done, at the same time it cannot get utopia by merely asking for it. He mentions the fact that the mass of men, not equipped to understand the ramifications of foreign affairs, attach themselves to such considerations:

> . . . the idea that democratic government is the best government on earth (irrespective of the particular situation of a given nation), or the idea that conquest is inherently immoral (without too sharp scrutiny of the American past in this regard), or the idea that it is wrong to negotiate in secret (though it is hard to see how diplomacy could be carried on if there were not at least some secrecy), or the idea that the state is bound by the same moral code as the individual, though this is a knotty question for philosophers.[21]

He notes that moral repugnance to imperialism might blind Americans to the injudiciousness of giving complete independence to nations not yet prepared for it, that publicity in international affairs sometimes makes compromise difficult, that naïveté about moral obligations of a nation might lead to quixotic action or to impossible righteousness. But in spite of all these weaknesses, he contends that foreign policy under popular government is no more susceptible to error than that under different types of regimes, especially those of totalitarian stripe. Alluding to the wars of the twentieth century in which no major democratic government has committed aggression, he questions the logic of blaming the ills of the world on those who seek to maintain peace by bringing about social adjustments of the international order.[22] The devotees of power politics have plunged the world into blood.

Professor Perkins answers the charge that to foreigners, America's lofty moral tone sounds like cant since this nation itself has

[21] *Id.*, *The American Approach to Foreign Policy* (Cambridge: Harvard University Press, 1952), 65. Hereafter referred to as *American Approach*.
[22] *Id.*, *Popular Government*, 21.

made deals. First he points out the reprehensible bargains which are exceptions to America's over-all record: [23] 1) Thomas Jefferson's attempt to bribe the French government to pressure Spain into ceding the Floridas, 2) the Taft-Katsura Memoranda of 1908 dealing with Korea and the Philippines, 3) the Yalta agreement on Manchuria at the expense of China. He replies that they should remember also that on occasion the United States *has* put ethical considerations ahead of national interest, narrowly defined.

Discrediting the argument that the economic factor is exclusive and decisive as a motive power in man, Perkins shows that man is swayed by faiths and loyalties, both religious and secular, which do not correspond to his pursuit of profit. Those who emphasize the role of sheer physical power apart from moral considerations in the activity of nations, miss the point that even the Soviet leaders declare their end to be betterment of the fortunes of the human race. While making no claim that American foreign policy is always altruistic, he stresses the fact that the citizens' belief that they are defending right and justice is one of the mainsprings of that devotion which brings victory.[24] Although all governments try to surround their foreign policies with the aura of an ideal, the difference between a Hitler and a Woodrow Wilson is that Wilson believed in what he was saying, and Hitler was cynically engineering a hoax.

In time of war it seems necessary in a democratic society to sublimate the issue. Lincoln dramatized his point in the Gettysburg Address. Wilson was equally justified, Perkins believes, since it would not have been easy to explain to the average man "what the ending of British rule on the sea might mean." The charge that America can wage war but not make peace, he answers by pointing out that permanent situations can seldom be created at the end of a war:

The new balance of power never expresses satisfactorily the aspirations and interests of both the victors and the vanquished; when the van-

[23] *Id., American Approach,* 78.
[24] *Ibid.,* 62–63, 82.

quished recover or new alignments are created, the chance for a new conflict arises. There will be lasting peace only when men devise machinery to alter the balance without violence, and believe in that machinery.[25]

However, he concludes that there is no evidence that the institutional approach to peace, as in a world government, is the best, and certainly that it is not the only one.[26]

Vera Micheles Dean

Vera Micheles Dean reminds Americans that morality and power are not necessarily irreconcilable; [27] power in armaments or money is in itself neither good nor evil, but becomes such by its use. She observes that in its new role of world leadership and its experience with *Realpolitik,* the United States has tended to assume that power must be divorced from morality, whereas in the past it has derived its strength more from moral principles than from physical resources or from weapons. The misunderstanding lies in confusing morality with moralizing—in the latter case, there has been a tendency to verbalize while assuming no responsibility for implementing the moral principles which could have had fruitful effects upon the world community.

Our national tendency to moralize—a tendency we share with the British—has caused us to see the world not in terms of geography, economics, military strategy, social clashes, and so on, but as a sort of Zoroastrian struggle between good and evil, between the virtuous West and the nefarious Russians (and only yesterday with the Germans and the Japanese). . . . The trouble with the crusading approach to world affairs, however, is that once the demons have been exorcised—as after the unconditional surrender of the Germans and the Japanese—and it

[25] *Id., Popular Government,* 18.
[26] *Id., American Approach,* 67.
[27] Vera Micheles Dean, *Foreign Policy Without Fear* (New York: McGraw-Hill, 1953), 180. Mrs. Dean is research director and editor for the Foreign Policy Association.

becomes apparent that the world continues to be plagued by many troubles, then the danger arises that we may simply throw up our hands in despair at human wickedness.[28]

She traces this defect to a lack of historical perspective. Americans do not anticipate that nations will act out of self-interest rather than altruism; they condemn all aspects of balance of power. The other friendly nations start with the premise "that every great power aspires to enlarge its sphere of influence and to gain all the economic and strategic advantages it can, by peaceful means if possible, by war only if all other methods fail." Though the others did not condone the German and Japanese gamble, though they did not approve Russia's absorption of the Satellites, they were not so shocked as were Americans.

Mrs. Dean outlines the following promises which America can make and the expectations of fulfillment they can hold reasonably.[29] Regarding political democracy, we cannot duplicate our own pattern in a country which did not inherit and gradually assimilate the institutions of western civilization, especially the Anglo-Saxon model. We can assist them to make the best of their opportunities, offer to share the experience of our teachers, social workers, business men, and labor leaders, but it is they "who must shape to their own ends such lessons as they wish to learn from us." Along economic and social lines, we may help to the extent of our ability in their efforts at land and tax reform, eradication of illiteracy, electrification, road building and sanitation. We shall also endeavor to facilitate their exports to the United States and to procure for them use of world markets. We should not assert prior claims to their strategic materials which they need for economic development.

We may view with sympathy their efforts at reform, but we must resist the temptation to move in as a clean-up squad. At least as much attention should be paid to the interests of labor as to those

[28] *Ibid.*, 8–9.
[29] *Ibid.*, 171–80.

of employers; the latter might be encouraged in countries receiving financial aid, to give workers a greater share in the fruits of expanded production, so that having a stake in the well-being of their nation's economy, they would have incentive to oppose Communism. In armament obligations, the United States should decide jointly with its allies, the means to check Russian aggression and internal subversion.

We must not expect them to fight or to man bases solely for our sake, any more than we help them solely for their own sake. But we can expect them to fight for the sake of maintaining a collective security system under the sponsorship of the United Nations, which they would regard as a form of insurance for themselves as well as for us.[30]

Singlehandedly, we cannot promise to rehabilitate and develop the economies of all underdeveloped lands which might block Russia, but a reasonable amount of aid might be promised to areas that are ready to introduce reforms which would make the grants useful. To forestall the attack of "imperialism," this aid should be channeled as much as possible through United Nations and its affiliated agencies.

Our main preoccupation in the next fifty years will not be to discover how we can transpose our way of life to other continents, by force, diplomacy, or financial inducement, but how we can fuse the civilization developed here with other civilizations of the world in such a way as to strengthen the fabric of international society. The variegated interests of men transcend the boundaries of nation-states. In the battle of ideas we shall not succeed if we plead for universal allegiance to the American idea. . . . We must be careful not to adopt a fundamentalist policy of perfectionism. We must not demand unconditional surrender and abject acquiescence.[31]

Foreign policy is but a reflection of a nation's philosophy of life. Domestic and foreign policies are but the faces of the same coin. It is

[30] *Ibid.*, 176–77.
[31] *Ibid.*, 179–80.

impossible to oppose change at home and press for it abroad; to carry the torch for anti-colonialism in Asia, Africa, and the Middle East, yet tolerate racial discrimination within one's own borders; to hedge the country with high tariff and immigration barriers, yet urge other nations to create free economic unions and to offer refuge generously to homeless people; to oppose feudalism in theory, yet help to perpetuate it in practice by economic and military aid to feudal goverments.[32]

Elsewhere, Mrs. Dean insists that the American-Russian ideological conflict is nothing unique since history is strewn with the clash of ideas.[33] She attributes the development of a cold war status to the fact that "other powers which might have cushioned the clash have disappeared or dwindled in strength." Obsession with Russian relationship as *the* problem of American foreign policy has inflated the Soviet out of proportion in the eyes of the rest of the world. Were Russia not a problem, there would still be the need for development of a policy based upon American principles and objectives, which were not merely a reflex to another country's maneuver.

Charles Burton Marshall

Charles Burton Marshall is dubious whether national interest is a conclusive guide in any policy problem; he prefers accent upon responsibility as the only way of serving national interest in these times.[34] Since ours is the position of greatest political strength and economic resourcefulness, the United States should assume the primary burden for discovering and developing an identity of interests among friendly nations. In the arena of responsibility the question is not *whether*, but *how*, to serve national interest. "The

[32] *Ibid.*, 25.

[33] *Id.*, "United States Foreign Policy in the Atomic Age," *American Scholar*, XVII (Winter, 1947–48), 90–91.

[34] Charles Burton Marshall, "National Interest and National Responsibility," *Annals of the American Academy of Political and Social Science*, XXVIII (July, 1952), 84–90. Mr. Marshall is former chief of the Policy Planning Staff, Department of State.

legitimate question of politics is not how to eliminate conflict of interest—a utopian concept—but how to organize society so that it can be adjusted rather than fought out." [35] Nations do have interests; sometimes they coincide, sometimes they harmonize, sometimes they are different but compatible, sometimes they are mutually exclusive. "It is useless to try to ignore this by talk about global harmony and the universal state." The resolving of these clashing interests in a higher synthesis requires of us the highest moral capacity in politics, "the capacity to be just in one's own cause, to be jealous of an opponent's rights as of one's own, and to suffer differences without permitting them to divide." [36] As Americans, he stresses, we must adjust our minds to "the reciprocalness of alliances and coalitions"—it is only fitting that we permit ourselves to be influenced by our allies.[37] To generate the consent necessary to maintain those coalitions, we must interpret our national interest on a wider basis than heretofore; if the image projected by the United States be impaired, freedom might be blighted everywhere, as the factors of security move against us. Successful leadership demands that our objectives be such that they seem important to those whom we lead. If we are so sure of being absolutely right, without need for listening to others, we lose adaptability. Great spans of time are required for the creative developments in world politics wherein a union of minds is sought. Patience will achieve more than force, since consent is a slow business.[38]

[35] *Id.*, "The National Interest and Current World Problems," *U.S. Department of State Bulletin*, XXVI (May, 1952), 699.

[36] *Id.*, *The Limits of Foreign Policy* (New York: Henry Holt, 1954), 98–99.

[37] *Ibid.*, 101–03.

[38] John J. McCloy, High Commissioner for Germany 1949–52, former president of the International Bank for Reconstruction and Development, and Assistant Secretary of War, shares with Marshall the conviction that national self-interest is not capable of counteracting the divisive influences at work today, and adds that the United States by its history and government is committed to a policy of law and morality. Noting the critical skein in the thinking of people whom we would befriend, he traces it to

Marshall makes interesting observations about the method of arriving at this working accord:

The projection of all differences into open debate, especially within the framework of an organization set up on the basis of a document enunciating moral and legal principles for the governance of world affairs, involves a very real danger of making the positions of disputants inflexible. . . . Moreover, the idea of having the whole world choose sides on every local issue may often tend only to make large problems out of small ones and to intensify world differences without doing anything whatever to help the parties immediately concerned on toward a solution. . . .

The peril of histrionicism [use of emotional elements and hyperbole to elicit public enthusiasm] is not new to international affairs but it has become exaggerated in the age of mass communication and the time of mass participation, whether real or sham, in the process of government. One of the drawbacks of microphone diplomacy—of the conduct of international affairs in large gatherings under full publicity —is the degree in which its usages encourage the theatrical attitude in world relations and tempt vain men and governments to try for grandeur by big talk.[39]

---

their combined reliance upon our protection, and fear of our immaturity. "Europeans are convinced that another war and occupation by a ruthless enemy, even if followed by re-liberation, would mean complete loss of their civilization, so complete that it could not be rehabilitated. Europe, exhausted and weary, simply cannot accept the idea of war. It fears the United States can." John Jay McCloy, *The Challenge to American Foreign Policy* (Cambridge: Harvard University Press, 1953), 20-25.

[39] Marshall, *Limits of Foreign Policy*, 115-16. Sir Alfred Zimmern, former professor of international relations at Oxford, co-founder and director of the Geneva School of International Studies, and Executive Secretary and adviser on UNESCO, had a favorable interpretation of the use of public debate: "For a foreign minister to know that in so many weeks time, he will be facing his opposite number in another country and must be ready to answer his points in public debate or in private conversation involves a most salutary discipline . . . in social behavior. If the League of Nations had done no more than that, it would already have rendered most valuable service." Sir Alfred Zimmern, *The American Road to World Peace* (New York: E. P. Dutton, 1953), 80.

Of the procedures of arbitration and conciliation, he makes these judgments.[40] Arbitration works well in settling disputes of matters deemed immaterial to the vital interests of the parties, differences expressible in terms of law. Conciliation, a formalized method of mediation, has not proved useful in a single instance; on the contrary, it has done harm in protracting the illusion that great world political issues may be translated into "questions solvable by legal and judicial means." It purports to strengthen peace by pretending that the factor of force is not really present. A treaty of pacific intention may express a factual situation among a small number of nations, but as a universal proposal, it states a fiction.

He respects the advice given to young Gladstone by one of his mentors—that politics is an unsatisfactory business and one must accept imperfect results.

I do not disparage the importance of objectives. Only in the light of ultimate purposes can one know how to proceed problem by problem in this field. Moreover, I do not believe that good is forever beyond reach, but I am sure that the way to it is difficult and long. . . . The never ending dilemmas inherent in measuring what we would like to do against what we can do impose great moral burdens. . . . The rebellion against that burden sometimes takes the form of an abdication of will, and relief is sought in a passive fatalism about the problems of national existence. Again the rebellion may take the form of resorting to the counsel of violence as the solvent for the difficulties and restraints which life imposes.

In either form the rejection is a rejection of life itself, for life imposes on nations, as on men, the obligation to strive without despair even though the way may be long and the burdens heavy. To recognize this is in itself a source of strength.[41]

As a practical example of enduring imperfect world conditions, he cites coexistence "with a great power that tries to lead a double life as a state and as a conspiracy"; without contemplating a per-

[40] *Ibid.*, 110–13.
[41] *Id.*, "The Nature of Foreign Policy," *U.S. Department of State Bulletin,* XXVI (March 17, 1952), 420.

petually frozen *status quo*, it chooses this as preferable to general war and its sequel. His explanation of the strategy here recommended, resembles the containment policy of George Kennan: "It rests . . . upon the assumption that the factors of position, population, talents, resources, and moral values redound to the ultimate advantage of the side of our interests, and that in the long pull it will be the adversary who must adjust his purposes." [42] The policy calls for improving our armed strength and that of nations in alliances with us, helping the depleted economies of our friends to recover and to improve, widening the area of peace by collaboration with former enemies such as Japan and West Germany, and avoiding losses in areas of sharp political conflict.

William Yandell Elliott

The composite opinions of a Study Group for the Woodrow Wilson Foundation represent a virile expression of Idealism.[43] They preface their stand with a glance at the distrust which the Founding Fathers had for unchecked power and for human frailty, at nineteenth century democracy's underestimation of the effects of original sin, at the unenlightened doctrine of inevitable progress. The lesson to be inferred from this is that democracies must take a more realistic view of the evils of human nature as well as of the potentialities for good.

The United States and the United Nations are essential to one another: our present national values will survive only if we can maintain support for them outside as well as inside the country, and the United Nations may be able to survive only if America is powerful enough. Thus power is a means to a moral end, the freedom of the world. They allude to the fact that "moralizing" in foreign policy [44] has provoked the extreme reaction of defining

[42] *Id.*, "National Interest and National Responsibility," 88–89.
[43] William Yandell Elliott *et al.*, *United States Foreign Policy: its organization and control* (New York: Columbia University Press, 1952).
[44] *Ibid.*, 15.

politics in terms of military force, but they deny the need for Machiavellian diplomacy as an antidote for the former escapism. Because moral values, like faith in a mission, govern the responses of human beings and supply the necessary dynamism, democracies must combine morality with power.

Without giving an unqualified condemnation of balance of power, they would accord it the place of a proximate objective in world politics today, "if the force representing freedom and resistance to imperialistic aggression is the weaker side and requires to be built up to a balance for sheer survival."

But a balance of power alone that does not aim at imposing restraints on future aggression of every order by establishing an over-balance to support a world system of law is surely not a solution. Indeed this so-called realism looks uncommonly like surrendering to the devil all the best tricks. . . . The concept of national interest which is limited to the protection only of those lines of action that promote the immediate satisfaction of a nation's economic requirements and the resultant political aims for protecting this type of national objective has very little chance of aligning on a state basis, sufficient power behind it to meet the challenge of powerful aggression bent on changing the world, such as comes from crusading communism. Moscow would be left with all the promises, to unite the world and to supply its own brand of "liberation" from the capitalists. . . . Any balance of power based on national interests alone also lacks the dynamic of a promise of either a secure or of a really free world.[45]

They promptly add that this does not justify the substitution of ineffectual performance for the necessary power systems— rather, it supports the need for recognizing a common line of interest among those who wish to assure their survival at the hands of totalitarian subversion and coercion. They also assure the doubting Realists that they would not foster self-determination for peoples who are completely unready. They would insist upon credentials for the aspiring nationalists, they would demand circumspect use of natural resources for world purposes as well as

[45] *Ibid.*, 20–21.

for native needs, and they would not concede "a legal fiction of sovereignty to tribes only slightly removed from savagery."[46]

Although Americans oppose the Marxist economic fallacy, they sometimes give the same primacy to the economic factor by stressing an increased standard of living as the adequate way to meet the Communist challenge; they would be chagrined to be labelled "materialists," the Study Group observes.[47] They accent the fact that wealth or technical superiority will not insure the health and survival of a civilization; they must be supplemented by belief in and practice of its value system, even at a heavy cost. To combat the non-Christian Marxism and Islamic nationalism, the United States must maintain its ideals, yet show leadership in power politics in which it is not well versed.

Whereas they favor development of an international regime of law, they would not favor a world government in which totalitarian systems like those of Russia and China were given

[46] *Ibid.*, 22. Clyde Eagleton, formerly a legal expert in the State Department and currently professor of international law at New York University, also stresses the necessity for criteria in this matter so as to serve the good of the community of nations. The apostles of fragmentation sometimes forget that the latter has rights and needs. The United Nations, representing the welfare of the whole, must question the intent of an ambitious group, the prudence of a weak or quarrelsome fledgling which might bring upon itself the attack of a covetous or injured neighbor against whom the UN would have to defend it.

Strategically located areas are danger spots if they are weakly held, or if their sovereigns cannot develop the natural resources which the general community needs critically. Should it have independence if it is unable to protect certain human rights, if it is unable to support itself economically? With the increase of infant states (three-fourths of the UN members are now incapable of contributing to the organization's military and economic support) each with a vote and little consequent responsibility, the burden of the stronger members becomes more disproportionate. "The duty of the United Nations to guard the welfare of the whole community appears to be in indirect conflict with its supposed obligation to produce more and more infant states and turn them loose upon the streets." Clyde Eagleton, "Excesses of Self-Determination," *Foreign Affairs*, XXI (July, 1953), 592–604.

[47] *Ibid.*, 17, 196–97.

weight according to their population. They were unanimous in labelling world federalism as utopian, but the members differed in their degree of emphasis upon NATO as compared to the entire United Nations.[48] In his personal comments, Mr. Elliott wished to register stronger feeling than the joint report did, that nothing was to be gained by concessions to Moscow which involved genuine surrender of principles, since such settlements prepare the world for an explosion as did Munich. He endorses Wilson's stand that moral community among nations must be the essential basis; yet today that is not true in the world forum. He suggests that we beware of those apostles of appeasement "who parade a tough 'realism' based on a calculus of power in the so-called 'national interest.' " These formulae overlook the fact that men's loyalites are the most important ingredient of real power. In order not to destroy the UN's moral claim to speak for all peoples, he recommends that only free nations be admitted in the future.[49]

Feller, Fox

In response to the neo-Realist charge that it is impossible to judge the conduct of states by moral criteria, A. H. Feller reminds them that the notion of inherent amorality of state conduct in-

---

[48] *Ibid.*, 28, 193. Clarence Streit might be representative of world federalism. In 1939 he proposed forming a nucleus of the fifteen democracies bordering the Atlantic; universality of world government would be their ultimate goal. The union would involve loss of power by national states, but the citizens themselves would suffer no relinquishment since they would simply shift certain rights from one government to another; both the state and the world governments standing alone would be incomplete. The state would transfer to the union its right to make war and peace, its right to regulate inter-state and foreign trade, its right to control the value of money and the media of communication. A person would be a citizen of both a national and an international community. Clarence Streit, *Union Now:* Proposal for Federal Union of Democracies of the North Atlantic (New York: Harper and Bros., 1939), 36, 88, 132–34, 179.

[49] *Ibid.*, 255–56.

troduced by Machiavelli is an aberration, not an immutable truth.[50] Although there must be compromises and adjustments of interests outside the legal realm, and the procedure of judgment must be different for a state from that followed in the case of an individual, still a standard exists. He objects to the fact that the Realists make the methods of diplomacy and institutions of international organization seem incompatible; conferences and treaties are part of diplomatic technique as much as secret meetings and dispatches by courier. He feels that the Realist substitute of "diplomacy" and "national interest" for moral principles is inadequate; it can never retain the allegiance of the mass of people who hope for a better world, and it will serve to make the nation the focus of hostility and fears.

> The Charter [of the UN] is no mere casual by-product of an American desire for "juridical tidiness." It is the embodiment of the deeply felt desires and needs of millions of people everywhere for peace, economic well-being, and respect for the development of human personality. . . . The objectives themselves are the common ground of mankind's will for survival with decency. It is the task of diplomacy so to conduct the adjustment of affairs between nations as to move toward the accomplishment of these goals.[51]

William T. R. Fox deplores the pessimism in Morgenthau's analysis, in which "Power, Evil, and Original Sin are three names for the same thing." [52] He labels the appeal as "neo-Calvinist" in its conviction that the kingdom of God will not prevail on earth

---

[50] A. H. Feller, "In Defense of International Law and Morality," *Annals of the American Academy of Political and Social Science*, CCLXXXII (July, 1952), 77–83. Mr. Feller was director of the Legal Department of UN from 1945 until his death in 1954.

[51] *Ibid.*, 83.

[52] William T. R. Fox, "The Reconciliation of the Desirable and the Possible," *American Scholar*, XVIII (Spring, 1949), 207–16. Mr. Fox is assistant director of the Institute of International Studies, managing editor of *World Politics*, and director of the Institute of War and Peace Studies, Columbia University.

in spite of man's efforts, and that "peace on earth and good will to men is something to be sung about in Christmas carols and not to be translated into actuality." While Mr. Fox censures also those whose faith in a particular design for universal peace would lead them to precipitate a third world war to make the Russians accept it, he would insist that firmness must be wedded to patience in the exploration of every avenue for peace.

Citing Morgenthau's judgment that war is never necessary for the upholding of a moral principle, yet a nation must be prepared to wage war in behalf of a national interest like security, territorial integrity, and basic institutions, he inquires whether one can decide what the basic institutions are, without consulting moral principle. If the Realist holds that the essence of the western state system is "respect for the existence and the individuality of its members," then he is recognizing the right of full development of *other* personalities and groups. The question remains, whether the national interest of a given state can be determined objectively except in terms of explicitly affirmed values.

Because the policy-maker must reconcile the desirable and the possible, he must weigh gains and losses, and not merely invoke moral principles in an irresponsible way, as Fox indicates that Cordell Hull did. Because there can be no escape from compromise, this fact makes politics a vocation for the mature man of prudence. Fox would challenge the sweeping phraseology of the Atlantic Charter and of the Truman Doctrine; he would deny that leadership in the UN and in the Marshall Plan are exclusively the result of America's belief in the brotherhood of man.

The European Recovery Program appears unselfish in a context in which material values alone are considered; but it is more correctly assessed as based on mutual interest, including the American national interest, once the non-material values of freedom and survival are also brought into the analysis. . . . That the American national interest seems to be in so little conflict with the interests of the other powers on the outer side of the Iron Curtain . . . shows that the national interest of the United States is in our time formulated in terms which can be supported by any other power whose diplomatic watchword is "live and let live." [53]

Jessup, Mowrer

Philip C. Jessup takes this counter-offensive to the Realists:

It seems to be the thesis of some who profess to be realists to deny the twentieth-century reality of anything which does not fit into a nineteenth-century mold. Nothing could be more unrealistic. The old mold is broken, and a realistic twentieth-century policy cannot be poured into it.[54]

The contrast to which he refers is that in the past the propriety of using force to vindicate rights and to promote interests was an unchallenged, normal aspect of international relations. But with the organization of United Nations, even the Great Powers renounced the unilateral resort to force.

Edgar Ansel Mowrer advocates that a good foreign policy is one which takes into consideration all of the relevant desires of the citizens, and a bad policy is one which "assumes that *homo politicus* can be sundered from *homo sapiens.*" [55] He parries against Morgenthau's proposition that national survival is to be pursued by statesmen above any considerations of morality, the demonstration that this would be true only if one of these spurious theses were correct: 1) Service of national interest promotes greater morality, 2) Patriotism is of a higher order than ordinary moral precepts, 3) Patriotism comes at the top of all moral values and must be the highest good of its own citizens.

[53] *Ibid.*, 214–16.
[54] Philip C. Jessup, "Ends and Means of American Foreign Policy," *International Stability and Progress: United States Interests and Instruments* (New York: Columbia University, The American Assembly, June, 1957), 33. Mr. Jessup, professor of international law and diplomacy at Columbia University, has served on the UN Security Council and General Assembly.
[55] Edgar Ansel Mowrer, "The Inevitable Compromise," *American Scholar*, XVIII (Summer, 1949), 378. Mr. Mowrer, a war correspondent, was director of the Office of War Information until 1943.

Louis J. Halle

As a preface to Louis J. Halle's plea for defense of civilization itself, these more cynical remarks would counter any suspicion that he is a utopian pundit. When government spokesmen announce that their policy reflects devotion to moral principles rather than expediency, he is reminded of the parallel suggestion that it is the florists' love of motherhood rather than love of money which prompts their Mother's Day ads.[56] The questions to be asked are whether the principle invoked actually determined the action, and whether the principle does in fact represent morality. He urges that not only fine moral policies, but also policies which will work, be adopted.

[Public opinion] hounds democratic governments with advice which may be wonderfully moral but which leaves them with their problems unsolved or aggravated. It is no wonder that a morality which overlooks the requirements of the problem sometimes seems cheap to those who, bearing the responsibility, are not free to overlook them.[57]

In his more profound writing, Mr. Halle states his premises about the nature of man for whom government is established. In accordance with the innate and equal dignity of creatures possessing souls and retaining a "spark of divinity," it was thought proper to their spiritual development that they should exercise freedom and self-government in this land; democracy was not adopted merely to produce a higher standard of living or any other material benefit.[58] Although inconsistencies between belief and practice "are inherent in the nature of man, that moral

[56] Louis J. Halle, "A Touch of Nausea," *New Republic*, CXXXVI (January 21, 1957), 15–17. Mr. Halle, a member of the State Department Policy Planning Staff until 1954, is research professor at the University of Virginia, and currently visiting professor at the Institute of Higher International Studies, Geneva.

[57] *Ibid.*, 16–17.

[58] *Id.*, *Civilization and Foreign Policy: An Inquiry for Americans* (New York: Harper & Bros., 1955), 22–25.

centaur, half beast and half god," the reality of the ideals is attested to by man's constant striving rather than by his failure of attainment. In contrast with the way life should be lived, he reflects:

It is hardly possible to avoid the conclusion that in our present thinking, man has become largely mouth and belly. Our aim, consequently, is no longer so much his moral improvement as the improvement of his living conditions. Our aspiration is for higher standards of living— better nourishment, better health, better housing, better clothing, better roads, better automobiles. When we seek to persuade others that our system of self-government under a regime of freedom is the best we no longer argue from the divinity in man or assert the rule of natural law. We point to standard of living we have achieved. "The more abundant life" has replaced "the good life" as the object of our self-government.[59]

His analysis of power is one of the most thorough. Showing that life, dynamic by nature and animated by kinetic energy, expresses itself in power, he denies that power can be estranged from life and considered as an evil in itself. It follows from this that the recurrent problem of politics, national and international, is to tame and control power within its legitimate channels.[60]

The arbitrament of what we sometimes called "naked power," power unsanctioned by law and unresponsive to ethics, piratical power serving the arbitrary ends of tyrants—this rather than power in itself was what we found offensive. . . . Believing that power politics meant war as well as tyranny, we undertook to illegitimatize rather than legalize them, to disenfranchise rather than regulate them, to denature power by solemn declarations and pledges to which it would submit, and to disarm the nations. . . . By refusing to accept power as a fact in international relations we ruled out any measures shrewdly designed to regulate it.[61]

He defines power as "the ability to get one's way" by use of eloquence, bearing, wisdom, knowledge, custom, or force. It is

[59] *Ibid.*, 28–29.
[60] *Ibid.*, 45.
[61] *Ibid.*, 47–49.

most secure when it has the willing consent of those who serve it. In evaluating what United States policy should be, he rejects both isolation and dominion.[62] Isolation would upset the present balance of power in favor of Moscow. With dominion, the American people, living like lords of the earth, would follow Faust in achieving immediate security by selling their souls; force would become the primary factor in the domestic community as well. The real issue today being between civilization and barbarism, these policies would both contribute to the spread of the latter.

To support his postulate that defense of civilization itself must be the United States policy, he says:

Our survival as the kind of nation we find we are requires us to defend our civilization as a whole, to associate ourselves with its other representatives in a defensive coalition, and to exercise the leadership of that coalition on a basis of consent. First of all we must put our civilization above our nation, if only because the nation is related to the civilization as the part to the whole. Even though we cared for nothing but the one room we inhabited in the mansion we would have to recognize that we could secure the room only by defending the building. And if we take a mature view we shall cherish Christendom, with all its historic glories and the promise of its vision, for its own sake.[63]

To show how this role would be exercised, he continues:

Then we must in this larger sphere as in the domestic, tolerate and even welcome diversity. We must not insist on the American way of life for others. . . . We must be willing to accommodate our particular interests to those of our allies even when that means a sacrifice on our part. If, for example, we open or close our markets to their production on the basis of our own economic interests only, without regard for the requirements of their economies, we must expect to find them the more reluctant to accept our leadership or entrust their welfare to us in any respect. And this will also be true if our military plans appear to encompass our defense at the price of theirs. . . . If we see a common problem one way and our allies see it another way we must not deal

[62] *Ibid.*, 206, 220–29.
[63] *Ibid.*, 231.

with them on the premise that right and wrong are settled by our own judgment, and that they must therefore acknowledge their error or stand convicted of willful perversity.[64]

Halle offers additional counsel about the management of this position of trust. Because he who wields power is tempted to make it his possession, there must be great restraint so as not to arouse antagonism. The nation must be wary of paternalism so as not to pauperize its allies with doles, treating them as poor relations, and thereby undermining their moral strength. There must be no discounting of the effectiveness of possessing adequate force and willingness to apply it as a means of deterring attack.

The requirements of this role of world responsibility would demand increased taxation and would place a check on the use of industrial facilities for luxury products. If Americans refuse to make the necessary material sacrifices, he predicts that they are rehearsing for a Carthaginian tragedy—like America, Carthage "enjoyed an incomparably high standard of living but would not take away from it for the sake of their own survival." [65] With the same eye to history, he recalls Thucydides' *History of the Peloponnesian War* as the best single book on international relations:

The tragedy of Athens, as Thucydides saw it, lay in her inability to live up to the moral responsibility that had come to her as a result of her moral excellence. She had achieved by sheer character, the prosperity that corrupts character. Power brought greed for power. She listened, now to evil counselors, the "realistic," and "practical" men of action in her midst, who said, in effect: "What thou wouldst highly, thou canst not have holily." The doom of Athens lay in that first act of despotism. . . . For once she had lost the confidence and good will of the Greeks by subjugating them she no longer dared to release them—and from that time on she found herself faced with the increasing union of her entire world against her.[66]

[64] *Ibid.*, 231–32.
[65] *Ibid.*, 257.
[66] *Ibid.*, 261, 266–67.

He recognizes that brave words cost nothing and bring plaudits from the people; a leader is tempted to brag about what the nation means to do, to be intractable in negotiation, but then to disparage the means of implementing the decisions if that entails sacrifice and is thus less palatable to the electorate. This policy of "bluster and a small stick" leads to great surrenders and great wars. Noting that the very same people are capable both of great nobility and of sordid abjection depending on the circumstances, he points to the need for inspiration especially in the form of living examples. But at the same time, he ponders whether a people too far sunken in depravity can generate effective leadership.

His outlook for the future contains no extravagant speculations; but in spite of our civilization's weaknesses, the opponents are closer to "primordial chaos."

What we can expect is that our present barbarian challengers, unable to prey on us, will have to make adjustments in their own disposition to our strength. We can expect the gradual restoration of a relatively stable balance of power in the world and the consequent creation of a situation in which such wars as occur may well remain limited because the antagonists have tacitly agreed to accept each other's survival as an alternative to mutual destruction. We can hope for, say, another century of troubled peace in which barbarism is frustrated and our nation finds itself gradually emerging on the high road of a more secure future. Beyond that one cannot see.[67]

Frank Tannenbaum

Frank Tannenbaum, whose attack on the Realists was cited in the introduction to that chapter, is exasperated by the fact that the Realists remain oblivious to the record of cooperative ex-

[67] *Ibid.*, 259–60. Halle's most recent book, *Choice for Survival* (published by Harper & Bros., in 1958), warns that the United States not allow itself to be trapped by the supposed choice of all-out war and all-out surrender. Whereas nuclear weapons may continue to be a deterrent to total war, specialized weapons may be adapted to limited conflicts. *Harper Books and Authors* (Social Studies), IX (March, 1958), 3.

perience among men and nations, and that they single out the relatively short history of the European state system as the exemplar of man's record, in order to depreciate the desirability of international institutions.[68] He discourages the use of a balance of power settlement, since it would lead our allies to conjecture that they are pawns in a game played at their expense. The existing partnership rests upon equality of members, no singular rights, and no sphere of influence. If we were to betray our friends, they would seek for a better bargain when the occasion presented itself. Were the United States to surrender its championing of equal dignity for small nations, it would eventuate in the forsaking of belief in the equal dignity of men.

In this current great debate about foreign policy, he finds deeper impact still than in that of the former contest between interventionists and isolationists. Both of the latter groups accepted the feasibility of international good will, the sanctity of treaties, adherence to international law, faith in the democratic devotion to human freedom. Not so the advocates of *Realpolitik*, who would convert the United States into a "centralized military empire," and would repudiate the American tradition of the "co-ordinate state," which reflects the experience of the federal system here, the Organization of American States, the British Commonwealth, and the Republic of Switzerland.[69] He sees that the opposing conceptions of international relations spring from different assumptions with respect to the nature of man and the role of human institutions.

While he admits that the United States is culturally a child of western Europe in its religious and political ideas, he stresses the absence of the feudal pattern in the shaping of that heritage into something unlike the original. There was no acceptance of the balance of power as a means of enhancing a king, and later a state. Here the government belongs to the people who made it, and

[68] Tannenbaum, *American Tradition*, 163. Mr. Tannenbaum, author and economist, teaches at Columbia University.
[69] *Ibid.*, xii–xiv.

they hold the governor and President to be their creation. The concept of equal sovereignty of states, or in other words, the concept of the co-ordinate state which is respected in spite of its wealth, power, size, population, or culture, justified the rebellion of the colonies against Great Britain and ordained American territorial policy. It was also the anvil for the Pan-American system, the evolution of the Monroe Doctrine into a multilateral policy, the Open Door in China, the League of Nations movement, the United Nations, the Truman Doctrine, and the defense of Korea. He declares that in their behavior the American people have either sought through isolation to escape from the rest of the world or to organize it on some sort of cooperative basis. When they have been guilty of denying their ideals by omission or commission, they have "made public confession of our shortcomings and put on sackcloth and ashes for the world to see." [70]

Tannenbaum draws up a body of unconscious commitments which have characterized the American people's attitudes toward life. They are committed to: the ordinary folk, the equality of men, individualism tempered by the common good, racial tolerance, democratic way of life, local self-government, nonhierarchical society, human well-being, religious tolerance, meeting issues as they arise, belief that evil is remediable, and rejection of utopianism, dogmatism, formalism, and fanaticism. [71] He interprets that beneath the dedication to democracy is the belief "that the voice of the people is the voice of God, that what the people want is what they need." [72]

---

[70] *Ibid.*, 11, 13, 29, 35–36, 57, 140.

[71] *Ibid.*, 16–28.

[72] Perhaps this bears traces of Rousseau's philosophy on this point, which might be summarized briefly. Since each man is by essence free and sovereignly independent, the renouncing of his liberty is forbidden to him; to make the state legitimate, therefore, the consent of individual wills must be its origin in the social contract, in which citizens totally abandon their rights in favor of the *general will*. Thus the people, always good and free, remain the source of their laws, guided only by the lawmaker. The *general*

F. S. C. Northrop

F. S. C. Northrop declares that a theory of foreign policy which is based upon power factors or economic aid alone is unrealistic and self-defeating.[73] Power, which is neutral with regard to moral and community responsibility, generates neutralism rather than allies. Only moral principles generate responsibility and thus give adequate insurance to allies. He credits George Kennan as being a "morally sensitive" individual, but explains his conversion to the power-politics theory out of his dissatisfaction with morally based foreign policy which reflected the living-law norms of only one nation, and consequently produced no peace. The cure for this mistake, he finds, does not lie in making foreign policy neutral with respect to ethical norms, but rather in basing that policy upon respect for the social institutions, cultural traditions, political parties, and domestic choices of other peoples. The living-law norms would be found in peoples' living habits, associations, and beliefs; international legal institutions should be harnessed to

will, which is then the permanently good movement of this "God-State," will tend toward the common good. Number does not create the _general will_, but merely indicates where it lies; the minority of necessity must have been deceived. The people, who are incorruptible, always want the general good, and need only guidance and clarification. When codified, the _general will_ is "the sole rule of justice and injustice for the state, and the sole measure of good and evil." F. J. Thonnard, _A Short History of Philosophy_, trans. Edward A. Maziars, C.PP.S. (Paris: Desclee and Cie, 1956), 749–50.

[73] F. S. C. Northrop, _European Union and United States Foreign Policy: a Study in Sociological Jurisprudence_ (New York: Macmillan, 1954), 111, 206. Mr. Northrop, professor of philosophy and law at Yale University Law School, demonstrates in his book how in the six years between the Hague Congress of the European Movement in May, 1948, and the Geneva Conference of April, 1954, the Truman-Acheson-Kennan policy of containment in both Asia and Eastern Europe, the Eisenhower-Dulles roll-back crusade against Communism, and the movement toward European Union affected one another.

these.[74] While economic aid is necessary, just as power is required for policing the world, experience in Europe with the Marshall Plan and Point Four, he feels, has made evident the fact that this aid alone cannot be the basis of an effective policy.

He would turn to culturalism as a stable basis of international collaboration; the successful experiment in this is the Continental European Community of six nations which achieved such a transfer of sovereignty because they approximated a common living-law; on the other hand, the Council of Europe consisting of fourteen nations did not accomplish this transfer because it lacked that basis of which regional proximity is no guarantee. The six nations can attain supranational positive law in matters economic, military, and political because they have accord in the normative content of their culture. Conversely, in the fourteen regionally associated states, where there are not common religious and political standards, a legal institution has been thwarted.[75]

From the above experience, Northrop derives the following implications for United Nations. In the immediate future the greatest practical compromise to be anticipated would be world confederation, not world federalism, since the diversity of living-law social norms among the eighty-odd nations of the world would make the latter prohibitive. However, both the Council of Europe and United Nations can achieve one specific transfer of sovereignty from the member nations—the right to have their unique living-law norms protected by the international community, if the states in turn would accept responsibility to contribute troops automatically to the police force. The principle of living-law pluralism would be the basis for international law and treaties among members; it would extend to economic, political, and philosophical norms for ordering communal relations. In NATO, he feels, the one specific transfer of sovereignty noted above, has been expedited successfully though the members do not possess common norms.[76]

[74] *Ibid.*, vi, 207–08.   [75] *Ibid.*, 111.
[76] *Ibid.*, 199–201.

Cook and Moos

Thomas I. Cook and Malcolm Moos in their joint work, *Power Through Purpose*, propose to steer between the extremes of utopian worldism and realistic nationalism. Because the United States as the holder of vast power is the heir and standard-bearer of the twofold culture strains of Graeco-Roman politics and law and Judaeo-Christian ethics and religion, they assign it the role of spreading ideals.[77] These revolve about man, the creature endowed with dignity for whose service earthly institutions exist, and for whom law is made to restrain excesses and to enable him to realize his goal. The understanding of national interest as exclusive and as the protegé of power politics would make us the victim of a united opposition we would beget. If nothing else, the facts of political and economic geography and the conspicuousness of our position demand the adoption of internationalism as national interest. They urge awareness that ethical appeal is the dynamo which generates power. The doctrine of national self-interest fails to make American foreign policy a fulfillment of the ethical purposes Americans have long pursued.[78]

They regret the fact that in the nineteenth century the teaching that law is the product of the state's will alone, gained repectability in the person of John Austin. The logic of this positivism eventuated in a denial of international law as true law; thence it was regarded as pious aspiration without effective restraining force. Governments considered themselves emancipated from the confines of ethics in foreign affairs. In contrast to this, Cook and Moos would envisage the only wise course to be that which fosters gradual harmonization between particular interests of different

[77] Thomas I. Cook and Malcolm Moos, *Power Through Purpose: the Realism of Idealism as a Basis for Foreign Policy* (Baltimore: Johns Hopkins Press, 1954), 206. Both authors are professors at Johns Hopkins University.

[78] *Ibid.*, 125–26.

peoples and the common good of humanity. The medium would not be moral principle unbacked by sanction, however; they recognize that the availability of force is necessary in politics. The method cannot embrace using other nations as means only; such "tough-minded unconcern for the well-being of other peoples," urged by narrow Realists, would preclude even the possibility of success.

Their definition of the international commitment of the United States is less cautious than that of the foregoing Idealists:

The international interest of the American social nation is a generous and humane tolerance. . . . It supports genuine cultural nationalism. It combats only that perversion of national distinctiveness known as integral nationalism, whereunder the nation-state seeks to embrace and absorb in its service all persons and all associations which function within its territory. . . . That commitment [to freedom] compels us to combat all types of totalitarian tyranny, by ideological warfare when possible, by force when necessary. It requires a refusal to ally ourselves with such regimes; a deliberate resistance to their expansion; and under certain conditions, even an intervention in their own lands to prevent oppression by them and to aid in their overthrow or transformation.[79]

They add that this does not mean imposition of American institutions nor the encouragement here of a false sense of superiority.

In discussing the ethics of intervention,[80] they insist upon the right and obligation of the United States to strengthen and hearten its friends who might be cursed with dangerous anti-democratic forces and parties; here the measure of intervention would be expediency. They relegate the post-Reformation doctrine of nonintervention to obsolescence. Today that tenet supports moral irresponsibility of governments which should be made to answer before the court of world opinion for the treatment of their own citizens; it also makes difficult the ensuring of personal rights on a world scale. The positivist rejection by a nation of the precepts of

[79] *Ibid.*, 130.
[80] *Ibid.*, 142–47.

natural law regarding man's rights, creates a presumption in favor of intervention, but the consequences of the armed action must be considered well, lest the "moral and material costs" to civilization outweigh the possible gains. However, if this nation abets a people in conspiring against their dictators, it must provide against retaliation at an unexpected moment.[81]

They conclude that the American tradition is nonstatist, that the people's loyalty revolves around institutions from the family outward, around regions, and around personal freedom—it is not identified with government as such. Thus "glory and aggrandizement of the nation-state are not, for Americans, synonymous with national interest." The old world stress on *Realpolitik* and balance of power are inapplicable in the new world situation.

Buell, Armstrong, Fenwick

Raymond L. Buell sees the operation of a Gresham's Law in international politics, as well as in economics—bad political methods tend to drive out the good.[82] Thus when power politics is dominant, democracies cannot compete with dictatorships unless they adopt dictatorial methods. He deduces from this that democracy is safe only when questions of foreign policy are settled by open methods of litigation and debate in international bodies of consultative and administrative nature, not by swift changes of diplomatic alignments.

Hamilton Fish Armstrong maintains that long-range problems cannot be handled by securing an isolated advantage here and a tactical success there.[83] The course must envisage the establishment of the principles of justice throughout world society; this

---

[81] *Ibid.*, 136–37.

[82] Raymond L. Buell, *Isolated America* (New York: Knopf, 1940), 453. Mr. Buell, a former professor, is a member of the Foreign Policy Association and an editor of *Time*.

[83] Hamilton Fish Armstrong, "Regional Pacts: Strong Points or Storm Cellars?" *Foreign Affairs*, XXVII (April, 1949), 355, 367. Mr. Armstrong is editor of *Foreign Affairs*.

corresponds to the highest interest of any state bent on retaining its freedom. This free and peaceful world society cannot be built, however, if the strong are neutral in the face of wrong. It is a lesser risk to play one's own role in the world fully with foresight.

Charles G. Fenwick elaborates much more upon the fact that neutrality for the United States in the twentieth century has been an "inherently illogical and paradoxical system," justified neither by history nor practical politics.[84] Announcement by the United States in time of peace, that it will treat lawbreaker and victim alike, has served as an invitation to lawlessness. Reliance upon neutrality was an easy way of escape from the moral obligation to distinguish between right and wrong. He demonstrates that the integrity of neutral rights seemed to depend upon the military power of the neutral, not upon the law-abiding attitude of the belligerents, so it was the part of prudence for the United States to use that same power to prevent war from breaking out. He deems the upholding of international law and order a vital national interest.[85]

Reviewing the history of neutrality laws, he notes that the great sixteenth century theologians, Vittoria and Suarez, "who sought to restrain the new 'sovereign' rulers by appeals to the fundamental rules of moral conduct and who both kept alive the conception of a society of nations," did not even discuss the status of neutrality.[86] Grotius' treatise on *The Law of War and of Peace*, published in 1625, foreshadowed neutrality, but he expected nations to "look to the merits of the controversy and to take sides accordingly." The appearance in 1758 of the study of the law of nations by Vattel, the Swiss diplomat and publicist, furthered recognition of neutral rights and duties. Vattel built his system of international law upon a "law of nature" very different from that of the School-

---

[84] Charles G. Fenwick, *American Neutrality: Trial and Failure* (New York: New York University Press, 1940), v. Mr. Fenwick, a political scientist, is a specialist on international law.

[85] *Ibid.*, 149–51.

[86] *Ibid.*, 9–11.

men. He argued that nations were living in a "state of nature," and in the absence of a supreme authority over them, each man must be permitted his own interpretation of the law of nations. Vattel's book, published shortly before the American Revolution, became the "textbook of the State Department and of the federal courts."

Bemis, Hinton, Sears

Samuel Flagg Bemis, while sympathizing with people who find their countries a possible battleground between two great powers, says that though they would strive for neutrality they finally realize that the contest is one of liberty against slavery.[87] To be neutral in such a "final Armageddon" would mean surrender of all the priceless human rights and constitutional freedoms from Magna Carta to the United Nations Charter.

In answer to the current misconception that the United States has not a well-thought-out foreign policy, he explains that the objectives have been constant, but the strategy has had to shift in relation to historical situations in the balance of world power.[88] In terms of security, that policy meant first the winning and pre-serving of independence; next, the expansion across a continent to make safe the area for republican and democratic institutions; finally, it means security for all free peoples against the new imperialism of today. Before the twentieth century, our prin-ciples extended to the new world mainly; now they reach out to the whole globe in a test of strength. Before World War II our policy rested upon a balanced Europe and a balanced Asia. This equilibrium has been lost by "defeat in victory" at Yalta, Potsdam, London, and Washington; therefore, through the Marshall Plan and the Truman Doctrine we are trying to encourage a new balance in Europe, in the southern part of the new world, and

[87] Samuel Flagg Bemis, "Shifting Strategy of American Defense and Diplomacy," *Virginia Quarterly Review*, XXIV (Summer, 1948), 335.
[88] *Ibid.*, 322–23, 334–35.

north along the Arctic. If the United States were not a great power defending those lines of freedom, the prospect would be an Iron Curtain for centuries.

Harold C. Hinton defines America's major interest as "preservation of its own liberty, stability, and prosperity," but these goals cannot be reached except temporarily unless the United States enjoys friendly contacts, cultural, diplomatic, and commercial, with as many governments and peoples as possible.[89] Because these relations can be maintained only to the extent that these nations are "free, stable, and prosperous," the United States must help as many as possible to become so or to remain so. Commenting on the fact that until the emergence of Communism our government had no comprehensive program for promoting the welfare of other people, but that Americans were content merely to draw profit, he does not think that we should expect gratitude in return for aid because our present concern for underdeveloped areas seems to them like pure self-interest.

Hinton criticizes the evident tactlessness with which some Americans think results can be achieved in foreign affairs. They would show moral indignation and have nothing to do with Communist regimes because Communism is evil. After spending money in aid, they retort, "Why aren't these people more grateful?" They favor threats of force because, "The only thing an Asian understands is force." Paralleling such conduct with private life, he shows that such means do not gain for one new friends, nor bind close the friends already won, nor serve as a protection against enemies. He agrees with George Kennan's axiom that diplomacy is more allied to gardening than to engineering, at which Americans excel. "Gardening takes patience, the creation of favorable conditions, and an understanding of the processes of organic growth." [90]

Lawrence Sears observes that American national interest will be served by dissipating the fears which are psychologically the

[89] Harold C. Hinton, "Axioms of Foreign Policy," *The Commonweal*, LXVI (August 9, 1957), 465. Mr. Hinton is a specialist in Far Eastern affairs.
[90] *Ibid.*, 466.

source of aggression in nations as in individuals; he approaches Communism as a symptom of deep-lying social maladjustments.[91] He assumes that peace rests upon reform, not merely recovery, so "until the TVA's have been built on the Danube and on the Yangtze, there will be the kind of poverty which breeds rebellion."

Price, Linebarger

Similar sentiments are voiced by Harry Bayard Price in *The Marshall Plan and Its Meaning*, where he stresses the fact that the government really endorsed what Secretary George B. Marshall said in the Harvard commencement address in which the program was announced June 5, 1947:

> Our policy is directed not against any country or doctrine but against hunger, poverty, desperation, and chaos. Its purpose should be the revival of a working economy in the world so as to permit the emergence of political and social conditions in which free institutions can exist.[92]

The newly established Policy Planning Staff, which drew up from previous State Department studies the recommendations contained in the Marshall Plan, stated that it did not see Communist activities as the root of the difficulties in western Europe; rather the difficulties seemed to spring from the disruptive effect of the war. Following the attack in Korea, however, public and congressional opinion demanded that economic aims be justified in terms of defense support. Nonetheless, the Marshall Plan precipitated the establishment of the first body within the European

[91] Lawrence Sears, "Walking Backward Into the Future," *American Scholar*, XVIII (Autumn, 1949), 479–80. Mr. Sears, currently professor of American philosophy and political theory at Mills College, taught at Princeton Center in Peking and at the U.S. Army University in Biarritz, France.

[92] Harry Bayard Price, *The Marshall Plan and Its Meaning* (Ithaca: Cornell University Press, 1955), 22–25. Mr. Price prepared this work under the auspices of the Governmental Affairs Institute, Washington, D.C.

movement, and this OEEC led to the European Payments Union, NATO, and the Schuman Plan. It probably forestalled a collapse of western Europe and the Mediterranean area, which condition would have invited Communist exploitation.[93]

Price does not overlook the shortcomings in the operation of this policy—they were the ignoring of moral and spiritual aspects of social development.

While the Communists were engaged in painstaking efforts to enlist the loyalties of peoples possessed of minds, ideas, passions, hopes, and prejudices, Americans though demonstrating good will at every turn, seemed curiously oblivious at times to the desire of peoples in Asia to rise from debasement of the spirit as well as wretchedness of the body. As a consequence they sometimes conveyed, for all their generosity and technological competence, an impression that Americans were superficial and materialistic in their approach to life. . . . In any event, the result was at least a partial failure to provide urgently needed—and wanted—moral leadership.[94]

This same oversight of appeal to the human qualities in the Asians is noted by Paul M. A. Linebarger who points out that poverty of prestige and of self-respect is greater than their poverty in economics:

They need to be needed. . . . There is nothing subtle or Machiavellian about a Communist propaganda which offers people honor as against American propaganda which talks in heavenly generalities about democracy, constitutionalism, free elections, good government, land reform, and similar problems. The Communist offer of honor may be made on the basis of the grossest deception and because of the most malignant motives, but . . . people who join the Communist side feel that they are needed, that the Communists want them. You couldn't join the American side if you were an Asian. There isn't anything to join. . . . No great crusade has ever been won on the basis of condescension and benefaction. . . . We are still, it can be argued, concerned with aggrandizing our self-importance by helping other people.

[93] *Ibid.*, 399, 404.
[94] *Ibid.*, 391.

. . . American psychological warfare cannot win with weapons alone
or with wealth alone. Victory can be found only in the discovery of a
truly common cause.[95]

Flannery, Fosdick, Murray

More penetrating is the analysis of Harry W. Flannery, who
would scuttle utilitarianism and sincerely recognize an obligation
in justice which redounds to a nation that possesses six per cent of
the world's population and fifty per cent of the world's produced
wealth, while it appropriates grudgingly fifteen hundredths of
one per cent of its gross national product for foreign aid.[96] He
discusses the report of Professors Millikan and Rostow on objectives of United States economic assistance before the Special
Senate Committee. They reasoned that it was in the national
interest to help the uncommitted countries to remain free and
independent by helping to develop their economies, as a means
of preventing further extension of Soviet power in the neutral
areas. Attacking their omission of any attempt to win the minds
and hearts of these people, he projects the idea that they would
be persuaded to embrace free institutions more readily if we
convinced them that one of our basic motivations in helping them
was that we had an obligation in justice to do so. In spite of our
superiority in material strength, political ideas, and social aspirations, we show feeble dedication to our ideology for lack of purer
moral impulse and universal spirit of self-sacrifice.

Communism . . . does offer them a positive ideology on the basis of
universal brotherhood with the downtrodden. This country, on the

[95] Paul M. A. Linebarger, "The Struggle for the Mind of Asia," *Annals
of the American Academy of Political and Social Science,* CCLXXVIII (November, 1951), 35–37. Mr. Linebarger, who worked in Korea on psychological warfare, is professor of Asiatic politics at the School of Advanced
International Studies, Johns Hopkins University.

[96] H. W. Flannery, "Foreign Aid: a 'New Look,'" *Social Order,* VII
(June, 1957), 266–75. Mr. Flannery, formerly a foreign correspondent for
CBS, was president of the Catholic Association for International Peace in 1959.

other hand, lets these people believe that our interest in them is only derived from our struggle with the Soviet Union; that if it were not for the "cold war", we would not be interested in their welfare . . . . to be paradoxical, it is in our long-run and perhaps our short-run, national interest to forget our national interest, and to help these people because we have a moral responsibility in the name of justice to do so . . . . this motivation, when realized by the people in the underdeveloped countries, would fuel our aid programs with a much greater chance of achieving their objectives. . . . It would seem almost indisputable that we as a people of the Judaic-Christian tradition, with such a disproportion of the world's wealth in relation to our population, have a moral responsibility to these impoverished areas; it is somewhat regrettable that this has not been more clearly and persuasively said.[97]

Dorothy Fosdick underlines another factor in foreign affairs where the feelings enter in. Americans should refrain from speaking as though this country has settled all its problems, since communication can be more genuine "between persons talking over their difficulties, than when one party to the conversation assumes he has none." [98] While not underestimating the role of technology in improving living standards and in furthering defense, she warns against overemphasis upon scientific propaganda. Pictures of students engaged in social and humanistic studies, directing technological progress to the greater benefit of mankind, would be more comforting abroad.[99]

Thomas E. Murray protests against the mad logic of total war dictating the decisions on military policies and weapons programs.[100] Even in an atomic age man can return to the civilized tradition of limited war. Though the bankruptcy of a policy of

[97] *Ibid.*, 275, 271.
[98] Dorothy Fosdick, *Common Sense and World Affairs* (New York: Harcourt, Brace, 1955), 170. Miss Fosdick was a member of the Policy Planning Staff of the Department of State, 1948–53.
[99] *Ibid.*, 179–80.
[100] Thomas E. Murray, "Morality and Security—the Forgotten Equation," *America*, XCVI (December 1, 1956), 258–62. A member of the Atomic Energy Commission, 1950–57, Mr. Murray delivered this address November 10, 1956, in Washington.

total war is evident, he rests his appeal upon the principles of justice. "The tradition [of civilized warfare] did not succumb to argument, but only to . . . the fact of man's passions." Because of international lawlessness today, he would not suggest renunciation of nuclear armament. His proposal is that American security does not reside solely in military power, but more in its moral strength of using power to serve the ends of justice.

We shall have no security as long as we are prisoners of the moral fallacy of totalization . . . as long as we cherish the empty illusion that our national security is totally reposed in massive military might. . . . The nation is secure in proportion to its fidelity to the moral norms that form the spiritual substance of the national life. . . . it is committed to a moral use of force, on penalty of self-destruction—I mean the destruction of its moral self . . . . we have forgotten that the methods of power when used in violation of the canons of justice, will undermine the basic moral security of the whole edifice of civilization which they should undertake to protect.[101]

[101] *Ibid.*, 261–62. So numerous are the books and articles dealing with these values in foreign policy, that thorough coverage is almost impossible. Among the most important recent works which have appeared since this chapter was completed are: Chester A. Bowles, *Ideas, People and Peace* (New York: Harper & Bros., 1958). Henry A. Kissinger, *Nuclear Weapons and Foreign Policy* (New York: Harper & Bros., 1957). Ernest W. Lefever, *Ethics and United States Foreign Policy* (Toronto: Longmans, Green, 1957).

* IV *

American History Evaluated
by the Idealists

WITHIN the ranks of the Idealist historians of American diplomacy, there are those who, like Frank Tannenbaum, would ignore the facts if they seem to imply anything but unblemished innocence for the country's record. There are others who question the motivation of the nation in specific instances, but do not endorse as good the evidences of national selfishness. There are those like Dexter Perkins who face the debits and the credits on the ledger, and conclude that the nation's frailties have not robbed it of wholesomeness. There are those like Robert Osgood whose estimate of political wisdom approaches the territory of the Realists, yet maintains more moderation in discounting the role of good intentions.

Dexter Perkins

Dexter Perkins' account can hardly be analyzed in strictly chronological order. The topical arrangement sheds more light, in his investigation of the attitude toward war, the attitude toward peace, the charges of imperialism, capitalism in foreign policy, etc. But in the period after the First World War, the plot of a story is visible.

Although Perkins would not approve present-day isolationism, he says of America's insistence on "plowing its own furrow" that "during the first hundred odd years of this country's history, the isolationist point of view corresponded with the interests of the United States, with the realities of international intercourse, and even with American ideals." [1] Since there were no general wars which threatened America's position, it was normal for the nation to concentrate on development of the continent. From its inception the United States was a child of fortune in gaining the country west of the Appalachians by the treaty with Britain, in buying the Louisiana territory, in the occupation of West Florida and in the Spanish treaty of 1819, in the settlement and annexation of Texas and Florida. To answer those who contend that had the United States not been so blessed, she would have engaged in war for acquisition of the domain, Perkins takes up a lengthy examination of the country's attitude toward war.

Though there has not been a long period of peace, he finds restraint prevailing; [2] America has never gone to war over an "incident" such as the XYZ affair, the *Leopard* and *Chesapeake*, the Mexican crossing of the Rio Grande, the *Maine*, or the *Lusitania*. Gathering irritation rather than sudden outburst char-

---

[1] Perkins, *American Approach*, 11. Cook and Moos make this same point clearer when they term the policy "continental insulationism." "We were not isolationist, in the sense of unconcern for Europe or a desire to enjoy higher standards of living in callow selfishness. We had indeed the vision of a better, freer, happier world to be created from a European heritage through America's liberating opportunity. With dignified humility, we saw that we could not aid or improve Europe directly; we would only . . . misuse our resources, and invite its intervention here." He contrasts this with isolationism, which "professes that a power which behaves like the proverbial ostrich deserves a comfortable world it never worked to make simply because it possesses the virtues of minding its own business and cultivating its own garden." Cook and Moos, *Power through Purpose*, 36, 38.

[2] *Ibid.*, 85–87.

acterizes the democratic nation which always has "a little of the water of appeasement in its blood." Even if there was somewhat of a goading to acquire territory in 1812, in the Mexican War, and in 1898, America has never plotted aggression directly, and the wars have been fought chiefly at the behest of economic interests.

Among the positive factors which have provoked United States' entrance into wars, Perkins notes that in three of the six cases, the avowed reason was violation of neutral rights—1798, 1812, and 1917.[3] The sense of national dignity and honor has been aroused by repeated assaults; there has been emotional repugnance to a way of life different from ours as in World Wars I and II. Concern about national security interests outside the national borders has been demonstrated: New Orleans in Jefferson's day, Florida in 1811, Patagonia in the sweeping sense of the Monroe Doctrine, possible German control of the Atlantic in the First World War, and dangers in the Far Pacific in the 1930's. The thesis of collective security has enlarged the area of American military interests to a sizeable part of the globe.

Dexter Perkins finds multiple explanations for America's predominantly peaceful bent.[4] By location the country has been physically safe. The rationalistic-optimistic view of human nature has influenced the peaceful sentiment. "If man is infinitely improvable and capable in time of using the power of reason to settle all his problems . . . then the appeal to force is a denial of an essential faith." Preoccupation with material progress has suggested the costliness and folly of war. In democratic forms of government, the necessity of debate reduces the opportunity for conflict, and popular government is unattuned to the militarist schemes of preventive war. The teaching of history in America he finds less nationalistic than that in most other nations; the guilt-complex on the part of some of its historians and other citizens shows how little inclined they are to glorify conflict. The fact that the nation did not build large armies and navies might

[3] *Ibid.*, 87–95.
[4] *Ibid.*, 98–109.

supply partial explanation for its recourse to arbitration settlements. Economic coercion has usually been preferred to war.

He agrees with the general American sense of satisfaction with its record of expansion. The term expansion he distinguishes from imperialism in this way: It is the process by which "the political control of a given nation is extended over territory which then becomes assimilated to and incorporated in the political and constitutional system of the expanding state."[5] While noting the criticisms which a severe moralist would render, he grants them limited validity. The adverse charges are: Napoleon's illegal act in the transfer of Louisiana, the annexation of West Florida in the wake of a revolution, Andrew Jackson's acceleration of matters leading to the Florida treaty, reproaches regarding Texas and the Mexican War, and shoddy details relating to the Gadsden Purchase. He replies:

It is possible to regard the expansion of the United States as a kind of biologic process which could hardly have been arrested, and which was carried on with less violence than often goes with such activities. . . . The territory acquired by the United States in the rounding out of the national domain was assimilated to the original area, that is, was endowed with the institution of self-government, and, with the exception of Alaska, constituted into states which were admitted into the Union. American expansion, in other words, involved none of the vexing problems which have so often followed in the wake of European wars of conquest. There were no resentful minorities, in important numbers, to whom American rule was obnoxious. There were no acute problems of assimilation.[6]

To make up for territory acquired by the sword, America has expressed disquiet of conscience by paying $20,000,000 for California; $20,000,000 for the Philippines; $25,000,000 to indemnify Colombia for her loss of Panama; and a partial remission of damages in the Boxer Rebellion.

[5] *Ibid.*, 30.
[6] *Ibid.*, 17–18

While admitting that America exercised a virtual protectorate over Panama after 1903, interfered in Cuba 1906–1909, and occupied for a longer time Nicaragua, Haiti, and the Dominican Republic, he would say that this rule was imposed with an uneasy conscience, with the conviction that imperialism for Americans must be a passing phase preparing the way for self-government. With regard to America's faith in the democratic process, he looks at the areas in the Caribbean over which the United States has exercised control—Panama, Cuba, Haiti, Nicaragua, and the Dominican Republic—and he doubts the universal applicability of the exported institutions. He questions whether much does not depend upon the political habits, the education, and the existence of a middle class desirous of peace and order, and practiced in the art of compromise so essential to democratic rule.[7]

Viewing the over-all record in Latin America, he notes that though the temptation was present between 1910 and 1917 for Americans to clean up a bad situation in Mexico, neither Taft nor Wilson attempted this, though Wilson engaged in something less than full-scale intervention with the occupation of Vera Cruz which led to Huerta's overthrow. Government by marines did not win popular response among the American people. Though Warren Harding in his 1920 campaign was moved by political motives more than by statesmanship, he criticized the intervention in Nicaragua, Dominican Republic, and Haiti. In the Kellogg-Briand Pact, the Senate limited the Monroe Doctrine. The New Deal's opposition to entrenched financial interests provided the circumstances for breaking with the imperialistic tactics of the past and launching into new Latin American relationships. Perkins gives this final judgment:

Whenever before, in history, has a nation possessing the material power of the United States deliberately, in a solemn international engagement, forsworn so explicit the use of force for the protection of its interests? . . . The policy of the American government in the last twenty years

[7] *Ibid.*, 31–34.

has been an example almost without precedent in abstention from policies of force in relation with weaker states.[8]

This restraint is evidenced in the lack of action when Mexico expropriated American oil interests in 1938, when the Cubans drew up a liberal constitution in 1940, and when at Bogota in 1947 the United States opposed even collective intervention.

Turning to an assessment of economic imperialism, he explores the advantages which have accrued to the inhabitants where American political control or supervision has been exercised.[9] In Puerto Rico and the Philippines, it is fair to say, capital would not have been available for their own development because Americans provided the investment only when they were assured of order and protection against arbitrariness. Progress was remarkable in the Dominican Republic, but not so noticeable in Nicaragua and Haiti. He acknowledges that the profits were amassed by a few men, but he would not dismiss lightly the fact that some fruits trickle down to the masses who receive higher wages and benefits from Americans than from native employers. With the expanding activities, jobs are created, and taxes are derived for use in public health, education, roads, and railway improvements. The increased domestic tranquility has relieved the peoples of constant plunder by revolutionary armies. In the case of the Virgin Islands, Puerto Rico, and the Philippines, the United States has expended its own funds to assist those economies.

Perkins faces the fact that American business interests have exercised substantial control over governments of states in which they have operated.[10] In the 1910 revolution in Nicaragua, American interests on the eastern coast of that republic instigated the trouble, and these interests had ties with the American State Department. In 1911, the Honduran revolution was financed from New Orleans. During the turmoil in Mexico 1910–1917, the oil

[8] *Ibid.*, 38.
[9] *Ibid.*, 41.
[10] *Ibid.*, 41–44.

companies had private armies backing the "constitutionalists" in the civil war. In Central America corporation influences was powerful enough to secure privileges from corrupt legislatures and to circumvent the law. But he would wager that such practices would be less likely to occur today because American business morals have improved, the Latin states have been protected against intervention since 1936, and in the past twenty years American administrations have not been sympathetic to extreme demands of American business abroad. Even in the light of the above evidence, he would ascribe little guilt to the American people as a whole, or to the government if corrupt or weak governments accede in this way. The practice of capital export is indispensable to world progress. Although the United States can make felt its displeasure, it cannot handle the situation effectively without resuming the practice of intervention.

Application of the word "imperialism" to such a recovery program as the Marshall Plan, he labels as distortion. The national independence of those countries has not been curtailed, but it is only reasonable that assurances be exacted regarding use of the grants for the purposes in view. Even more ridiculous would be the imputing of "imperialism" to Truman's Point Four which he lauds as one of the most beneficent ideas ever advanced by a powerful nation, and as "an attempt to translate some of the values of our advanced technology into economic progress outside our borders." [11] Perkins gives this over-all evaluation of so-called American "imperialism" in the political and economic spheres:

On the whole, the record, by the comparative human standard, is not one for which we need to apologize. Powerful nations, by the ineluctable necessities of international politics, almost inevitably make that power felt. The question is, how do they exert it? Do they exert it with ruthlessness, as Germany has often done? Do they assert the universal validity of the principles on which their own governments are founded as the Russian government does today? Or are they led toward

[11] *Ibid.*, 44.

tolerance, as the United States has clearly been in accepting the doctrine of non-intervention with regard to Latin America, and as it has shown in its attitude toward other forms in other parts of the world, until some issue of national security was involved? Do they grant economic assistance on generous or harsh terms? The answer to these questions suggests that, in the moderation which ought to go with strength, the United States has played and is playing a creditable role.[12]

Perkins challenges the assumption that because America is a land of business, its foreign policy represents the interest of the capitalist class, and that in a sinister way.[13] He observes that various capitalistic groups do not even have the same interest and that within one group there is disagreement about where self-interest lies. In reviewing the facts, he admits that commercial interests were evident in the Federalist administration, in the Tripolitan War, in aspects of the Monroe Doctrine, in the 1880's in the Open Door, in Secretary Hull's diplomacy, and in a limited way, in American reaction to the rising imperialisms of Japan and Germany with their trade restriction. In the Caribbean, this was part of the motivation in encouraging internal stability of those governments, and in sponsoring the 1907 and 1923 agreements not to recognize a government of revolutionary origin. Whereas the purpose was to protect property in the interventions in Cuba and Puerto Rico, it is probable that strategic interests were more telling in Haiti, the Dominican Republic, and Nicaragua. He would not explain the widespread national sentiment in the Spanish-American War, however, on such restricted grounds as commercial interests alone. There were times when the administration was not solicitous about the capital-exporters: Taft and Wilson refused intervention in Mexico, Coolidge's administration blustered but became more conciliatory, Franklin D. Roosevelt made only a mild protest about Mexican oil expropriation.

In this order, he classifies the influence business groups have

[12] *Ibid.*, 45.
[13] *Ibid.*, 46.

had upon foreign policy: 1) commercial interests, 2) American investors on foreign soil, 3) bankers.[14] While granting that the stake of bankers and traders in an allied victory was an influence in America's entry into the First World War, he emphasizes that the real cause of war was German submarine warfare. That Wilson should have taken his position on submarine attacks because of financial interests, trade, or loans he finds to be inconsistent with his character and contrary to the testimony given by the chronology of his statements on the submarine. In 1915 the American conscience was genuinely shocked by that type of devastation; it was not a generation as yet habituated to horror. He discovers that the backing which Franklin Roosevelt received for his departure from neutrality was drawn from all classes in the nation and rested on "detestation of totalitarian states, reprobation of treatment of minorities, and on democratic principle."

Refuting the Marxian interpretation of foreign policy, Perkins charges that they "have argued from false premises to debatable conclusions." [15] When tracing the fighting among nations to their economic organization, the Marxians overlook fighting in noncapitalist ages, and by-pass something intangible in the nature of man. The explanation of underconsumption and consequent conquest for markets seems to stand refuted by the vitality of the American home market. Instead of fighting against one another, the capital-exporting nations today are coalescing against the danger of Soviet power. He counters Stalin's charge that there is danger of collapse in capitalist countries, which collapse will result in Fascism and in war against nations with other economic organizations, with the reminder that the seat of political power in America is not Wall Street alone; this is one factor to which must be added the role of labor, of the farmer, and of large and small business. When evaluating economic determinism, the question is not whether economic factors exist, but whether they are decisive.

Before the advent of Woodrow Wilson, the democratic ideal

[14] *Ibid.*, 54–57.
[15] *Ibid.*, 59–61.

was prominent in foreign policy debates.[16] In 1794 men like Jefferson and Madison placed primary concern in ideological and moral sympathy with the French, when British friendship in terms of imports was more in line with self-interest. In Henry Clay's previews of Pan-Americanism in 1818, he stressed similarity of institutions in Latin America, while John Quincy Adams looked at the selfish aspects. President Monroe failed in his efforts to inject a strongly ideological element into the Doctrine, with a sympathetic reference to the Greeks and a commentary on the suppression of constitutional government in Spain. However, the Europeans recognized the ideological significance in the Monroe Doctrine—Metternich bewailed this separation of the New World from the Old. In United States press comment, the distinction between American and European institutions outweighed recognition of any immediate peril. The moral factors were expressed in sympathy for the Second French Republic in 1848, in the representation President Taylor sent to Hungary, in the reception of Kossuth after the Hungarian revolt, in support of the Juarez regime, in refusal to recognize Huerta, in the holding of democratic elections in Latin states at the conclusion of intervention, and in partiality for the allies in World War I.

The apogee of diplomacy colored with the democratic ideal is found in Wilson's war message of April 6, 1917, when he made the central issue of the war a struggle to destroy autocracy and to establish an international peace organization. Of Wilson's propagation of democracy everywhere, Perkins says:

In a passage more remarkable for its rhetoric than for its prescience he welcomes "the great naive Russian people" to the ranks of the democrats, and actually in his optimism and exaltation, goes so far as to say that the autocracy which "crowned the summit of Russian political life" was "not in fact Russian in origin, character, or purpose." Idealism could hardly go further than this. . . .

The avowed theory of his speeches [regarding Germany] was that not the German people, but the rulers of Germany, were to blame for the

[16] *Ibid.*, 68–69.

war, that if the democratic forces in Germany could be liberated, a new nation, to all intents and purposes, would arise. And insistence on this point of view was certainly a factor, and a very important factor, in bringing about the flight of the Kaiser and the establishment of a re-public in the Reich. It may be that, in this respect, Wilson's policy was not entirely wise; it is possible to argue that a constitutional monarchy would have opposed a more successful resistance to the madness of National Socialism than the republican regime could have done.[17]

To Wilson's diplomacy at Versailles, Perkins accords the tribute of integrity of purpose and success in some important respects. He grants that Wilson wavered in pressing his standards of recti-tude in regard to self-determination for the Sudetan Germans, but he remarks that men before him have failed and men after him will continue to show human frailty. Noting that a mood of disillusionment inevitably follows in some degree a period of war, he judges that "to many unsophisticated Americans, un-accustomed to judging the questions of international politics on a realistic basis, they [the compromises] bore the aspect of a series of sordid deals, or unworthy concessions." [18] Many groups were bound to react against Versailles—the Germans, Italians, Irish-Americans, and American traditionalists.

Perkins finds the 1920's a curious compound of international cooperation and isolationism.[19] Evidences of the former are the Washington Treaty, the Dawes Plan, participation in many League activities, and the Kellogg Pact. Indications of isolationism are the immigration restriction, the insistence upon payment of allied war debts, the tariff wall, and the avoiding of commitment to keep the peace by economic or other action. He has little respect for the "legend" of the 1930's, that the United States "had been swept into the World War by incompetent leadership, by the pressure of financial interests, by the subtle propaganda of the Allies," nor does he find wisdom in the so-called neutrality legisla-

[17] *Ibid.*, 72.
[18] *Ibid.*, 25.
[19] *Ibid.*, 26.

tion designed to keep the same thing from happening again. The evolution of American policy in the twentieth century to involvement in European affairs he finds to correspond with the shifting of the balance of power and the changes in the European scene.

The material power of the United States was now adequate to the assumption of great international responsibilities. Its own place in the world at large was challenged as it had never been challenged before. That there should be an immense alteration in the American mood was a foregone conclusion in the circumstances.[20]

He describes America's gesture in the Nine-Power Treaty as one of faith; that if she divested herself of physical power in the Far East, this would pave the way for more moderate policies on the part of the rivals. Instead the Great Depression merely accelerated the rise of Japanese militarism to power. While it was clear in the Manchurian crisis that force alone could restrain Japan, the President and the majority of public opinion favored only moral pressure. He concludes, "It is difficult to see how American action did aught but exacerbate a far from easy situation." [21]

However, Perkins gives credit to the prevalence of the ethical motive in reaction to the Sino-Japanese war of 1931, for appeasement might have served self-interest more thoroughly because the investment and trade ties with Japan were greater than those with China. He suggests that prudential considerations might have pointed to a gentler handling of Tokyo at the time the situation was becoming more serious in Europe, since the Japanese had made clear they would seek a way to evade obligations to Germany under the alliance of September, 1940. His comment on Cordell Hull's reaction to Hitler's seizure of Austria, etc., before Munich is that the Secretary of State wrote "more sincere homilies" than usually flowed from the pen of a diplomat.[22]

[20] *Ibid.*, 28.
[21] *Ibid.*, 21.
[22] *Ibid.*, 81.

Perkins admits that the democratic nations in the thirties were slow to check the tide of violence. In America there is an especially strong tendency to underestimate the role of force, to hope for compromise of conflicting views, to be optimistic about the reasonableness of human beings. But he traces the ineptness of foreign policy in the 1930's to the Great Depression which occasioned an absorption in domestic restoration. He counsels that one not use the thirties as a vantage point in viewing the capacity of a democracy to cope with problems. He would select the year 1945 and compare American policy with the *Machtpolitik* of Hitler, Mussolini, and Tojo who had brought ruin to their people.[23]

By 1939 the United States was recognizing the potential peril which a victory for the Reich would mean even on this side of the Atlantic. The fall of France was a shock to complacency, and public opinion echoed the President's decision of assistance to the democracies. Of Roosevelt he says, "The President himself proved a resolute and imaginative leader, sometimes moving in advance of the people, sometimes merely interpreting their desires, but always clear as to his own and the nation's ultimate purpose." [24]

To those who say that the statement of "unconditional surrender" in World War II was a handicap, he replies that it did not prevent a German plot to overthrow Hitler in the summer of 1944, it did not forestall concessions to Japan at the end of the war, it did not prolong the Italian resistance in the summer of 1943, and it was never a savage demand for the extermination of the German people.

Instead of concentrating on the errors made by the United States after the Second World War, he would advert more to the folly of the Kremlin in 1945–48 when it could have won the friendship of the West and have worked at domestic reconstruction, but when it chose instead to alienate public opinion in large parts of the world.[25] He has genuine misgivings about the wisdom

[23] *Id., Popular Government and Foreign Policy*, 22–26.
[24] *Id., American Approach*, 27.
[25] *Id., Popular Government*, 36–41.

of American policies in China after the war. Miscalculating the strength of the Chinese Nationalists and failing to see that only a degree of intervention which would be resisted and resented by Chiang could prove effective, the United States wasted its assistance from 1945 to 1949. He considers the American action in Korea, Indo-China, Matsu, and Quemoy to be in accord with wisdom and restraint. Though the intervention in Korea had to be costly because of the weather and the handicap of fighting with their backs to the sea, he approves their decision based on principles of international morality. He labels Russia's error in Korea as monumental because the attack of the North Koreans galvanized the United States into action in both the East and the West.

His judgment of Roosevelt at Yalta is not complimentary.[26] While he recognizes that the President's military advisors felt it essential to bring the Russians into the battle against Japan, and while he is aware that the Chinese Nationalists later accepted the arrangements in Manchuria, he finds it disconcerting that this "deal" was not recorded in the Archives of the State Department and that the public objected when the terms were revealed. The secrecy suggests that Roosevelt feared reprobation. Perkins denounces the personal diplomacy and the self-assurance in "bargaining" away the rights and interests of a third party. Naïveté about the possibility of getting along with Russia he attributes to the American people as well as to the President; public opinion polls registered two out of three affirmative answers. He finds no indication that things would have been different in 1945 had the country been less naive, since Russian strength was based on their military position. He deems it quite remarkable that the nation learned its lesson so quickly—within a two-year period.[27]

In the dilemma faced by America in wishing to withdraw from the affairs of Germany and Japan, Perkins mentions both the obligation to nurture the "tender democratic plant" in the former enemy states, and the adverse effects of propaganda which stated

[26] *Id., American Approach,* 79, 144.
[27] *Id., Popular Government,* 32–33.

that America was preventing a true expression of popular will in not allowing them to choose Communism if they wished. "Our answer lies in the historic record, and in the fact that the choice for the people whose territory we continue to occupy lies between a wide degree of self-rule under American occupation, and a tyranny which may and probably will imply complete subservience to a foreign power." [28]

Perkins does not agree that the Kremlin is a more dangerous foe than Hitler, and that the war accomplished nothing.

There is a world of difference between a paranoiac and a calculating foe. Russian foreign policy certainly aims at objectives which we cannot approve and indeed must oppose. But it has been, in the main, cautious, advancing only when it sees an opportunity to advance without serious danger of challenge, highly intellectual in its technique, rather than brash and reckless. . . . Hitler, on the other hand, was a monomaniac. . . . His elimination was an international necessity. And, with it, as a matter admitting no choice, went the elimination of imperialist Japan.[29]

He commends the fact that American diplomacy did not try to bargain with the Soviet by leaving the latter free to pursue its course in Eastern Europe in exchange for concessions to American interests in Western Europe. On the contrary, the United States sought to prevent the enveloping of the satellites. But as to current policy, he makes this recommendation:

It may perhaps be questioned whether a sound sense of political realism dictates abstention from diplomatic intercourse with governments whose origins or whose principles we disapprove. It may be that it is wise to keep the channels of communication open, and hope that some breath of freedom will penetrate from the outside world. . . . It may be, for example, that the best hope of the future in our relations with China is in the emergence of a Chinese Titoism, rather than in a fixed hostility to the new regime set up in that country; but the force of

[28] *Id., American Approach*, 40.
[29] *Id., Popular Government*, 27.

American opinion makes it very difficult to act on any such hypothesis.[30]

Reflecting on the course of American foreign policy, Perkins discovers a certain rhythm of pacific and bellicose instinct. This theory tends to "exorcise the romantic, and not particularly useful, superstition that man is automatically advancing along the road to permanent peace, and that Americans are, in the very foundations of their national character, leading this advance."[31] From his analysis these conclusions are gleaned. Periods of peace have been longer than those of belligerency; the nationalistic feeling stimulated by war dies down rapidly. The rise of bellicosity seems to coincide with recovery from economic disturbances. Because changes in economic mood are reflected in the political mood, he would hope that a more peaceful era could be attained by moderating the oscillation in the economy. To effect a more stable economy he would favor: 1) enormous government spending which is less subject to fluctuation; 2) the sustaining of buying power by price supports, unemployment insurance, and public works; 3) control of the stock market and of installment buying; 4) high wages and trade union growth; 5) the narrowing of profits and the cutting of hours rather than the cutting of employment; 6) recognition of the importance of international trade.[32]

Whereas Americans have often taken a romantic view of the international scene, he does not criticize their dreaming of a world regulated by law, so long as they do not lose touch with reality.[33] Admittedly they did lose touch with reality in the rapid demobilizations at the end of the World Wars, in the Kellogg Pact, in neutrality legislation in the thirties, and in failures of military intelligence (regarding Japan and Korea). But by painful experience the present generation has come to the conclusion that

[30] *Id., American Approach*, 74, 183.
[31] *Ibid.*, 114–15.
[32] *Ibid.*, 127–28.
[33] *Id., American Approach*, 110–12; *Popular Government*, 44–45, 52–55.

force is a factor in international affairs which they cannot afford to disregard. He credits the United States with realism in its support of United Nations, its proposals on nuclear disarmament, and its executive agreements in NATO.

In his conclusions about America's record as champion of liberty and independence, Perkins writes:

In the Orient with its relatively recent and somewhat naive nationalism, it may be possible to represent the policies of the United States as imperialism in disguise, and to succeed in impressing many persons with the validity of this view; but this canard is hardly likely to succeed in Europe, and it is certainly not mere chance that where the voters remain free, and governments truly representative, there is, on the part of the great majority, a preference for a close association with the United States as compared with a communist revolution.[34]

Robert E. Osgood

As an introduction to Mr. Osgood's historical treatment, one should bear in mind this remark:

If this interpretation of the realities of international relations seems to underestimate the role of ideals in shaping national conduct, that is because of my belief that in the historical circumstances with which it deals the American people have been prone to overestimate the role of ideals and underestimate the role of national power and self-interest.[35]

He criticizes the exaggeration on the part of both Realists and Idealists in the early twentieth century, the period with which his study begins.

The Realists, in order to rationalize a self-assertive national egoism, exaggerated the force of aggressive national self-interest in international society and posited the existence of an inexorable struggle for power which men were incapable of altering, while they interpreted ideals according to a romantic conception of moral duty that sanctioned a

[34] *Id.*, *American Approach*, 185.
[35] Osgood, *Ideals and Self-Interest*, 10.

free exercise of national power but did little to encourage self-restraint. Idealists, on the other hand, distorted reality to fit their desires by exaggerating the efficacy of supranational ideals in national conduct and belittling the forces of national egoism, in Americans as well as nations in general, while they viewed the fulfillment of universal ideals as a task involving no particular political responsibilities or distasteful expediencies but simply the conversion of the unenlightened by means of America's beneficent example. Thus idealism was actively propagated by those most ignorant of the role of national self-interest and power in world politics, while realism remained the province of those least inhibited by ethical restraints upon the assertion of the nation's power and self-interest.[36]

From the turn of the century till the 1930's he finds American foreign relations marked by the "impulsiveness, instability, and ineffectiveness," in which time the nation enthusiastically undertook commitments which it would subsequently repudiate in the midst of bewilderment and disillusionment.[37]

In the Spanish-American War he depicts the American people as moved equally by a spirit of knight errantry and national self-assertiveness.[38] After the navy, the interest group most anxious for battle was Protestantism which deplored Spanish inhumanity and yearned for missionary activity in the Orient. He finds economic consideration an integral part of the "gospel of naval strength" and strategic territories. Albert J. Beveridge was blatant with his avowal of material interest when he deduced from the existence of farm and factory surpluses the conclusion that fate had thus decreed that world trade should be ours.[39]

Osgood does not judge the imperialist rationale to be completely in accord with a "realistic view of world politics," because it was chiefly "the product of a strong temperamental and emotional bias against idealism and its values of love, reason, humility and self-

[36] *Ibid.*, 106.
[37] *Ibid.*, 17–18.
[38] *Ibid.*, 44.
[39] *Ibid.*, 45.

denial." [40] Imperialism sprang from aggressive, combative instincts, and was oriented toward national egoism in espousing the primacy of self-interest in the acquisition of power.[41] The anti-imperialists, who were equally strong at the time, stressed "motives of love and sublimated the urge for power into the drive for prestige and moral influence." They placed a higher estimate "on the ability of reason and morality to transcend selfishness," they trusted America's mission to the efficacy of good example, and they opposed imperialism as contrary to traditional national interest and "incompatible with liberal and humane principles" upon which the nation was founded.[42] The latter group felt that imperialism had distorted the original purpose of the war and was a "travesty upon the national mission."

John Hay and the Open Door policy are exposed by Mr. Osgood more severely than he would probably have chosen, simply because the public thought "with a single stroke of his pen he had saved China from exploitation and forced the great nations of the world to observe American treaty rights."

. . . it appeared to be simply the brave deed of a strong and independent nation, acting in accordance with the long-standing concern of missionary and religious groups for Chinese welfare. The public did not suspect that Hay had so little regard for his pronouncement as a principle of beneficence that in November, 1900, under pressure from the War and Navy departments, he directed the American minister at Peking to seek free and exclusive use of Samsah Bay—a project that was defeated only by Japanese objections.[43]

The Peace Movement of the early 1900's does not receive many laurels either. In its missionary spirit, he likens it to imperialism, for both movements combined "a new-found sense of national power and prestige with an old desire for a world of liberty,

[40] *Ibid.*, 47.
[41] *Ibid.*, 87.
[42] *Ibid.*, 47–49, 87.
[43] *Ibid.*, 74–75.

brotherhood, and prosperity"; both were convinced of America's "superior endowment of Christian ethics and the attributes of civilization," both were impressed with "the lure of national destiny" and with "responsibility for extending to the less fortunate peoples of the earth the blessings of democracy, order, and progress." [44] He quotes one of the peace movement giants, Andrew Carnegie, with statements to the effect that international law has no material force behind it, and is thus a proof of the "supreme force of gentleness." This same industrial titan discouraged preparedness as the First World War wore on by saying of a possible invasion, "They would make themselves at home and learning the advantages of staying with us, would become applicants for citizenship, rather than our opponents in warfare." [45]

Osgood explains the decline of the imperialistic spirit by the end of Theodore Roosevelt's first term in this way:

The fact is that in these years the American people lacked the only incentive which, under the circumstances, could have sustained a consistent regard for the nation's position in world politics; and that was the preservation of America's territorial integrity and her fundamental institutions. . . . Fear, however, was conspicuously absent from the American outlook.

When traditional conceptions of national interest reasserted themselves and when domestic reform and the international peace movement siphoned off America's crusading energy, neither patriotic nor philanthropic fervor sufficed to sustain the leadership of the Realists who had planned and guided America's entrance into the arena of world politics. Moreover, because the Realists' active concern for power politics became associated in the public mind with a discredited militarism and imperialism, a realistic calculation of power politics became synonymous with Machiavellianism. Realism had kept bad company; therefore, it shared the opprobrium.[46]

[44] *Ibid.,* 86.
[45] *Ibid.,* 94, 204. Quotes from *New York Times Magazine,* December 6, 1914.
[46] *Ibid.,* 78, 84.

He declares Theodore Roosevelt's public pronouncements to be a good barometer of the pacific trend in America; he could rail only in private against the mollycoddles and against irresponsible Idealism.

The little difficulty which Theodore Roosevelt experienced in leading the country to the most active international participation since the days of the French Alliance he attributes to the President's political genius in directing the aroused nationalism into new channels.

By bold deeds, such as "taking" the Canal Zone, composing the famous "Perdicaris alive or Raisuli dead" telegram, and sending the great white fleet around the world, he was able to capture the public imagination and dramatize the emergence of the United States as a great power, capable of inspiring awe and respect in all parts of the world. The popular response to Rooseveltian diplomacy would have been of quite a different sort had the general public been cognizant of the extent of their President's involvement in what they would have considered strictly European and Asian affairs.[47]

Because Osgood's literary style makes his interpretation especially convincing, it seems justifiable to risk the charge of quoting excessively. Roosevelt's desertion of the cause of an international peace organization and his violent support of active intervention in the First World War are recorded by the author in colorful language.

Because Roosevelt found in Wilson's high-flown moral leadership and deprecation of brute physical force the epitome of that pacifist temperament and utopian view of international relations which had been his nemesis for a quarter of a century, he felt compelled to rally all his crusading fervor and high animal spirits behind an appeal to principle, beside which an appeal to mere national expediency paled into insignificance . . . putting peace above righteousness, preaching the gospel of feebleness for the sake of mere safety from violence was utter selfishness and crass materialism; neutrality between right and wrong was sheer poltroonery. . . . However, Roosevelt's visceral reactions

[47] *Ibid.*, 75.

cannot be considered apart from his deep-seated ideological and intellectual antipathy toward Wilson's self-denying idealism. . . .[48]

Almost a third of *Ideals and Self-Interest* is devoted to Woodrow Wilson's diplomacy. Here there is space for only a brief summary of some aspects of the President's moral tone, and greater attention to Osgood's evaluation of the period. He notes that the application of moral principles to foreign relations was a counterpart of those same tenets in industrial and social legislation under the name "New Freedom." Self-denial was paraded in the unorthodox procedure of communication to the press as a means of proclaiming the end of dollar diplomacy, in the Mobile Speech disavowing material interest in foreign policy, in the plea for repeal of Panama Canal toll exemptions, and in the thirty "cooling-off" conciliation pacts. Osgood proposes that "the logic of geography and strategic interest" receives testimony in the fact "that this moral-minded administration, largely out of solicitude for the security of the Panama Canal, found it necessary to carry out more armed interventions in Latin American than any of its predecessors, to impose upon Haiti and the Dominican Republic prolonged military occupations without treaty sanctions and against the protests of the native governments, and almost, but for the Senate's refusal, to convert Nicaragua into a protectorate."[49] Yet he recognizes that Latin America's unequaled trust in his good will is a tribute to the power of ideals and to his "obviously benevolent intentions."

Osgood describes Wilson's altruism as a virile thing:

He was determined not to indulge his emotions lest he reach a decision that might seem unworthy in the cool light of history, for his conception of morality was the product of solid intellectual conviction, not a thin rationalization of emotional inclinations. . . . He wished America to perfect her international behavior to fulfill the mission of uplifting the rest of the world by exemplifying the ethical standards applicable among individuals. He believed America should no longer live isolated

[48] *Ibid.*, 140, 142, 152.
[49] *Ibid.*, 105.

from the world; it was American character and ideals, not American wealth or military might, that the world needed. In that lay her power.[50]

Wilson's position on neutrality is not portrayed in a derogatory fashion, though Osgood cites failures in perfect impartiality. Noting that the President's critics accused him of "timidity and moral myopia," Osgood credits his understanding of neutrality with meaning "self-control and service to humanity." [51] Wilson could not grasp how it would be possible for America to serve as an impartial peacemaker if she used national expediency rather than "Humanity as her guide." Unlike Lippmann's thesis, Osgood's explanation of America's entry into the war is the unrestricted submarine warfare against neutral as well as belligerent ships. He finds that the government was on shaky ground when it declared Britain's armed merchantmen to be carrying defensive armament and forbade Germany the right to attack such merchantmen without warning.[52] He denies that the threat of a German victory to American security was even a consideration of the President. Wilson would have ranked this as expediency "while his aversion to the balance-of-power system and to all elements of force in international relations caused him to depreciate strategic calculations as a basis for national action." [53] He thought that he could keep the nation free from war without jeopardizing its security. For a man of this temperament "war had to be holy in order to be justifiable." Osgood distinguishes from Wilson's crusade for democracy against autocracy, the Realists' contention that there should be a concert among the democratic nations for the sake of securing power and vital interests.

Among the supporters of the League to Enforce Peace, organized officially on June 17, 1915, Osgood discerns different purposes on the part of the advocates. Militant Idealists wished to renounce

50 *Ibid.,* 176–77.
51 *Ibid.,* 180.
52 *Ibid.,* 183–84.
53 *Ibid.,* 191.

isolationism in favor of a league which would protect the supremacy of the large democratic powers over the "have-not autocracies." The pacific Idealists, on the other hand, would envision a league as "the supreme expression of America's altruistic spirit of service to humanity, a means of replacing the outmoded diplomacy of the balance of power with the new, enlightened diplomacy purged of national selfishness and the preoccupation with physical force." [54] He points out that Henry Cabot Lodge supported the idea of a league conditionally until Wilson adopted a universal association as a national aim. Lodge distinguished his views from the Wilsonians in stating that selfishness as an attribute of human nature is almost never controlled by the nobler emotions in masses of men as distinct from individuals.[55] He would control, not abolish, physical force, and he would not combine plans for a future peace with attempts to end the war. Not until December, 1916, did a prominent political figure of either party take an anti-league stand, with the exception of Bryan who would not use force to oppose force and who would not approve of American soldiers being ordered around by European monarchs.[56]

Osgood marks the continued psychological defeat of Germany in not providing even a moral pretext for its acts of expediency and in violating the public sensibilities with the destruction of Louvain and Rheims, the execution of Edith Cavell, the deportation of Belgian and French labor, etc. Exposés of the schemes of ultranationalists Bernhardi, Nietzsche, and von Treitschke were used against the Germans to exemplify the contempt of international ethics attributed to their rulers.

German propaganda, with its customary inefficiency, instead of identifying Germany's cultural traditions with American tradition, seemed intent upon stressing the peculiar philosophical superiority of German Kultur, its greater profundity and intellectual purity.[57]

[54] *Ibid.*, 244.
[55] *Ibid.*, 245.
[56] *Ibid.*, 249.
[57] *Ibid.*, 237.

When Germany was opposed on the basis of a suggestion that international struggle for power is a civilizing influence, America's most ardent national egoists were the leaders of the idealistic attack. The latter comprised a circle of Roosevelt's admirers: General Wood, Elihu Root, Colonel Stimson, and Senator Lodge.[58]

He shows how important were Wilson's exalted war aims in convincing pacific Idealists of the noble democratic and peaceful ends to be won by intervention in the war. The reconciliation of this group "consecrated America's second crusade as an altruistic mission." [59] But those who accepted the war only on the assurance that the Fourteen Points would produce a brave new world, were in the vanguard of disillusionment when the new order was not produced.

In evaluating the intervention in World War I and the disillusionment afterward, Osgood writes:

The American mission, divorced from a conception of fundamental national self-interest, seemed to have been futile at best, false at worst; and the nation's scholars, journalists, and politicians set to work fixing the blame for intervention upon this group or that individual, as though to purge the nation of its guilt by indicting the selfishness, hypocrisy, or gullibility of a few. . . . If Americans had been more realistic, they might have tempered both their egoistic and idealistic inclinations with the discipline of enlightened self-interest and a sober estimate of the role of morality in international affairs.

If Woodrow Wilson erred, it was not because he led the United States into war but because he failed to do everything in his power to prepare the people to see their entrance into a foreign war as an act consistent with imperative principles of national self-interest, as well as with national ideals and sentiments. . . . If Americans, as a whole, supported intervention for insubstantial reasons, it was not because they were wrong in their idealism, their moral indignation, or their lively sense of national pride and honor. . . . It was, rather, because they failed from the first to guide and restrain their aspirations and sentiments with

[58] *Ibid.*
[59] *Ibid.*, 274.

a realistic view of national conduct and a prudent regard for the practical consequences of specific policies.

Armed intervention might well have been the wisest alternative from the long-run standpoint of American ideals and interest, but the great majority of the people did not choose war upon mature deliberation; they simply drifted into war, guided largely by impulses—some noble, some mean. . . . America's vaunted moral leadership revealed itself once more as the irresponsible outburst of a nation physically mature but emotionally and intellectually adolescent—a quick-tempered, good hearted giant of a nation . . . never quite comprehending either the circumstances or the consequences of its erratic behavior.[60]

To George Creel's Committee on Public Information, Osgood attributes the fashioning of "verbal magic" which raised the "American Messiah" to a position of unprecedented world leadership in the record of the presidency, and which attracted the German people with the lure of a millennium. But he denies that this crusade reflected a concerted intention of the people as a whole either to abandon isolationism or to sacrifice any sovereignty for the sake of a league.[61] In the press' reception of the Fourteen Points, he notes that the League was ignored in their preoccupation with territorial terms. As in the case of the Open Door notes,

. . . the American public was basking in the sunshine of its own righteousness, drinking in the gratifying spectacle of the United States advising the unenlightened nations how to straighten out their affairs; but if there was a general desire to undertake any concrete political commitments on behalf of Wilson's pronouncements, the press did not reveal it. Wilson's mystic faith in his identity with the common people of America was encouraged by the obvious popularity of his war leadership . . . he was filled with a certain naive assurance that the great mass of Americans were as fervently and consistently altruistic as he and, therefore, equally attached to his program of international organization. . . . American enthusiasm for a league was, in large part,

[60] *Ibid.*, 261–63.
[61] *Ibid.*, 277–78.

enthusiasm for a world in which the nation could escape a recurrence of its present involvement in the toils of world politics. To this extent the desire for a league arose from the very sentiments that made acceptance of new international commitments unlikely.[62]

The President's defense of America's entrance into the League as a purely philanthropic gesture, he notes, gave strength to the nationalists' argument that if they were offered nothing but an opportunity to aid others, they should be able to determine the extent of their own generosity.[63] In citing the cases of European selfishness relative to the peace, Osgood says: "Evidently hundreds of millions of peoples of conflicting hopes and ambitions regarded Wilson as the Messiah of their special national concern and theirs only." Wilson's appeals for the League seemed to disillusion still more the Idealists who wanted perfection, and they antagonized the champions of nationalism. "In the American outlook, political isolation stood for national comfort, ease, and security. Only a broader conception of self-interest could have prevented a reversion to America's traditional habits of conduct." [64] Only a challenge to their survival would have altered their outlook then.

Osgood observes that Wilson was more ready to compromise with the peacemakers at Versailles than with those in Washington. Eighty-five per cent of the Senators who voted on the treaty on November 19, 1919, were willing to accept American membership in the League; those who wished reservations could combine with those who wished none, against the minority who opposed any league.[65] "Ironically, the President's own confidential reservations, which he gave to Senator Hitchcock to use as he saw fit, were substantially the same as Lodge's reservations relating to Article X, the Monroe Doctrine, domestic questions, and withdrawal from the League."

In the spirit of disenchantment with the League, Osgood finds

[62] *Ibid.*, 278–79.
[63] *Ibid.*, 286.
[64] *Ibid.*, 113.
[65] *Ibid.*, 293–94. He cites T. Bailey, *Woodrow Wilson and the Peace Makers* (New York: 1947), II, 154 ff.

a "sullen and peevish paranoia," a "nationalist xenophobia," and a contempt for the "intractable obstacles in the path of perfection." [66] He concludes that neither the United States nor humanity as a whole gained anything by the failure "to reach a compromise on a pragmatic basis."

Whether the Versailles Treaty had reservations or not, America's position in world politics was made no more secure by her withdrawal from the potential center of collective security and her rejection of the best instrument of an Anglo-American accord; and, on the other hand, America served the material and spiritual welfare of mankind no better by withholding her force and her moral reputation from the world's best hope for the reconstruction of peace. . . .

It must be said that President Wilson's leadership throughout the period of war and peacemaking, though it was eternally right in its moral objectives, could not have been deliberately calculated to defeat its own ends more surely. . . . Wilson demanded an impossible and unnecessary performance, encouraged the postwar repudiation of the very objects he sought, and obscured the one basis upon which a more realistic view of national conduct could have been created . . . enlightened self-interest. . . . There was a vast area in which American ideals and American interests coincided; indeed, in which they were indispensable to one another. The popular realization of this fact and the will to act upon it realistically was born in the adversity of a second world war.[67]

From the standpoint of winning the war, he can see that it made little difference "whether Americans entered it to redress the balance of power, to vindicate their honor and rights, to make the world safe for democracy, or to achieve a democratic association of nations." [68] But it made a big difference in America's postwar role, and "altruistic service to humanity was the most difficult of all ends to pursue or to achieve through warfare." The paucity of the crusade's rewards seemed out of proportion to the tremen-

[66] *Ibid.*, 295, 298.
[67] *Ibid.*, 302–04.
[68] *Ibid.*, 195.

dous hopes which had been raised and the enormity of the sacrifices. Just as in the aftermath of the Spanish-American War, American altruism proved fleeting.

From the attempts to safeguard the uncertain peace by limiting armaments and outlawing war through the moral pressure of public opinion alone, he sees the dangerous consequences in the failure to meet the struggle for power in the Far East.[69] Disarmament was advocated most by women's organizations and by churches. In the Washington Disarmament settlements, he notes the futility of the limitation when not supported by an effort to balance and mitigate the conflicts of national power of which the accumulation of armaments was a symptom. The hollowness of the Kellogg-Briand Pact is evident in Osgood's account of its origin.[70] Aristide Briand had originally proposed that France and the United States mutually outlaw war for the secret purpose of strengthening the bilateral nonaggression pacts with which he had been encircling Germany. Later, when Secretary Kellogg suggested its multilateralization, Briand tried to get out of it, but was unsuccessful.

Osgood is not sympathetic to America's handling of the Manchurian incident. He chides the government for assuming a moral position that was politically irresponsible; it remained unwilling to back up its stand with national power since "Japan's threat to international morality did not seem to endanger fundamental interests." [71] He recognizes that it was the beginning of an imperialist thrust in the East in which more was at stake than Chinese territorial integrity and American commercial interests; but he remarks coolly that had the United States no more to lose than equal opportunity for trade in an area of little American business, then regardless of international morality, the nation should have contented itself with ordinary diplomatic devices. Secretary Stimson's moral chastisement and rejection of commit-

[69] *Ibid.*, 307.
[70] *Ibid.*, 347.
[71] *Ibid.*, 353.

ment to coercion did not vindicate the moral wrong, or protect American interests in the Far East, or avoid war.

It actually worked to defeat all of these objectives by arousing Japanese resentment, fixing conditions for a settlement which the Japanese could never meet and at the same time, displaying a weakness which encouraged the radical element in Japan to pursue their imperialist ambitions. Ideally force should have been combined with measures that would have given Japan a sense of economic and political security.[72]

With a sense of relief that it finally happened, Osgood describes America's conversion to Realism in the early days of the Second World War. He traces it to a recognition of the primacy of national self-interest and of the necessity of facing power configurations, all of which came of the inter-war disillusionment and the later threat to American survival. He deems this political Realism "a vital balance wheel needed to restrain and give direction to the nation's egoistic and idealistic impulses." [73]

At first, self-interest seemed to lie in isolation and non-intervention, but as Americans read the hard lesson of survival in the fate of Europe, the great majority became convinced that their own survival was inextricably bound up with the interest of Great Britain and France in preventing German domination of Europe. This remarkable transformation in the American outlook might not have come so readily had not the overwhelming majority of the nation felt that America's practical advantage coincided with a compelling moral purpose, but it was the international flux of power, not the dictates of morality, that proved to be the decisive factor in the actual course of action which the nation adopted.[74]

Although he rates Franklin D. Roosevelt as a spiritual descendant of Woodrow Wilson in many ways—in his sense of America's moral responsibility to promote peace, democracy, and a better way of living throughout the world—yet he notes his "grasp of the stuff of world politics, a respect for the imperatives of power,

[72] *Ibid.*, 356.
[73] *Ibid.*, 19.
[74] *Ibid.*, 404.

which Wilson never attained or sought." [75] Without being an advocate of *Realpolitik*, Roosevelt was able to perceive "that the domination of either Europe or Asia by a hostile and aggressive power would be a disaster for America's hemispheric security." Osgood judges that in order to appease an isolationist minority, he defended America's step-by-step involvement in the world struggle for power too much in terms of neutrality, non-intervention, and altruism. Roosevelt's claim that America was "the great arsenal of democracy" was the most extreme interpretation of the American mission in terms of tangible commitment; he believes that self-preservation, not missionary fervor, moved the nations to respond. [76]

Roosevelt was probably as sincerely dedicated to America's mission of world peace and freedom, as profoundly convinced in the cause of international organization, as Wilson, but his thinking reflected the temper of his times, and in 1941 he was absorbed in the nation's immediate task of self-preservation rather than in the problem of preventing future wars. . . . The mood marked America's passing from the age of innocence. [77]

Osgood considers that Americans assumed a responsible world leadership only when circumstances demanded that political isolation be abandoned. Under the discipline of adversity they acquired "a new respect for the exigencies of power politics, a more sober view of the penalties of impulsiveness . . . a conception of American idealism more in accord with the hard facts of human nature and international life." [78] However, Americans are still prone to anticipate a standard of perfection in international diplomacy that exceeds the bounds of real possibilities. Their willingness to act internationally still fluctuates with the presence of threat. As an example, he cites the Marshall Plan which was based upon economic and social factors which were urgent regardless of the

[75] *Ibid.*, 410–11.
[76] *Ibid.*, 416.
[77] *Ibid.*, 424–25.
[78] *Ibid.*, 431.

Soviet's military power, but he doubts that Congress would have passed the measure had the specter of the enemy been dimmer.[79]

He reproves any attempt to equate the practice of collective security today with Wilson's ideal of "a system of international organization in which all nations would recognize an obligation to combine against any nation guilty of aggression, as determined by impartial procedures and laws." [80] Today, he says, no nation in its right mind would subordinate "its special security interests to a hypothetical general interest in maintaining a stable international order." It must choose the aggression it opposes and the method "according to the calculated effect of alternative courses of action upon its power position." Otherwise, it would squander its capacity even to defend its vital interests. He analyzes the operation of collective security both in a regional organization like NATO and in the United Nations as a whole.

NATO is a military alliance against a "particular potential aggressor" with narrowly defined obligations to serve a common security interest.

This is precisely the kind of entangling alliance, designed to promote a particular alignment of power, that President Wilson hoped would be replaced by a universal concert of nations.[81]

In his analysis of the United Nations, the writer of this study frankly acknowledges that Osgood stands in the Realist, not the Idealist camp. That his heart remains with the latter can be seen, however, in his hasty retreat at the end of the journal article when he implies that the improvisations might be temporary and when he appears to retain a fondness for the "symbols of universality." He seems to manifest dual yet conflicting loyalties—to his academic training on the one hand, and to an ineluctable voice from within, on the other hand.

In the functioning of United Nations, he demonstrates that it

[79] *Ibid.*, 434.
[80] *Id.*, "Collective Security and the Lessons of History," *Confluence*, V (Winter, 1957), 343–44.
[81] *Ibid.*, 345.

has depended actually "upon the few nations who possess a preponderance of world power displaying unanimous approval of, or at least common acquiescence in, measures for dealing with the situation at hand."

Great power unanimity or acquiescence have, in turn, depended not upon the dictates of universal legal and moral obligations, but rather upon the existence of an alignment of interests and a distribution of power such as these nations have found it to their self-interest to support, or at least not actually to resist, measures taken in the name of the international organization.[82]

The United Nations has added new dimensions to power politics by establishing new procedures and institutional arrangements through which the traditional struggle for power must operate. If it is true that not legal and moral obligations, but accompanying configurations of power and interest are the decisive element, then the breakdown of international order which led to the Second World War could be properly attributed to failure of the United States to join the League.

And by the same token, the containment of the Soviet Union will depend primarily upon the way in which we manage our power and prestige in competition with the Communist bloc, rather than upon the rights and wrongs of national conduct according to the UN Charter.[83]

Nevertheless, he admits that Wilson's concept of collective security is more in keeping with "the traditional image of America's role in the world than the policies we are compelled to pursue in reality." To bring harmony between the two points mentioned above, two types of self-deception are practiced: either to read the current practice into Wilson's statements, or to read Wilson's conceptions into the contemporary outlook. While it might be possible to rationalize that Wilson was swayed more by the imperatives of national security than his generalities on internationalism indicated, Osgood prefers to maintain that Wilson's ideas

[82] *Ibid.*, 346.
[83] *Ibid.*, 348.

were not implausible then in terms of America's experience and assumptions about world affairs.[84] Wilson's concept was firmly rooted in nineteenth century liberalism and twentieth century progressivism which professed that democratic institutions, trade, and commerce would draw nations together in better knowledge of their harmonious interests and that they would eventually come to observe the same standards of reasonableness and good will that existed among individuals.

In contrast to Wilsonianism, he terms the current approach to collective security as "sophistication," which was common only to the early years of American independence and to the last decade or two of its history. It stresses that the observance of universal legal obligations depends upon a favorable balance of power. To give the blessing of a philosopher to his conclusions about power politics, Osgood cites Christian Wolff's explanation that the balance of power would be unnecessary if states acted perfectly reasonably and fulfilled the obligations which the law of nature imposes upon them. Because he believed people could not attain the state of reasonableness Wilson envisaged, Wolff sought to mitigate their wars by obliging them to use force "as the impartial application of legal rules might prescribe." [85]

Osgood pinpoints the ambiguity in America's present approach to collective security. When expediency and the United Nations Charter obligations coincide, Americans assure themselves and the rest of the world that they are determining their policy objectives in accord with universal law and justice in behalf of the international community. In dubious cases they "try to get the best of both worlds by talking—and to some extent thinking—in terms of Wilson's conception of collective security, while making concessions to power politics on an *ad hoc* basis." [86]

But one may wonder what difference it makes if we console ourselves with a myth as long as we are compelled, in practice, to conduct our policies as the realities dictate. The only answer is that our longing

[84] *Ibid.*, 348–49.
[85] *Ibid.*, 352.
[86] *Ibid.*, 353.

for the myth may inhibit our adjustment to the realities. The problems of the cold war, the problems of containment, cannot be resolved in terms of the general good of opposing aggression and upholding collective security. . . . Our commitment to the ideal conception of collective security becomes a liability only when it conceals this necessary basis of action and leaves us straddled awkwardly between two worlds—the one, a world of aspirations; the other, a world of power politics—bridged only by a succession of pragmatic improvisations to meet a series of unanticipated crises. We shall be in a better position to avoid this liability when we can retain Wilson's conception as an ultimate aspiration but repay our debt to History with a candid acknowledgment that we live in a world he never envisioned.[87]

Osgood's final judgment on America's orientation to foreign affairs is that the people "have shown the ability to grasp the hard realities of world leadership and yet retain the moral enthusiasm nourished during isolation and innocence." [88] America's sense of mission has lost its youthful buoyancy but gained soberness and humility which enhance its stability.

Frank Tannenbaum

Perhaps Mr. Tannenbaum oversimplifies American diplomatic history by reducing it merely to commitment to the ideal of "the co-ordinate state." He has a tendency to dismiss unpleasant realities and to make Uncle Sam a blood relative of Pollyanna. One gives limited credence to any thesis which takes a strand of truth from a plaid fabric and presents it as a miniature of the whole pattern. Had Alfred T. Mahan defined the role of sea power, had Charles A. Beard explored the place of economics, had Hans J. Morgenthau revealed the importance of power in international relations —without any of them claiming that his specialty was the determinant in the affairs of men or nations—each would have made a valuable contribution to scholarship. Likewise had Frank Tannenbaum

[87] *Ibid.*, 354.
[88] *Id., Ideals and Self-Interest*, 452.

avoided their fault of exaggeration of one aspect in a complex subject, his book would not have been labeled "jejune" by his critics.

He hails as the initial American commitment to the ideal of the co-ordinate state the Northwest Ordinance of 1787. "The decision to divide this vast area into separate states and admit them, each in turn, upon a footing of equality with the old states was not only something new in territorial policy but was an act of the highest political wisdom." [89] This principle of union based upon equal sovereignty is contrary to the concept of a colony; it was applied in the lands of the Louisiana Purchase, of the Spanish Treaty area, and of the acquisitions resulting from the Mexican War.

Tracing the co-ordinate principle in operation, he sees evidence that John Quincy Adams and Henry Clay were prepared to broaden the Monroe Doctrine to a multilateral policy as early as March, 1826. [90] Though the Doctrine did not contain a self-denying ordinance, successive assertions have given assurance the United States did not mean to indulge in practices it condemns in others. He singles out the annexation of Texas and the war with Mexico as the single real deviation in this regard, but he is consoled that John Q. Adams, Abraham Lincoln, Daniel Webster, and Henry Clay expressed opposition to it, and that the majority of American historians are ashamed of the aggression.

They do not believe in the current doctrine that might makes right, nor do they teach that security requires the powerful state to oppress the lowly one. The American historian has not fallen victim to the newer doctrines of power politics. That is why what they have said about the Mexican War is so important. [91]

He notes that Richard Olney, after his statement in the Venezuelan boundary dispute that a fiat of the United States is law on

[89] Tannenbaum, *The American Tradition in Foreign Policy,* 51.
[90] *Ibid.,* 58. He cites J. A. Richardson, *Messages and Papers of the Presidents,* II, 235 and *International Conference* (Government Printing Office, 1890), IV, 123.
[91] *Ibid.,* 83–84.

this continent, did not "contemplate interference in the internal affairs of any American State." [92] With Theodore Roosevelt's twisting the Monroe Doctrine beyond its historical intent, he finds no argument for the right of permanent intervention. Of the hypocrisy displayed by the United States and the adverse reaction of Latin America in regard to repeated interventions in the Caribbean as well as in the Mexican war, he judges:

The policy of force was always initiated by the executive, and always, with the exception of the war with Mexico, in the end defeated by the Congress and the people. . . . If we did not follow the alluring path of empire, it was because the American people recognized that they could only do so at the sacrifice of their own liberties, grounded in constitutional federalism, and in denial of their most cherished beliefs.[93]

Of the treaties and agreements negotiated under the Roosevelt Corollary of the Monroe Doctrine, he records that they were usually denied ratification by the Senate as an attempt "to foist an imperial policy upon a recalcitrant Congress and a strongly critical nation." [94] Senators made repeated efforts to attach riders to naval bills in order to prevent payment of Marines stationed in the Caribbean area. Theodore Roosevelt's boast, "I took the Canal," he finds less impressive than the fact that Panama was encouraged to become an equal member of the family of nations —the rebellion was comparable to the secession of West Virginia during the Civil War.[95]

Turning to the Far Eastern imperialism, he reproves the notion that imperialism was the purpose rather than the result of the Spanish-American War.[96] He believes that Senator George Frisbie Hoar's opinion on the intended annexation of the Philippines echoed the original theme in American foreign policy:

[92] *Ibid.,* 63.
[93] *Ibid.,* 70–71.
[94] *Ibid.,* 76.
[95] *Ibid.,* 81.
[96] *Ibid.,* 74.

We will acquire no territory; we will annex no people; we will aspire to no empire or dominion, except when we can reasonably expect that the people we will acquire will, in due time and on suitable conditions, be annexed to the United States as an equal part of a self-governing Republic.[97]

He observes that the bill for annexation of the Philippines passed with a majority of only one vote, and that victory was generally assumed to reflect the news of the rebellion which reached the United States on the day before. Tannenbaum documents America's record of virtue in the Philippines with statements of President McKinley and Governor-General Taft:

The Philippines are ours, not to exploit, but . . . to train in the science of self government. . . . Whether an autonomy of independence or quasi-independence shall ultimately follow in these islands ought to depend solely on the question, Is it best for the Philippine people and their welfare? [98]

While he adverts to the fact that the difficulty of defending the Islands, the consequent expense, and their meager commercial importance were considered in the discussion, he judges that if these points had been considered primary, the Philippines would have received immediate independence. Instead the Senate preferred to give them greater internal political autonomy and prepare them for full freedom.

In America's relations with China he finds only one line of action worthy of rebuke, the Taft-Katsura Agreement of 1905 and the Root-Takahira Agreement of 1908, which gave Japan a free hand in Korea and Manchuria. These were executive agreements, not submitted to the Senate for confirmation, and both occurred under Theodore Roosevelt who caused so many other aberrations in American foreign relations.[99] He mentions with

[97] *Ibid.*, 75, quoted from Fred H. Gillett, *George Frisbie Hoar* (New York: Houghton Mifflin, 1934), 208.
[98] *Ibid.*, 74.
[99] *Ibid.*, 101.

satisfaction that when William Howard Taft, Roosevelt's personal representative in the 1905 incident, became President he sought to safeguard China against further ravaging. The President suggested to Great Britain that China be given a loan to purchase the Manchurian Railroad, and in 1912 he approved American bankers' participation in the International Consortium. Bryan's protest against the Twenty-One Demands in 1915, the Lansing-Ishii Agreement of 1917, the Nine-Power Treaty of 1921, and the Stimson Doctrine of 1933 all showed the opposition to Japanese control. He observes that the Americans carved out no sphere of influence in China because they would not support a war to claim for themselves territory which was Chinese. The terms insisted upon in the November 20, 1941, meeting with the Japanese Ambassador were further evidence of America's respect for China's integrity; America accepted the risk of war and this had nothing to do with commercial advantage.[100]

Tannenbaum gives this explanation of America's entrance into World War I:

It may express our innocence, our naïveté, our childish lack of experience in the world, but to the American people the only thing that justified the war was the extirpation of German militarism, which was the great visible evil. . . . For with us, security is only conceivable in a just world. . . . Power derived from conquest, exploitation, and abuse is insecure just because it is unjust, and is bound to fail when the crucial test arrives.[101]

Wilson's failure at Versailles and the rejection of the League he explains in terms of pure Idealism:

When Wilson found himself faced with the realities of Europe, he compromised with the evil he had taken the American people into the war to destroy. He compromised in bitterness and unhappiness. . . . For in the League, at least, there was the promise that in the end the ideals of the American people would be fulfilled. . . .

[100] *Ibid.*, 108.
[101] *Ibid.*, 114–15.

The American people, however, defeated this effort because Wilson had destroyed their faith when he yielded to European diplomacy. Had Wilson stayed at home, or had he abandoned the conference and declared in the ringing words he was master of, that he would not bargain with evil, that the American people had not gone to war to rescue the Imperial powers and guarantee them in their possessions, that he had not taken the people of the United States to war to destroy the German people but to save them and their conquerors as well from the dangers of future wars, he would not have lost his leadership, and he might have won both the League of Nations and an acceptable peace.[102]

While he nods at factors like Wilson's stubbornness and the effort of Lodge and the Republican party to discredit the President, he stresses the element of bitter disillusionment among the people when they found themselves misled by their allies and confronted with a League which sanctioned an unjust peace. The failure of collective security under the League of Nations he attributes to the fact it was not based upon the principle of the co-ordinate state; had the members had equal voice, effective economic and military sanctions would have been employed against Italy for the attack on Ethiopia. In reply to the charge that the small states would have committed the large powers to a war in which the former would have borne a minor part, he answers, that to have acted that way would have been to avoid a greater tragedy. He would enforce these beliefs:

. . . that in the modern world there are no separate interests for the small or the large state, that their destinies are collectively involved in each other, and the violation by war and oppression of the independence of even the smallest power is, in the end, the denial of the possible survival without war even of the largest power.[103]

Tannenbaum interprets the Good Neighbor policy as moral and spiritual, not merely as political and economic.

It stands for the old American ideal of the dignity of man and the equality of the states. It seeks to resolve the persistent conflict between

[102] *Ibid.*, 117–18.
[103] *Ibid.*, 165.

the large and the small Powers by accepting a multiple universe, all the members of which were of equal juridical status, possessed of equal privileges and similar responsibilities.[104]

With the approach of the Second World War he finds the Americans determined to stay out of the "European mess" because after the surrender by France and England at Munich there was a voluntary yielding of the principle of "national integrity and political equality" for which Americans had fought in the First World War.[105] The statements of equality, freedom, and independence implicit and explicit in the Atlantic Charter, Lend-Lease, and the North Atlantic Treaty gave World War II the crusading flavor of 1917.

Of the settlements in the Far East he expresses doubt that the national interest was served by the destruction of Japan "as a counterpoise to Russia," nor would it have been so expensive to have Japan "control and develop China," but because the United States must support the survival of free and independent nations, the decision of Hull and Roosevelt was inevitable as "the decision of the American people." [106]

The reversal of an American policy within five days of its announcement—the policy of the United States' having three votes in the General Assembly to match Russia's quota, he traces to the strength of opposition to this violation of equality. Recalling the criticism to which the veto power has been subject from the beginning, he suggests that it has lost much of its weight since vital questions may now be transferred to the Assembly. He is pleased by the fact that this transfer of jurisdiction occurred in the effort to protect Korea's integrity, "an eloquent testimony to the soundness of the historical American tradition of the co-ordinate state."

America wants peace with Russia, but will not buy it at the expense of other nations. The American tradition has no room for a settlement

---

[104] *Tannenbaum*, "The Anvil of American Foreign Policy," *Political Science Quarterly*, LXIII (December, 1948), 527.
[105] *Id., The American Tradition in Foreign Policy*, 125.
[106] *Ibid.*, 110.

which would divide the world into spheres of influence. . . . The only kind of peace acceptable to it is based on collective security—again, the principle of the co-ordinate membership of all states in the family of nations. . . . We are not quarreling over economic interests, political doctrines, or her [Russia's] internal policies, even if we do not like them. . . . Our quarrel is not about Russia, but about her contempt for the independent sovereignty of other nations.[107]

Never would he go along with those who say that United Nations has failed and that the North Atlantic Treaty Organization is the true substitute. The latter is merely a temporary defensive organization to implement the ideal of the United Nations and "has nothing to do with the balance of power idea and less to do with dividing the world into spheres of interest between Russia and ourselves."[108]

In the conclusion of Tannenbaum's study of how the American federal relationship conditions its expectations and demands upon the outside world, he summarizes the occasions when the United States denied its own beliefs:

The traditional twisting of the "British Lion's Tail" is but one example of a species of irresponsibility in international relations; Theodore Roosevelt's interference in the arbitration of the Alaska boundary dispute; his "I took the Panama Canal"; Wilson's intervention in Haiti and Santo Domingo; the Platt Amendment; the arbitrary senatorial action on Japanese migration; the almost century-long bullying of Mexico; the numerous landings of American marines in Central America; the indifference to the feelings of foreign nations often expressed in Congressional debates; our constant preachments and moralizations; the subordination of our foreign policies to domestic policies; the support of "big business" and American investors in foreign countries, sometimes without due regard to the legitimacy of their claims; the lack of sensitivity to foreign culture and foreign values, and since the Second World War, the conscious but faltering support of colonialism, are all part of the story of our failure to abide by our own commitments.[109]

[107] *Ibid.*, 136–37.
[108] *Ibid.*, 166.
[109] *Ibid.*, 140–41.

⋆ V ⋆

Catholic Principles Relating to Man and to the State

MANY of the writers in this controversy between the Realists and the Idealists admit that the disagreement springs from a different approach to the nature of man, the effect of original sin, the purpose of the state, etc. Therefore, it is necessary to give much attention to these preliminary understandings before presenting the Catholic principles of international relations. But even these aforementioned fundamentals must be prefaced by something else —an explanation of the Thomistic theory of knowledge, since the controversy raises the questions, "What is reality?" and "How do you arrive at truth?" Because *a priori* reasoning from abstract moral principles is challenged by the empiricists, we must make clear the steps followed in forming a practical judgment, with reference to prudence and feasibility.

Thomistic Approach to Truth and Reality

Not only does everything in the creature belong to God, but its very existence is a "way of imitating God, a way of being God-like." [1] This is not to say that the creature is God Himself, since it remains finite and participates in, but is not identified with, the act of existing. Since its whole reason for being is God, the ultimate standard of truth is the intellect and will of God—in conformity of the thing to that standard, one finds truth.

Man is aware that he knows the truth when he knows that the propositions he forms about reality are conformed to things as they are. Truth is grounded in being. . . . The act of being, according to St. Thomas . . . is not merely the act through which being exists as a substance; but it is also the act through which being rests in its end once it has found it.[2]

Thomistic realism holds to the real existence of things independent of men's thinking or knowing them.

There are three types of certitude: [3] 1) metaphysical certitude, which is possessed when the matter for judgment bears on the act of existing—in this certitude there is no possibility for the truth of the opposite; 2) physical certitude, found in propositions about the steadiness of being and action in the physical world observed over a long period of time; 3) moral certitude, grounded in the way men usually act under given circumstances. Since natural law ethics will be mentioned repeatedly, it is well to note that Natural Law receives general acceptance only in periods when metaphysics is dominant; it suffers an eclipse in periods when morality and law are separated, when essences are viewed as unknowable.

Dr. Vernon Bourke expresses succinctly the Thomistic theory of knowledge, which serves to restore to a position of respect in this debate universals and abstraction.

Thomists stress the difference between sense perception as a knowing of individual aspects of things, and intellectual comprehension as a

[1] Frederick D. Wilhelmsen, *Man's Knowledge of Reality:* an Introduction to Thomistic Epistemology (Englewood Cliffs, N.J.: Prentice-Hall, 1956), 137.
[2] *Ibid.*, 139–40; Thomas Aquinas, *De Veritate*, q. XXI, a. 2.
[3] *Ibid.*, 166–71.

knowing of the *universal* meanings of things. Universals are not thought to be real existents in the Platonic sense (exaggerated realism) nor are they regarded as mere fictions of the mind (nominalism). Rather, universals (treeness, greenness, humanity) are concepts (as they exist in the intellect) with a real foundation in reality . . . extramental realities are held to exist whether known or not.

The intellectual act of abstraction provides a link between our sensory knowledge of individuals and our intellectual understanding of their universal natures. Abstraction is not understood as getting away from reality. It is an intellectual penetration into the depth of existing things. . . . The principle of causality may be used to reason to the existence and something of the nature of immaterial things. This principle and that of non-contradiction are held to be indemonstrable but known through intellectual insight.[4]

In their theory of reality Thomists differ from materialistic philosophers who attempt to explain all real events and actions by the laws and properties of bodies.

[The acts of rational thinking and of willing] require the existence of beings with operative potencies which are different from material powers. Hence we now make an important negative judgment: a being does not have to be material in order to exist. . . . In itself, being includes all essences and everything existing. . . .

Metaphysics is indispensable for the work of the philosopher. This philosophy of being distinguishes first of all, between *what* things are (essences) and *that* things are (existence). Essences may be partly grasped through simple apprehension, but existence is revealed in judgment. Being is both essence and existence.[5]

Man, a composite of material and immaterial being, is a unity to whom acts are attributable as to an agent. The soul is immaterial because it gives rise to immaterial actions. Intellectual cognition,

[4] Vernon Bourke, "Thomism," *American Philosophy*, ed. by Ralph B. Winn (New York: Philosophical Library, Inc., 1955), 147–48. Dr. Bourke is professor of philosophy at St. Louis University.
[5] *Ibid.*, 148–49.

an operation of the immaterial faculty, starts where sensation leaves off. It is explained graphically by Dr. Bourke:

The intellect which makes the abstraction works something like an infra-red light which reveals hidden writing on an old manuscript. The light does not make the writing, or change the parchment, but it enables one to see more than is ordinarily visible. Similarly, the act of intellectual abstraction enables one to grasp more of the nature of reality than is visible to the senses.[6]

Because true cognition consists in the agreement of the assertion expressed in the judgment, with the actual reality or ontological truth, continual experience and self-orientation toward reality are important. Heinrich Rommen observes that the real distinction between realism and empiricism is not that the latter prefers inductive experience and the former holds to deductive speculation. Rather, empiricism notes only what is in the foreground and realism pushes beyond the "cheerfully affirmed actuality" to what is in the background, the essence and their laws of being.[7] The doctrine of the immutability of Natural Law rests upon the fact that the essential forms of things are unalterable because they are "ideas of the immutable God."

The divine reason by thinking creates the essence of things. The divine will brings them into existence either immediately as first cause or indirectly through secondary causes. . . . These lines of thought are of importance because the principle that law is positively something pertaining to reason and not mere arbitrary will depends upon this realistic epistemology. . . . The principle that law is arbitrary will is founded upon a nominalist or purely empiricist theory of knowledge.[8]

---

[6] *Ibid.*
[7] Heinrich A. Rommen, *The Natural Law:* a study in legal and social history and philosophy, trans. Thomas R. Hanly (St. Louis: B. Herder, 1947), 165–66. Dr. Rommen is professor of political science at Georgetown University.
[8] *Ibid.*, 168–69.

Man's will is a special faculty of intellectual appetite. This power which inclines toward intellectually known objects, universal goods such as justice, peace, beauty, goes beyond the sensory appetite. Man is able to assent to this attraction, yet not all will acts are free.[9] It should be noted that though man is a means for the glorification of God, he is also an end in himself, so much that after endowing him with freedom, God cannot make him an instrument except by man's own volition. The priority of the intellect over the will in both God and man, the knowability of the essences of things, and the ordered hierarchy of values must be noted because these are the supports of natural law ethics.

Since nominalism is evident in this debate on national interest, we might advert to its historical background. The doctrine of the will as the nobler faculty is the root of nominalism, which is directed to the "individual particular thisness"; in its extreme form it denies the knowability of essences, which are related to the intellect, and declares universals to be but vocal utterances. Thomas Hobbes (1588–1679), a nominalist, held that reason is unable to know universals; their expression consists in mere names which reason assigns to them arbitrarily "without any foundation in fact and reality, for the purpose of introducing order into the chaos of sense impressions." [10] Positivism, which flows from this nominalism, assigns prominence to empirical knowledge of individual things; as a philosophy of life it reduces itself to materialism. "The state itself is not recognized as a moral collective person . . . there is no external justice, nor is there an unalterable moral law." [11]

Much of this confusion can be traced to Duns Scotus (c. 1278–1308) who emphasized the primacy of the will over the intellect. With William of Occam (c. 1300–1349) there set in an evolution which would lead to moral positivism and even to nihilism since "oughtness" would be without foundation in reality. He stated that the goodness and rightness of certain actions are not found in

[9] Bourke, "Thomism," 151.
[10] Rommen, *Natural Law*, 82.
[11] *Ibid.*, 126–27.

their conformity with nature, but in the absolute will of God who would be considered free to prescribe the opposite course of action. Suarez (1548–1617) resolved this difficulty by pointing out that "as the light of natural reason indicates by way of judgment the inner agreement or internal contradiction of actions with rational nature, it likewise indicates in the very same act that this corresponds also to the will of God, the Author of nature." [12]

Before stating the method of arriving at practical judgment, we might note remarks of Professors Land, S.J., and Klubertanz, S.J., on the Natural Law. "According to St. Thomas, the 'natural law' exists only in a mind, though it has a basis in the natures of things. . . . Moreover, according to St. Thomas, the natural law is not of itself a complete and completely detailed rule of human action." [13] While conscience is not the source of moral laws, it is the immediate application of them. Because the objects of human action are contingent, the data of experience and judgments of prudence enter into practical reasoning. When judgments are arrived at by a simple application of first principles of the practical order, the deduction has a minor premise drawn from experience. Still other judgments are made "in dependence upon a full consideration of diverse and changeable circumstances." This relative factor is stressed in other statements of these scholars:

The situation in which men stand relatively to one another rather than human nature in the abstract—the relationship in which they concretely exist—establishes many ethical arguments . . . . the common good (a social gain achieved by the complementation and supplementation of individual activity) is, in turn, the work of given men of a given time and place. [14]

[12] *Ibid.*, 197.
[13] Philip S. Land, S.J., and George P. Klubertanz, S.J., "Practical Reason, Social Fact and the Vocational Order," *The Modern Schoolman*, XXVIII (May, 1951), 239. Professor Land, formerly a member of the Institute of Social Order, now teaches the economics of underdeveloped regions at the Gregorian University, Rome. Professor Klubertanz is dean of the College of Philosophy and Letters, St. Louis University.
[14] *Ibid.*, 242, 245–46.

Particularizing factors are technological stage, state of education, and cultural development, etc. Among the determinants for St. Thomas of the ideal state were: "a) the condition of the people and the objective sought, b) the virtue of the people, and c) the virtue that can be expected in the available rulers." [15]

Criticizing *a priori* legal codes as rigid and inflexible, these same writers accuse them of generalizations derived illegitimately "from the particular contingent situations which fit into the lawmaker's conception of how things ought to be." The qualities needed to obtain perfect ethical insight demand that it be based upon reason, be unhindered by passions, be mature, informed, and dynamic. Deductions from principles often need to be completed by points of empirical evidence to justify the implications. Feasibility, in distinction from pragmatism, is a criterion of *means*, whereas pragmatism judges *ends* by their results, their practicality, their satisfyingness. [16] Regarding the principle of feasibility, once the end is established, one must decide how best to achieve it morally under the present circumstances. The role of the state in moral matters is to exercise prudence, not abstract perfectionism.

The Nature of Man

A political philosophy consonant with Catholic thinking begins with creation as the origin of human nature, for there is no other explanation of the immaterial soul. Since we know of no way in which such an immaterial thing may come to an end—it cannot disintegrate into parts—the only conclusion is that human souls are immortal. [17] Man depends first upon God, and then on whatever superiority he has from God by nature or grace. Man can have but one final end which fills up the measure of his capacities. Since all men have the same nature, they must have the same end.

[15] *Ibid.*, 248; Thomas Aquinas, *Contra Gentiles*, III, 3; *Summa Theol.*, I^a–II^{ae}, q. 97, i; I^a–II^{ae}, q. 105, a. 1, ad 2.
[16] *Ibid.*, 259.
[17] Bourke, "Thomism," 151–52.

God's purpose in creation is the communication of His divine reality; man has a principle of activity which moves him to his appointed end, "a limited participation in and a manifestation of, the divine excellence. . . . To insure the creature's movement toward the divine purpose, the Creator implants in each a natural appetite for its proper good." [18] Man's essential beatitude is in the knowledge and love of God. This happiness is actually realizable because it would be contrary to divine goodness to lure man on by this conscious appetite for that which could never be satisfied. Since the universal experience of mankind testifies that mortal happiness is imperfect, his life here must be preparation for happiness hereafter. Moral values have supremacy over all else because each human act has meaning only in so far as it leads man to his final end. Man is responsible for those acts of which he is master. Factors modifying culpability are ignorance, passion, habit, and violence.

If one admits with Aristotle that "what each thing is, when fully developed, we call its nature," then it follows that man is a political animal, for in his state of complete development one finds him as a citizen. It is incorrect to assume any natural opposition between the individual and the political community; historical instances of it were not of nature's making, but were the result of one's self-centeredness or of unwarranted pretensions by those representing the authority of the state.[19] Man is by nature a social being impelled to live in society by virtue of need, fitness and inclination toward it. This attraction is rational, not instinctive;[20] he is able to attain knowledge of particular things necessary for human life by reasoning from natural principles. However, by his

[18] Thomas J. Higgins, S.J., *Man as Man, the Science and Art of Ethics* (Milwaukee: Bruce, 1949), 15. Professor Higgins teaches ethics at Loyola College, Baltimore. Hereafter referred to as *Man as Man*.

[19] John F. McCormick, S.J., "The Individual and the State," *Philosophy of State*, 11–12.

[20] Thomas Aquinas, *On Kingship*, trans. Gerald B. Phelan, rev. by I. Th. Eschmann, O.P. (Toronto: Pontifical Institute of Mediaeval Studies, 1949), Book I, ch. 1, 4–5; *Summa Theol.*, I^a, q. 96, a. 4; II^a, II^{ae}, q. 109, a. 3 ad 1.

own individual reason, he cannot arrive at knowledge of all these things; he must live in a multitude so that he has the benefit of others' discoveries, for example, in medicine. The term *social* is wider than the term *political,* for a man can depoliticize himself and still remain a man, but no one can cut himself off from all social relations, their rights and duties and still remain human.[21]

Mankind constitutes a single family, regardless of race, color, language, or nationality. All men are descended from a single couple; they are children of the same divine Father in heaven; they are redeemed by the blood of the God-man and they are called to incorporate themselves in His mystical body.[22] Natural morality creates reciprocal duties of justice and charity for all human beings, who must contribute according to their means to the material and spiritual conditions favorable to the full development of the human race and to the maintenance of the common good of mankind. Assertions about the dignity of man and his inalienable rights have meaning because he is made to the image of God, with an immortal soul which transcends any secular value. Natural rights are inviolable and inalienable; rooted in "existential" human ends, man cannot free himself of these rights though he may delegate some functions.[23] The exercise of the rights may be impeded, but this does not annul them. Rights are connected with duties on the part of the one in question, and they require respect from other men. It would be inconsistent to speak of "man-made inalienable rights, or of state-given inviolable rights. What man has made he can destroy; what the state has given it can take away." [24]

[21] Emmanuel Chapman, "The Relation Between Ethics and Politics According to Aristotle and St. Thomas," *Philosophy of State,* 178. Hereafter referred to as "Relation Between Ethics and Politics."

[22] John Eppstein (ed. & trans.), *Code of International Ethics,* compiled by International Union of Social Studies, revised by Malines Union (Westminster, Md.: Newman Bookshop, 1953), 44. Hereafter referred to as *Code.*

[23] Johannes Messner, *Social Ethics,* trans. J. J. Doherty (St. Louis: B. Herder, 1949), 152–53. Dr. Messner is professor of political economy in the University of Vienna.

[24] Thomas P. Neill, *Weapons,* 192.

Limitation is inherent in the rights of men because human beings must live with others similarly endowed.

There can be no real conflict between the rights of the individual and the rights of society, because the rights of the individual emanate from a being that carries within itself as a constituent part of its nature the destination to be incorporated in the social order. An order is impossible between beings invested with absolute rights and complete independence. . . . At their very origin individual rights are circumscribed to that extent that they will not nullify the purposes of the social order; otherwise we would have to admit a basic contradiction in man's nature. . . .[25]

Man has social freedom as a means of self-determination in respect of his natural ends. "Freedom is based on rights, not rights on freedom; this erroneous view was the fundamental fallacy of individualism." [26] Because of man's "existential" ends, he has "rights that are anterior to any arbitrary will and therefore not subject to any social contract, majority principle, public opinion or poli." Compulsory law enforces such standards of behavior as are necessary for the existence of the community; state intervention grows as man's social and political virtues stagnate in the atmosphere of narrow self-interest. Hence the more man is ethical, the freer he is.[27]

The Catholic view of man's life in society is not utopian. Human nature, though impaired, is still rational in its impulse, still possessed of the knowledge of good and evil. But man must struggle toward the good, beset by evil inclinations, his intellect and will lacking the governance of the preternautral gift of integrity. His weakness and perversities must be reckoned with in the examination of society. Because of this realism, the duty of social reform

[25] Charles P. Bruehl, *The Pope's Plan for Social Reconstruction:* a Commentary on the Social Encyclicals of Pius XI (New York: Devin-Adair, 1939), 42. Hereafter referred to as *Pope's Plan.* Professor Bruehl teaches sociology at St. Charles Seminary, Overbrook, Pennsylvania.

[26] Messner, *Social Ethics,* 220.

[27] Rommen, *The State in Catholic Thought* (St. Louis: B. Herder, 1945), 288–89. Hereafter referred to as *The State.*

is urged and original sin is acknowledged in the maxim that "politics is the art of the possible." Messner shows this synthesis of realism and idealism, and makes careful distinctions of what they are not.

Political realism so regarded is the very opposite of political opportunism with its facile rule of choosing the line of least resistance. For natural law ethics makes it a moral duty of the community to put forth the utmost effort to achieve "the possible," and thus carries with it the most inspiring and potent social idealism. . . . Any policy must fail which expects the automatic improvement of men merely through the reform of the social system.

This realism of natural law ethics is as far removed from Manichean, Lutheran and Jansenist pessimism as it is from Pelagian and rationalist optimism in the interpretation of man's nature. Luther, in particular, sees in the Fall a radical deflection of human nature toward sin and evil: man has become incapable of realizing the moral order in personal and social life and can only rely upon grace. . . . The optimism of the Enlightment, on the other hand, attributes to reason an unlimited ability to attain the true and the good by its own powers; hence the belief in unlimited human progress, intellectually and materially, which marks nineteenth century humanitarianism.[28]

Since much of this controversy hinges upon the effects of original sin, further distinctions in the matter may be profitable. In Catholic teaching, original sin is not something positive, but rather the privation of those supernatural and preternatural gifts which were gratuitous blessings given to the human race in the person of Adam. This does not imply that reason is unable to recognize Natural Law and the will to strive for it, as taught by Luther and Calvin, in the context of depravity.[29] Farther still would it be from Spengler's pessimism in which progress is considered a fake, and justice and equity made meaningless except as instruments for political might.[30]

[28] Messner, *Social Ethics*, 82–83.
[29] Rommen, *The State*, 63–66; Calvin, *Institutio*, Book II, ch. 3, 1.
[30] *Ibid.*, 88.

Pope Pius XII warned against the opposite extreme of ascribing all of man's perverse inclinations to functional weaknesses which of themselves can be cured as soon as he knows fully the laws to which he is subject in his relations with the world about him.[31] This tendency breeds softness, indulgence, and aversion for just punishment. In order of being, human nature is good; good is the object of every appetite,[32] but the inferior faculties sometimes tend, even in their first movement, to oppose the order of reason. The nineteenth century idea of progress was profoundly secular and optimistic; it envisioned the evolution of man's socio-political life from a crude form of animal existence to a future earthly paradise in which the god-like man would need no compulsory laws, political authority, or churches.[33] It represented the triumph of Rousseau's political doctrine; it was a secularized form of the Christian hope of perfect life hereafter in union with God, not attained by man's natural powers alone. An earthly millennium is not the goal of history; the goal is, rather, the final supernatural redemption of all creation. Because the Christian is aware of sin and of passions adverse to peace and progress in his political life, he must exert himself incessantly to bring about the slow perfection of "the City of Men" where he works for the salvation of souls.

The Origin of the State

We turn now to an investigation of how society is organized for man's political existence. The state, not being a substance, does not exist outside or above its citizens; it exists only in and by the individuals who are the "matter" of the state; its form is the moral end expressed in its laws and constitutional organization.

[31] Pius XII, Christmas Message, 1956, *The Pope Speaks*, III (Spring, 1957), 335–36.
[32] Thomas Aquinas, *Summa Contra Gentiles*, trans. English Dominican Fathers (London: Burns Oates & Washbourne, 1928), III, 7.
[33] Rommen, *The State*, 86–89.

The common purpose unifies and organizes the individuals into a distinct community. The end of the state is not absolute, for it is subordinated to the end of all creation, the glory of God. Of man's rising above the body politic, St. Thomas says, "Man is not ordained to the body politic according to all that he is and has; and so it does not follow that every action of his acquires merit or demerit in relation to the body politic; but all that man is, and can, and has, must be referred to God." [34] This political society, required by nature and attained by reason, is the most perfect of temporal societies.

St. Augustine laid the foundation for future Christian thought with his concept of the state originating in human nature by virtue of the divine will. It was not original sin which gave rise to the state, for even had Adam not sinned men would have organized themselves in a state; only the aspect of physical compulsion is the result of sin. The state remains necessary for the redeemed since "grace does not destroy nature or make its essential socio-political institutions superfluous, as some sects think." [35] Luther was the first to consign the state wholly to the realm of fallen nature. There are within man "potentialities of perfection which cannot ordinarily be actuated apart from other men or through mere casual contacts with them but only through stable, peaceful, orderly association with others; that is, through social life." [36]

Professor Kennedy explains the origin of the state in this way:

The proximate, juridical cause of its existence is the consent, express or tacit, instantaneous or gradual, of the multitude of families proximately disposed to form such a society; but its end and its essential attributes are determined by the law of nature. . . . States as such and political

[34] Thomas Aquinas, *Summa Theol.*, trans. Fathers of English Dominican Province (New York: Benziger Bros., 1947), I^a, II^{ae}, q. 21, a. 4, ad 3, p. 688. (Reprinted from the *Summa Theologica*, Benziger Brothers, Inc. Publishers and Copyright Owners.)

[35] Rommen, *The State*, 76; Messner, *Social Ethics*, 499.

[36] Paul V. Kennedy, S.J., "The Principles of Democracy," *Philosophy of State*, 168–69. Professor Kennedy teaches philosophy at West Baden College.

power as such are immediately from God, but *this* state, *this* government depend on the choice of the community.[37]

Robert Bellarmine (1542–1621) explained the method by which the authority was communicated.[38] Whether it be monarchy, aristocracy, or democracy, the political power comes from God. Willing or unwilling, men must be ruled by someone if they do not wish the human race to perish. The power resides immediately in the collected body, since Divine Law gives it to no particular man. Since the state cannot of itself exercise this power, it is delegated by the multitude to one or to several. Independent forms of government depend upon the consent of the people, who with legitimate cause may change the form. As in all other things which pertain to the law of nations, God uses here the medium of human wisdom and choice. In the individual state, nearly everything is the result of historical development: the exercise of political authority, the structure of institutions and social systems, the national character influenced by inherited physical and mental qualities and environment.[39]

Catholic political philosophy is at variance with the contract theories which arose in the post-Reformation period.[40] Thomas Hobbes (1588–1679) thought that man, intrinsically evil, was driven by the "war of all against all" into acceptance of a contractual order of law, which would have to be upheld by a concentration of might in the hands of the sovereign political power to which all individual rights were transferred. Unlike Hobbes, John Locke (1632–1704) and Jean Jacques Rousseau (1712–1778) believed that the transition into political status was not necessary;

[37] *Ibid.*, 169–70.
[38] Roberto Francesco Bellarmine, *De Laicis:* treatise on civil government, trans. Kathleen E. Murphy (New York: Fordham University Press, 1928), ch. VI, 24–27; Suarez, *De Legibus*, Lib. III; *Defensio Fidei*, Lib. III.
[39] Messner, *Social Ethics*, 493–94.
[40] Pope Leo XIII discusses this in two encyclicals, "Diuturnum" and "Immortali Dei." The various contractual theories are analyzed in Rommen, *The State*, 60–61, 125.

they identified the natural man with the autonomous primitive, motivated by self-interest, who took refuge in the political community to escape the difficulites involved in individual self-sufficiency. In this state rights and duties would not be based upon nature, but upon revocable contract; the end of the state would be individual self-interest, not something objective and transcendent to the individuals.[41]

The Catholic theory of consent differs from that of the contractualists in the understanding that the state is a natural, not artificial, society, and that man has a moral obligation to form it. Individual rights come from God and nature, not from the Social Contract. Authority is derived immediately from God, not from the will of many individuals; when this authority is transferred to a ruler it may not be recalled arbitrarily, since obedience is due the ruler who is more than a paid agent of the Sovereign People. The welfare of the people demands that sovereignty be stable.

The Common Good

The purpose of society is the advancement of good living, which is another way of saying a life of virtue among its members.[42] Man is unconditionally ordained to God as his ultimate objective end; his ultimate subjective end is the possession of God. Society is concerned with divine things indirectly, through its constituents; it has an obligation to do nothing which would impede the individual in the acquisition of his true end. The common good is the intermediary end of each individual as a citizen of society; he is obligated to the promotion of the common good which in turn is ordained to the perfection of the individual as an individual. The common good cannot be purchased at the expense of human

[41] Higgins, *Man as Man*, 460–62.
[42] Thomas A. Joyce, O.P., "The Metaphysical Basis of Political Action," *Philosophy of State*, 118–20. Professor Joyce teaches philosophy at the Dominican House of Studies, Catholic University of America.

personality. By its very nature, the agency of political action must be centralized so as to obtain the common objective; thus sovereignty exists as the right to rule and direct; coordinated effort is impossible without subordination.

The common good and the individual good coincide, though they do not absorb each other:

The actual good order is the best guaranty of the private good of the individual; and the righteous realization of the private good by the citizen is to the advantage of the common good. . . . Though man's social nature reaches its perfection in his becoming a citizen, man does not become a mere part of the state, but as a member retains his inalienable personal independence, his substance. . . . The common good is to be conceived like the health and the vitality of the organism, which are different from the members but are of benefit to each of them as something animating them, connecting them so that each participates in it and still no member has it wholly and separately.

The common good is the directive rule and the last unappealable norm of the acts of the sovereign power. . . . It turns the external amorphous mass, the mere conglomeration of individuals into a solidarist body of mutual help and interest, into the organically united nation. . . . Under no circumstances can it be conceded that public authority, the end of which is to serve the common good, should be put into the service of private interests.[43]

The common good must take precedence over the individual good "when both belong to the same order, but when the good of the individual is of a higher order then it takes precedence over the temporal common good," [44] as in the case of his freedom and spiritual perfection. There is a sense in which the human parts are greater than the social whole:

For a society is temporal and mortal; a man is eternal and immortal. No man could be compelled to sacrifice his supreme good nor even to risk it, even though he would confer the most tremendous benefits

[43] Rommen, *The State*, 310–11, 327.
[44] Chapman, "Relation Between Ethics and Politics," *Philosophy of State*, 179.

on any society. However, certain societies such as Church and State are so necessary to all men, so completely equipped to promote man's real good that there never could be a true conflict in which an individual would have to choose between his supreme good and the genuine good of one of these societies. That which promotes the real good of these societies must eventually promote the good of the individual.[45]

If there is a real conflict between the interests of the greater number of persons or a group of persons and the supposed common good, it is a sign that the order has become unjust. The salvation of man's soul must prevail against a conflicting positive demand of the state. In the realm of "quantitative conflicts," even a just war may not be continued if it requires the destruction of "seventy per cent of the male population." There can never be demanded from all the citizens that they renounce basic rights of family life, that they forego freedom to direct the education of their children, that they sacrifice religious obligations, because the state was produced to enable them to pursue these things together in peace and security. "Reason of state" as something outside morality is hostile to the Christian idea of the service character of the state; this Christian contribution differs from the Greek concept.[46]

The common good must be realized on every plane: the spiritual, the cultural, the social, the political, and the economic. Although spiritual values are beyond the end and the power of the state, they are not unimportant for political life, since life is not compartmentalized. The jurisdiction of the state in moral matters is restricted to public morality. The virtue of justice in all its forms —legal, distributive, and commutative—is directly the concern of the state; other virtues are its concern only as they are actually related to the common good and to justice.[47]

From the fact that the common good constitutes the supreme law of the state there follows the primacy of politics or of the political community "to assign their places to the various groups with their particular interests and claim to power and by so doing

[45] Higgins, *Man as Man*, 362.
[46] Rommen, *The State*, 308–09.
[47] *Ibid.*, 329–30.

to prevent the exploitation of some groups by others." [48] This is a process of absorbing the interests into the dynamics of progressively realizing the common good. In spite of the efforts of organized interest groups, the government must be strong enough to protect the "objective pre-eminent interests," rather than make politics the domain of factional quarrels. These other associations have a primary right to self-help; the state's secondary function is to secure for them the possibility of realizing their purposes on their own responsibility within the framework of the common good.[49] Catholic political philosophy differs with the individualistic school of utilitarianism which sees the common good as the utility of the greatest number or the sum of individual goods.[50] Politics is not merely the art of achieving and retaining social power for some selfish end; it is rather the "architectonic art" of building institutions and protective forms for more perfect realization of the good life by coordination of free persons and associations.

Employing some of the vocabulary of the Realists, Messner says this about the accomplishments of politics:

The actual common good can never be more than an approximation. The function of bringing about the common good must therefore mean doing what is most expedient in the circumstances. Hence reason of state enjoins a policy of "the possible." The statesman who, neglecting the realities of political forces, however idealistic his motives, lends himself to measures which bring the state into unnecessary danger, acts in fact against the common good. Reason of state can command the more imperfect in order not to make the more perfect impossible. That the true realistic policy as prescribed by reason of state has nothing in common with opportunism, has already been explained. . . .[51]

Seven correlative elements in the common good are unity, order, stability, security, freedom, peace, and progress.[52] Of these elements, St. Thomas seemed to give priority to peace which is the

[48] Messner, *Social Ethics*, 579–80.
[49] *Ibid.*, 594.
[50] Rommen, *The State*, 314; Thomas Aquinas, *Summa Theol.*, IIa, IIae, q. 38, a. 7; q. 31, a. 3.
[51] Messner, *Social Ethics*, 644.
[52] Charles G. Walsh, "Economics and the Common Good," *Thought*,

tranquility of order.[53] Justice prepares the way for peace by removing the obstacles, but charity really brings it about. Prudence, meanwhile, guides the intellect in its arrangement of all things.

A twofold union is involved in peace. One is the union of the different appetites of the individual, the other is the union of the appetites of one man with those of another. Now charity effects that twofold union, the first kind in so far as we refer all things to God. Thus all our appetites are directed towards one thing. The second union is effected in so far as we love our neighbor as ourselves, from which it follows that a man desires to fulfill the will of his neighbor as his very own.[54]

Pope Pius XII emphasized this unity of order to be found only in return of the human mind and heart to God, as a means of stemming the disintegration brought about by materialistic egoism.

. . . by working for the universal good, each of you will work for the good of your country and for the welfare of your family, precisely because order is one: it can reign in souls, in nations, in the whole of humanity, only if everything is in its proper place; and therefore, only if God everywhere occupies the only place which is proper to Him: the first. And thus finally, in the stability of order, there will descend upon the earth that peace, which is so much sought after. . . .[55]

Church-State Relationship

Since spiritual values were considered in the promotion of the common good, we may briefly investigate the role of the Church

---

XXIX (Spring, 1954), 7–31, citing the explanation of Moorhouse Millar, S.J., *Labor and the Common Good* (New York: Fordham University Press, 1940).

[53] Thomas Aquinas, *On Kingship*, I, 5, 15; *Summa Theol.*, Iª–IIªe, q. 29, a. 1 ad 1; a. 3 ad 3.

[54] Joyce, "The Common Good," *Philosophy of State*, 121.

[55] Pius XII, Address to the International Union of Catholic Women's Leagues, April 14, 1939, in Harry C. Koenig, *Principles for Peace:* Selections from Papal Documents Leo XIII to Pius XII (Washington: National Catholic Welfare Conference, 1943), 562. Hereafter referred to as *Principles*.

with reference to political society. Pope Leo XIII in "Immortali Dei," referring to the primacy of the spiritual power, said that the judgment of the Church should extend to "whatever in human affairs is sacred, whatever pertains to the salvation of souls or the worship of God." [56] The primacy of the spiritual power is derived from the fact that it deals with what has primacy in all human affairs, the relationship of man to God and to his own supernatural destiny. Pope Leo XIII did not explain how the Church was to exercise its right to correct affairs in their religious and moral aspects. John Courtney Murray, S.J., provides a useful interpretation when he suggests that the spiritual direction must be accomplished "from within the temporal order itself, through the agency of its own institutions, and not from without—not therefore by the efficiency of the Church as such; for the Church as such stands outside the political order, transcendent to it." [57]

Professor Murray feels that Leo XIII really did put forth the principle of solution when he said that the rule of Church and State is over the same man who is both a citizen and a Christian.

If therefore there is conflict and not harmony between them, the conflict is felt in the depths of the personal conscience, which knows itself to be obligated to both of the powers which are from God. Their harmony therefore is required by the unity and integrity of the human personality. . . . Leo XIII was implicitly saying that the human person by his action as Christian and citizen ought to be the instrument and agent of establishing this harmony in actual fact. . . . It is only through him and through them [institutions of popular rule responsible to the citizens] that the Church can reach the temporal order. . . . The action of the Church on him terminates at conscience, forming it to a sense of its Christian duties in all their range and implications for temporal life . . . . the Church is a reality for the state because she is

[56] Leo XIII, "Immortali Dei," November 1, 1885, in Koenig, *Principles*, 27–28.

[57] John Courtney Murray, S.J., "Contemporary Orientations of Catholic Thought on Church and State in the Light of History," *Theological Studies*, X (June, 1949), 219. Professor Murray teaches at Woodstock College and is editor of *Theological Studies*.

a reality for its citizens—a reality in a higher order, in which the state as such has no competence.[58]

The fact that the American constitution provides for a state which is lay in finality and function does not mean that it is theoretically secularist, "animated by the doctrine that the natural, terrestrial and temporal are All That Is; for it recognizes that there is a 'spiritual power' in society that must be free . . . . indirectly to achieve the due temporal incarnation of the spiritual." Pope Pius XII expressed the role of the Church thus:

Her work is done in the depth of each man's heart, but has its effects, extending throughout his life, in all his activities. Through men thus formed the Church prepares for human society a basis on which it can rest securely.[59]

Norms of Morality

In contrast to those who admit that there are only "mores," and deny that there are universal, immutable laws of morality everywhere valid, Catholic tradition holds ethics to be a philosophical science applying to all men and establishing the moral order of human acts; it treats of ultimate causes of human conduct and bases its conclusions on unaided reason.[60] All schools of ethics accept the fact of moral consciousness, but then they diverge, as the empiricists, for instance, who hold that this fact can be reduced to man's self-interest in doing good. Catholics hold that morality is the correspondence of human conduct with right reason and with "existential" human ends; man tends toward the good, not by compulsion of instincts, but by the impulsion of the mind recognizing the "ought." Messner states, that the demands of morality are nothing else but the demands of reality itself; in other words, that being and good are convertible. Hence what is proper to essential

[58] *Ibid.*, 220–24.
[59] Pius XII, Allocution to the College of Cardinals, Public Consistory, February 20, 1946, in *Catholic Mind*, XLIX (April, 1946), 195.
[60] Higgins, *Man as Man*, 8.

nature is morally good." [61] And the nature of things is based upon God.

The correlation between reality and morality in the social sphere could be delineated thus:

> Nothing that is morally wrong can in the end be economically right; or as to politics: What is politically right is morally good, is as true as the principle that nothing which is morally wrong can be politically right. Both these propositions imply the condition: that economics and politics get down to true reality without binding themselves by 'scientific' or party dogmatisms . . . . genuine ethics does not and cannot force any moral principles from reality itself. . . . Only the good can be real; evil cannot become an ultimate reality. For evil is deficiency of being, of the fullness of being demanded by nature.[62]

Social utilitarianism or altruism, the doctrine held by Pufendorf, Bentham and Comte, states that the happiness of mankind is the norm of morality. It is correct in its contention that an act is good if it leads toward happiness, but its notion of happiness is false in holding either the "here and now" theory, or in making humanity an end in itself; a variable standard of the "useful" is no standard at all, for it is in perpetual flux.[63] To say that morality stems from emotion as do Shaftesbury and Rousseau is to deny that in man's nature appetite should follow reason.

The specific morality of an act depends upon what a man does and why he does it. The result of the act—desired, achieved, or approved—is the moral object of the will act and its primary aspect. There are moral objects which are good, bad, and indifferent. Circumstances modify the morality they already possess, but if the object is bad, no amount of good intention will render the act good.[64]

---

[61] Messner, *Social Ethics*, 46–47.

[62] *Ibid.*, 47. Augustine expressed this thought about evil as a deficiency of being in *The Confessions of Saint Augustine*, trans. Edward B. Pusey (New York: Random House, 1949), VI, 134–35.

[63] Higgins, *Man as Man*, 48, 53–54.

[64] *Ibid.*, 69–70.

Natural Law and Positive Law

Since the Natural Law will be the frame of reference for much of the political analysis, it would be well to explain what it is, how it is known, and how it applies to positive law. St. Augustine defined it as "the mind and the will of God commanding the natural order of the universe to be observed, forbidding it to be disturbed." [65] St. Thomas called it the rational creature's participation in the Eternal Law.[66] As "oughtness" it appears in the rational nature of man both as natural impulse and as the command of nature's Creator. Conscience, while not the source but the application of moral laws, is a practical judgment of the goodness or badness of an act which has been or is to be performed. Intellect is the faculty of which conscience is the act; the latter is not intuitive, but is rather the result of a reasoning process in which a syllogism is implicit, though the operation is usually instantaneous.[67] Because conscience is the subjective norm of morality, each person must make his conscience correspond with the objective norm or law. The Divine Law promulgated in the Decalogue only directs man toward that which human nature itself demands from him.

According to some scholastics, moral obligation can be summed up in St. Thomas' words, "Good is to be done and sought for, evil is to be avoided." [68] The good is that which is fitting, but not every possible good must be done—only "every good the omission of which would be evil." [69] If moral truths were innate in man, there could be no dispute about them. Instead man has the aptitude to grasp them, but his faculties require training and proper social environment. There are some self-evident truths, but these do not form a detailed code. These principles become better under-

[65] *Ibid.*, 82, citing Augustine, *Contra Faustinus*, Lib. XXII, cap. 27.
[66] Thomas Aquinas, *Summa Theol.*, Iᵃ, IIᵃᵉ, q. 91, a. 2.
[67] Higgins, *Man as Man*, 126–28 .
[68] Thomas Aquinas, *Summa Theol.*, Iᵃ, IIᵃᵉ, q. 94, a. 2.
[69] Higgins, *Man as Man*, 116–17.

stood as the mind experiences reality; this experience is not their source, but rather the occasion for the human mind to grasp them. The need for some temporal sanction to enforce the Natural Law is filled by positive law, which is valid only if it is based on Natural Law.

Of the primary principle of Natural Law, no man whose reason is developed can be ignorant. He might be inculpably ignorant, however, of the tertiary principles, since knowledge of these exacts involved reasoning for which some people would not have the ability or the opportunity in order to arrive at truth independently; some authority is needed to declare these principles.[70] Divine revelation is required for the more complicated areas of human conduct. The Natural Law does not explicitly indicate how its precepts apply to all cases.

Contrary to the notion that human nature is gradually changing into something else in which social and economic conditions compel revision of the laws governing human conduct, Catholic tradition holds that Natural Law is one, universal, and unchangeable, both intrinsically and extrinsically.[71] Because all men have the same specific nature, it places them under the same obligation, though it may not actually oblige this or that individual because of insanity or lack of development. By study and by the occurrence of undreamed of circumstances man can learn more about the law, but the precepts will not be new; they have always been in nature's code. Persons conclude that there are exceptions to the law either because they misunderstand the precise meaning of the precept or the nature of an *intrinsically* evil act.

To place natural law doctrine in a clearer perspective, we might investigate some of the deviations regarding the origin of law, in contrast to natural law theory which places it in the ends of human existence. In the Realist-Idealist controversy, some of these deviations are employed. The various schools of political and legal theory attribute the origin of law to the social contract, the social

[70] *Ibid.*, 117.
[71] *Ibid.*, 109–12.

"institution," the autonomy of the individual, the will of the people, the folk spirit, social experience, individual or social utility, effective command, coercive power, the mode of production in material life, social function, the Hegelian objective spirit, the sense of justice, and to the fact that law is identical with its actual effects.[72]

We have referred previously to William of Occam's error in reducing natural moral law to positive law expressed as the divine will. These conclusions could be derived from that:

. . . sin no longer contains any intrinsic element of immorality, or what is unjust, any inner element of injustice; it is an external offense against the will of God. . . . Hence there exists no unchangeable . . . natural law that inwardly governs the positive law. . . . The identity of this thought structure with *The Prince* of Machiavelli, with the *Leviathan* of Hobbes, and with the theory of will of modern positivism (the will of the absolute sovereign is law, because no higher norm stands above him) is here quite obvious. . . . The absolute power of God in Occam's doctrine became at the hands of Thomas Hobbes the absolute sovereignty of the king.[73]

In the philosophy of Hobbes and Baruch Spinoza (1632–1677), human nature is governed by passions rather than by reason. In the *status naturalis* man has no obligations or duties, might is right, and the power to instill fear is the gauge of authority and the governor of obedience. Because Hobbes denied that man has a natural inclination toward mutual help and love, the order of law cannot be derived from human nature; it must become the work of the sovereign. Since man's nature is ferocious, the state becomes good, and the supreme norm of justice.[74] The force theory of moral obligation, held by Hobbes, Spencer, and Oliver Wendell Holmes, is a denial of the freedom and dignity of man's nature.

[72] Messner, *Social Ethics*, 150.
[73] Rommen, *Natural Law*, 59–61.
[74] *Ibid.*, 85–86; Hobbes, *Leviathan*, Part I, ch. 10.

After the time of Grotius, the presentation of Natural Law was influenced by Deism and became a secularist theory of ethics and politics in which the social contract was the basis of normative content. John Locke (1632–1704) regarded Natural Law as a "nominalistic symbol for a catalogue or bundle of individual rights that stem from individual self-interest." [75]

David Hume (1711–1776) declared there was no method for determining what is intrinsically good or bad in passions. Since moral principles were not founded upon objective truth or reason, the morality of an action was determined by the sentiment of approval, with virtue defined as the "quality which gives to a spectator the pleasing sentiment of approbation; and vice the contrary." [76] He felt that through education life in common could develop a social habit of reference to common interest, although the latter was but a nominalist symbol for the sum of tangible individual interests.

With Immanuel Kant (1724–1804) the autonomous, self-sufficient human reason became the measure of things, as he banished the objective basis of the order of things and the eternal law. His alleged achievement in individualist-rationalist Natural Law was the separation of ethics and law, of morality and legality.[77]

Inner freedom, the moral autonomy of the individual person, is the sphere of morality. "A person is subject to no other laws than those which he (either alone or jointly with others) gives to himself." External freedom, according to Kant requires coercive laws. . . . The motive of moral legislation is duty, derived from the autonomy of reason and appearing in the form of the categorical imperative. . . . not enforceability but external physical force is directly and necessarily included in the concept of law.[78]

[75] *Ibid.*, 89.
[76] *Ibid.*, 112–14, quoting D. Hume, *An Enquiry Concerning the Principles of Morals*, Appendix I, 1; Hume, *Selections*, ed. by Charles W. Hendel, Jr. (New York: Scribner's Sons, 1927), 241.
[77] Rommen, *Natural Law*, 101; Messner, *Social Ethics*, 244.
[78] Rommen, *Natural Law*, 101; inner quote is from I. Kant, *Introduction to the Metaphysics of Morals*, trans. T. K. Abbott, IV, 24.

The romantic movement in legal philosophy, called the historical school of jurisprudence, insisted that law was a creation of the spirit of a people, working in an irrational manner, revealing itself in their legal conventions. The time-honored customary laws emerge from the mysterious soul of the nation which "grows like an organism and is not deliberately fashioned." [79] Theirs was an attack on the abstract thinking of the age of rationalism.

Nineteenth century positivism rejected theology and deductive reasoning. Nose-counting and type-grouping was the positivists' method of inductive reasoning; their doctrine of humanitarianism was made a religion in Auguste Comte's sociology.[80] More moderate positivism laid stress upon law as the will of the state duly promulgated; inherent justice in positive law was considered irrelevant. Professor Higgins calls attention to the fact that modern legalism almost denies that God's authority which is invisible, is genuine and effective, since it contends that nothing can be called law "which does not issue from a supreme visible authority capable of enforcing its commands." [81]

The materialist natural law theory of Karl Marx and Nicholai Lenin is found in dialectical materialism; the development of man and society is determined by physical laws and particularly by technical modes of production. Other materialist views of Natural Law are the evolutionism of Julian Huxley and the naturalist psychology of Sigmund Freud.[82]

Heinrich Rommen points out that the environment is once again favorable to the idea of Natural Law, even though it might have been pronounced dead by early twentieth century jurisprudence:

For World War I and its consequences, to say nothing of World War II and its effects . . . have brought men to recognize more and more openly the questionableness of philosophy without metaphysics, of an

[79] *Ibid.*, 110–12.
[80] Neill, *Weapons*, 108–09.
[81] Higgins, *Man as Man*, 87.
[82] Messner, *Social Ethics*, 244–45.

epistemology without certainty of truth, of a jurisprudence without an idea of right.[83]

Christopher Dawson, commenting upon the loss of prestige and spiritual significance in Natural Law, notes that it retains disguised reality in the vernacular under expressions like "Fair Play" and "Decency," though it has disappeared from their ideology.[84]

Positive law, based on Natural Law, is necessary because man's intellectual limitations impede his knowledge of parts of the Natural Law, and his moral tepidity interferes with his observing the law consistently when no physical penalty is attached to its violation. Although a positive law be unjust (though not at the same time contrary to Natural Law, as an unjust tax burden) it might be correct to obey it because the natural law norm enjoins in some cases sacrifice of a particular good to a more general good—security under an external order of peace in the community.[85] While Natural Law has an indirect sanction which works the deterioration of a people who disregard the law of moral living, a more immediate threat is needed because the propensity to disorder is just as strong, and sometimes stronger in man, than his rational longing for order.

It is precisely the object of the positive law to render the citizen virtuous. It is not merely a question of maintaining order, or external peace; the law should rather act as a medium of popular education to transform those who live under common legal institutions into perfect citizens.[86]

Especially in the light of the above, it must be emphasized that if mere arbitrary will of the state could create the justice of law, national self-interest and expediency would be the only rule. The eternal law of God is protector of man's liberty in civil society:

[83] Rommen, *Natural Law*, 39.
[84] Neill, *Weapons*, 184, citing Christopher Dawson, "The Papacy and the New Order," *The Dublin Review* (April, 1942), 112.
[85] Rommen, *Natural Law*, 55.
[86] *Ibid.*, 54.

For, once ascribe to human reason the only authority to decide what is true and what is good, and the real distinction between good and evil is destroyed; honor and dishonor differ not in their nature, but in the opinion and judgment of each one; pleasure is the measure of what is lawful; and given a code of morality which can have little or no power to restrain or quiet the unruly propensities of man, a way is naturally opened to universal corruption.[87]

The Role of the State

Although the author does not maintain throughout this discussion Jacques Maritain's terminology in distinguishing between the "body politic" and the "state," his explanation would serve a purpose in showing the relationship between the person and the state, and in dispersing the Rousseauan concept that the state has absorbed the individual wills which die mystically in order to resurge in the unity of the "General Will."

The State is only that part of the body politic especially concerned with the maintenance of law, the promotion of the common welfare and public order, and the administration of public affairs. The State is a part which specializes in the interests of the whole . . . . it is a set of institutions combined into a topmost machine: this kind of work of art has been built by man and uses human brains and energies and is nothing without man . . . . the State is not a kind of collective superman; the State is but an agency entitled to use power and coercion, and made up of experts or specialists in public order and welfare, an instrument in the service of man. . . . The human person as an individual is for the body politic and the body politic is for the human person as a person. But man is by no means for the State. The State is for man . . . . the human person is both part of the body politic and superior to it through what is supra-temporal or eternal, in him, in his spiritual interests and his final destination.[88]

[87] Leo XIII, Encyclical "Libertas Praestantissimum," June 20, 1888, in Koenig, *Principles*, 43.

[88] Jacques Maritain, *Man and the State* (Chicago: University of Chicago

The *Code of International Ethics* refers to states as true moral persons endowed with all the rights their mission requires both in regard to their own subjects and to other national societies.[89] Their rights and duties, no more absolute than those of individuals, were not created by the will of man, but were derived from the nature of states. International agreements merely determine their mode of application. Because the state's function is fundamental for the performance of man's tasks in the material and cultural spheres, it has a high moral value. St. Thomas along with Aristotle described it as the most excellent creation of human reason and accorded politics the highest place among the arts.[90] This would surely be contrary to individualism and collectivism of the rationalist sort which deprives the state of dignity and makes it a servant of individual economic interest, not recognizing its connection with man's moral existence.

Messner separates truth from error in the Hegelian idea of the state in this way:

The state is not in itself the reality of the mind and not "the reality of the moral idea," but rather the agency by which the mind can subdue the social dynamic of the irrational forces in human nature and hence the agency for realizing the moral idea, the moral principles which are indispensable to the life of society.[91]

The state may demand from the individual the sacrifice of his life in order to protect the state because the state "as the objective

---

Press, 1951), 12–13, 148. (Copyright 1951 by the University of Chicago.) Mr. Maritain has been professor of philosophy at Princeton University since 1948. Maritain makes this distinction in his definition of terms: The body politic or political society is the whole of which the state is only the topmost part. The body politic "contains in its superior unity the family units, whose essential rights and freedoms are anterior to itself, and a multiplicity of other particular societies which proceed from the free initiative of citizens and should be as autonomous as possible," 10–11.

[89] Eppstein (ed.), *Code*, 55–56.
[90] Messner, *Social Ethics*, 500–01.
[91] *Ibid.*, 502.

framework of the good life for all, is more than one individual's private good." [92]

Catholic tradition accepts the organic concept of the state, that it is a living structure in which the distinct parts each with its separate function are joined to the others by a unifying vital principle.

According to the organic view, law is neither the sign of the power of the stronger nor a device by which a balance is achieved between liberties of one individual and the self-interests of the others in the political order without arbitrary interference by authorities. . . . Law is the order in which and by which the faculties, the external acts of the individuals, and their natural and free associations and groups recognized by the law but not created by it, are directed toward the common good. . . . Law rests far more on moral free acceptance and consent, on reason and confidence, than on actual compulsion and menace.[93]

Political pluralism, or the existence of groups in the community with separate interests, is in keeping with the organic arrangement. Even though there is a condition of amity and unity, the existence of conflicting interests involves the state in balancing, in compromise. Because the state is a community of the whole people, one group is not to identify itself with the state and forcibly exclude others from its management as happens when one party declares itself to be the state. Marxism in its assumption of the classless society misconstrues the tendency in human nature toward pluralism.

The principle of subsidiary function outlines the actual common good in the state. The state is the institution for coordinating the individual functions for the good of all; the upper form does not take over and make superfluous the lower ones. Its office is not to eliminate the use of ingenuity by individuals and groups. Man comes to self-realization through exercise of responsibility. It is a miscalculation to say that the community is best served when

[92] Rommen, *The State*, 284.
[93] *Ibid.*, 142.

a small number of government planners are commissioned to think for everyone else.[94] This could be a squandering of the mental capital of the nation.

Nevertheless, the nature of the state is not exhausted with the preservation of law and order; it has a welfare function:

The state must not only create the legal basis for social cooperation, but also see to it that all citizens can obtain their proportionate share of the fruits of social cooperation, materially and spiritually. Admittedly, society shares with the state in the full performance of these tasks of justice. Nevertheless they belong largely to the political sphere, and to the departments of economic and social policy, spheres in which the state was denied competence by the laissez-faire principles.

Today the true idea of the state is challenged from the opposite direction: the new conception is that of the "provider state." The latter regards it as its function to provide directly, by central planning and controlling of social cooperation, for all the material and cultural needs of the citizens and to supply them with everything necessary for every eventuality of life. This idea of the state is what lies at the root of modern movements for state-planned economy and society as exemplified in all socialist and communist theories.[95]

Professor Neill delimits the state's welfare function in this way:

[The state] may do only those things which clearly aim at the perfection of men and thereby at the common good; it cannot, moreover, make use of means which themselves are harmful to man or destructive of his integrity. Thus the state cannot rightly offer him physical protection and material security by denying him his human freedom and human responsibility. It cannot rightfully protect him as though he were a little child. It cannot guarantee him a full dinner pail by denying him the right of responsible human labor.[96]

[94] Messner, *Social Ethics*, 574–75.
[95] *Ibid.*, 486–87.
[96] Neill, *Weapons*, 195. Pius XII in "Summi Pontificatus," October 20, 1939, also stated that the standard should not be primarily the material prosperity of society, but rather the harmonious development and natural perfection of man (NCWC publication, 24).

Indirectly, paternalism would lessen the importance of the family, and it would be contrary to the Natural Law for the state to take direct, complete, and perpetual care of citizens in general. The state ought to offer all a fair opportunity for self-help. "The manner, measure, and mode of social opportunity to be provided by the State will depend on many factors of time, place, climate, custom, level and complexity of economic development." [97]

Social reform is not sufficiently justified by the utilitarian explanation that mitigation of economic woes is dictated to ensure against social upheaval which might destroy the system they cherish. Social reform is a duty because the common good has been distorted by parts of the whole being deprived of participation in the abundance and being slighted in personal recognition.[98]

Yves Simon raises the question, "Is there any ground for the proposition that government activity should be at all times kept down to a minimum, no matter whether circumstances demand that this minimum be high or that it be low?" [99] While granting that government is necessary and good, he replies:

It is perfectly obvious that there is more life and, unqualifiedly, greater perfection in a community all parts of which are full of initiative than in a community whose parts act merely as instruments transmitting the initiative of the whole . . . . direct management by the whole is preferable only when the difference with regard to fulfillment of a task is very great. . . . The history of all nations shows that states have a tendency to take over, whenever they can, functions that used to belong to smaller units of public administration. . . .

To save society from state absolutism, it is not sufficient, he feels, to incorporate checks and balances, constitutional guarantees, or even the control of the people over the governing personnel.

[97] Higgins, *Man as Man*, 437.

[98] Rommen, *The State*, 147–48.

[99] Yves Simon, *Philosophy of Democratic Government* (Chicago: University of Chicago Press, 1951), 128–29, 132. (Copyright 1951 by the University of Chicago.) Professor Simon formerly taught philosophy at Notre Dame University and is now at the University of Chicago.

Democratic forms would soon disappear if they were not supplemented by institutions external to the state apparatus: freedom of the Church, freedom of the press, the private school, the independent labor union, the autonomous cooperative, private ownership, and free enterprise.[100]

To distinguish the foregoing philosophy of state from the many aberrations, we might review several of the latter. Kant formulated the *laissez-faire* view of the state by maintaining the complete cleavage between an internal moral order and an external juridical order.[101] The Manchester economic liberals adopted his idea that the state as external force should merely protect the individual rights of citizens. In the "liberal watchman state," guardianship of commutative justice was the only function of government. It seems absurd that a natural institution should have but a negative function. The accent was on the successful *homo economicus*. That society of the survival of the fittest accepted efficiency as the measure of truth and utility as the measure of good. It demanded "initiative, alertness, daring, speculation, a sharp legalistic mind, and jealousy for all the rights of the individual." It scorned "charity, unselfishness, social restraint, contemplation, and fidelity to ethical ideals." [102] This liberal theory which devalued the state made economics rather than politics the perpetual task; it allowed the bourgeoisie to rule the community for itself. Economic success, not unselfish service to the community, became the standard of social reputation.

Equally false is the socialist-totalitarian concept in which individuals are mere marionettes whose objective ends are submerged in society or the state and its ends. Once the transcendent end of the individual is denied, this dilemma results:

Either the state and the common good are mere names for the individuals taken together, and these latter are the only reality; or it is a mere biological organism, where the individual is nothing but a mem-

[100] *Ibid.*, 136–37.
[101] Higgins, *Man as Man*, 432.
[102] Rommen, *The State*, 339–42.

ber, having no reality and independent value separate from that organism.[103]

The Nation and Nationalism

The terms "nation" and "state" are often used synonymously in this study, but for the sake of investigating the right to self-determination and the role of nationalism, we must here approach "nation" in its more specific meaning. Sociologists have commonly attributed these factors to nationhood: territorial unity, natural environment, common habits of life, similarity of language, kinship by blood, common history and culture. That a nation's "spiritual fellowship" can exist without the unity of language, however, is evidenced by multilingual nations.

The decisive moment in the emergence of a nation occurs when a people becomes conscious of itself and thus finds its soul. . . . This consciousness is stirred especially through the experience of being linked by a common destiny. It is stirred especially through the experience of being linked by a common history, of common tribulations, wars, and victories, of heroic figures of the remote and recent past, warriors, saints, statesmen, who have been able to rouse the people to the service of common ideals. . . .

[Ego consciousness] is realized by the people's will to foster its own character, to assert it in the community of peoples, to prove the value and strength of the nation and thereby to establish its claim to status and respect in the family of nations, pointing to a function of its own in the social and cultural progress of mankind. . . . Nations' consciousness of their own individuality is a modern phenomenon. . . . With the rise of modern democracy the peoples begin to act as units. . . . This process of individualization, although the fact is often overlooked, is indispensable for the existence and real development of a real community of nations.[104]

Messner notes that sovereignty is an essential element of the state, but not of the nation which is a social entity; to exist, a nation

[103] *Ibid.*, 327.
[104] Messner, *Social Ethics*, 384, 388–90.

needs some degree of political autonomy, but it need not be state sovereignty as the principle of national self-determination implies.[105] In the nineteenth century absence of an efficient international order, however, the nationality sought this guarantee of status. He distinguishes between the function of state and nation: the former is to organize peace and order, the latter is to make fruitful its culture both for its own members and for other nations. He warns that the state can hinder the nation's realization of its mission "if it makes itself the nation's schoolmaster and drill sergeant, and if it wishes the nation to live its life chiefly in the political arena."

Rommen offers this criticism of national self-determination:

It is wrong to contend that political unity is possible only on the basis of exclusive uniformity in religion, race, and national culture, just as it is not necessary to build political unity upon economic and social equality. What a state needs is justice in a concrete order of law, and that presupposes only moral unity in the zeal for the common good; it does not presuppose either economic, religious, or "national" uniformity. Where history and the circumstances of geography and providence have cooperated to produce a nation-state, it is well; where history, geography, or historical settlement or migration has not produced a framework for a nation-state, the nonnational state, with political liberty and justice and moral unity even though without national uniformity, is the better thing. If the principle of national self-determination should mean the right to political sovereignty by any group that feels itself to be or claims to be a distinctive national unit, such self-determination would become disruptive and revolutionary.[106]

Where there are small national groups unable to establish independent states strong enough to withstand the political pressure of powerful neighbors, Rommen contends in the interest of peace that such dispersed groups should live in comparative cultural autonomy in a nonnational or multinational powerful state able to afford protection, "rather than that a vacuum of power be created by the existence of small nation-states, jealous of one

[105] *Ibid.*, 393–94.
[106] Rommen, *The State*, 696–97.

another and therefore an easy prey for an expansive neighboring power with its natural attraction of small states into its power orbit." [107]

Professor Higgins offers the reminder that nationality as the basis of the state is not a precept of the Natural Law; the nationality might be a "remote dispositive factor" to consent, which is the juridic cause of a particular state, but other considerations might be stronger such as proximity, mutual need, and long-enduring habits of acting together.[108] Nationality is often so vague. But the above must be balanced by the statement that a nationality group has a right to equitable treatment at the hands of the dominant part, and it must be allowed to preserve its religion, language, and national characteristics. These minority rights are really the individual, personal rights of human beings.

The *Code* states the case cogently with regard to the rights of both the minority and the parent state:

But if, under the pretext of preserving its unity, the State oppresses the minority by a policy of assimilation and uniformity, it is betraying its trust, and the separatist activity of the oppressed nation may be justified, as long as there is no other means of redress and the international common good is safeguarded. If on the other hand, the authorities do not arbitrarily identify the State and nationality, and confining themselves to their task of security and general assistance, leave the racial groups under their care freely to exercise their cultural mission within the State, the secessionist claims of the minority are quite groundless. But in no case can the mere advantage which a minority would find in becoming an independent political body or in uniting itself to another national State ever justify the unilateral severance of the bonds which unite it to a rightly organized political society . . . . a close bond of solidarity has been created between all the members of the community, and no one has the right to reject it, lest grave damage be caused to its associates.[109]

[107] *Ibid.*, 697.
[108] Higgins, *Man as Man*, 551–52.
[109] Eppstein (ed.), *Code*, 58.

Patriotism and nationalism, though not identical, are connected in one sense.[110] The moral virtue of patriotism leads one to love his country with filial piety as the cradle of his race and the home of those who share his culture. Nationalism too is concerned with a community of blood and race, but often it goes beyond state boundaries to *irredenta*, and is found also among nomadic peoples and among the Jews when they had no country. When internal dissension threatens to divide the social body, patriotism changes into nationalism in its rally for unity; in a multinational state the drive for absolute autonomy of minorities might be contrary to patriotism. Though nationalism may be good and sound in itself, it becomes a lawless passion when national culture is made an absolute value. This exaggerated nationalism sacrifices the cultural values of the other nations and will even subordinate to itself human rights, morality, truth, and religion.

In the light of the extremes to which nationalism has tended rather consistently, Dr. Neill makes these observations:

One of the most formidable barriers to the creation and successful operation of any world government is modern nationalism, which indeed is the most formidable single obstacle to peace of any kind. . . . When the skepticism of the Enlightenment pushed the God of the Christians aside, it made room for other gods. And the national state was quickly placed in the niche formerly occupied by God. . . . This secular religion is made possible largely by the void in men's hearts and minds created by the wide rejection of all supernational religions.[111]

He reiterates the sentiments of Lord Hugh Cecil spoken in 1919:

Patriotism is morally quite a different thing from nationalism; they differ as love does from hatred, for while patriotism makes a man love his country nationalism makes him hate other countries. If, indeed, patriotic sentiment be suffered to feel itself independent of the moral law it will grow into nationalism.

110 *Ibid.*, 176–78.
111 Neill, *Weapons*, 168–69. The Lord Cecil quote is from *Nationalism and Catholicism* (London: Macmillan, 1919), 30.

Recent popes have spoken about exaggerated nationalism. Pope Leo XIII in a letter "Pervenuti," March 19, 1902, lamented the system of jealous egoism which had arisen among nations who regarded one another as rivals, if not objects of hate. Pope Pius XI in the encyclical "Ubi Arcano Dei," December 23, 1922, deplored the debasing of genuine love of country to a condition of extreme nationalism which was atomizing the great human family. That same Pontiff in an address "Le Missioni e Il Nazionalismo," August 21, 1938, said: "There is room for a fair and moderate nationalism, which is the breeding ground of many virtues, but beware of exaggerated nationalism as of a veritable curse . . . . for it breeds constant division and the threat of war." [112] Pius XII in the encyclical "Summi Pontificatus," October 20, 1938, stated that the wise development of a nation's genius and qualities does no harm; thus he distinguished between unity and uniformity.

Rommen mentions that the more nations turned to nationalism, the more they destroyed their common Christian heritage. Untempered by the restraint the latter would have counseled, this materialist cause was blind to the immaterial values which are by nature international. To redeem nations from their narrowness today, he would champion education which aims at understanding of other nations with the end of cultivating what we have in common, since a community cannot be a negative thing.

In the era of materialism the nations have tried to build the city of men upon the so-called solidarity of economic interests, upon the secular fraternity of man, upon the socialism of the international proletariat, all this to little avail. . . .[113]

He offers as the solution for a new state of peace, the direction of men's lives to the moral and intellectual perfection of man as the image of God, and the deliverance from the use of material success

[112] Pius XI, Address to Students of Collegio de Propaganda Fide in Rome, in Koenig, *Principles*, 545.
[113] Rommen, *The State*, 688, 700, 708–09.

as an absolute criterion. Instead of holding religion to be the enemy of civilization or merely a subordinate aid, men must return to the conception of religion as the "very soul and end of civilization."

The Concept of Power

Power is an essential element of the state under two aspects: as an association for the establishment of law it must have the concomitant right of physical coercion, and as the agency of preserving the country against aggressors it must be armed for defense. The function of ordered power is to combat destructive power from within and from without the state. Since power is one of the strongest primary impulses, it is liable to perversion either in the hands of a ruling class which might utilize state power for personal glory, or in the designs of a state which uses power for expansion and aggression.

Messner strikes a sane balance between extremes of optimism and pessimism in evaluating the role of power:

All of these manifestations of the power element in the state belong to its actual nature just as the partial perversions of other instincts belong to the actual nature of man. But as the latter do not make up the essential reality of man, the former do not make up the essential reality of the state. By its very idea of man's nature, natural law doctrine must show how in the actual reality of the state the dynamic of natural law counteracts the dynamic of the irrational elements, and how the latter challenges the human spirit to assert itself against them and overcome them.

Thus the realistic conception of human nature and its partial perversion preserves the natural law doctrine from the optimistic belief in any final elimination of the problems arising from the existence of irrational elements in the state. That conception also preserves natural law doctrine from any tendency toward a pessimistic theory of the state which speaks only of an ineluctable tragedy in which state and community of nations are ultimately delivered over to the dynamic power.

That, however, the sheer dynamic power does not constitute the whole nature of the state, must be understood from the historical experience that no state can base its existence exclusively on force. . . . Power must seek justification before the will of the community which demands the minimum of the common good necessary for human existence, and thus the human mind forces its law upon power, though with varying success. . . . The endeavor to subdue the power element inseparable from the state is no less a part of the reality of the state than the power element itself. . . . Thus the perversion of power compels reason to organize power for the purpose of securing peace and so to moralize power. . . . Thus we arrive at the conclusion that the human mind does not find itself impotent in face of the irrational forces of power politics.[114]

In his evaluation of the thinkers who contributed to the amoral concept of power in the state, Messner concludes that their thinking dominates the modern political world, which judges that the state consists fundamentally in power and therefore may pursue its interests to the limit of its strength, with its policies cloaked in justice.[115] Nietzsche erred in overestimating the power impulse, saying all other impulses were derived from it. Marx went astray in underestimating its elementary character and in ignoring those motives which do not depend upon the class structure of society. Supporters of the "power state" derived a moral pretence of justification from Hegel's identifying the state with the "ethical idea." Maritain remarks that foreign policy based upon *raison d'Etat* with its particular interest as the supreme law of activity, goes back to the Hegelian myth of the state as a super-human person, but that modern states were actually Hegelian in practice long before Hegel and his theory.[116] With von Treitschke's making the power essence of the state a means for a cultural end, moral standards became relative.

[114] Messner, *Social Ethics*, 473–76.
[115] *Ibid.*, 478–79.
[116] Maritain, *Man and the State*, 192.

The State Bound by Moral Law

Since natural societies originate in the Natural Law, it would be absurd to maintain that their activities are free from that law. The state could be regarded as a moral person with obligations in the same sense that a corporation must be humane to its workers or a municipality must honor its bonds. The fulfillment of these obligations devolves upon particular men. Sovereignty means that in the sphere of temporal social jurisdiction the state has no superior in the law of another state.

If men, who are of immortal value, are so subject, the State, which is only a means to men's temporal perfection, must likewise be subject. . . . If men, acting for the State, were not obliged to conform their public actions to the Natural Law, some deliberate acts of men would be free of moral law.[117]

Pope Leo XIII in the encyclical "Longingua Oceani," 1895, said: "That which is not permitted in private life is no less prohibited in public life." [118]

Messner admits that the "existential" ends of human beings, in so far as their fulfillment depends on the state's rendering of social functions, confer a moral priority on the necessities of the common good. But that fact does not raise the conduct of the state above the universal moral order.

The general moral principles apply without restriction to the acts of the state, although the practical consequences to which they lead may differ from those which would ensue for the individual . . . . acts that are immoral in themselves are therefore immoral in politics also. The principle that the end justifies the means cannot be a principle of true reason of state.[119]

[117] Higgins, *Man as Man*, 555–56. Similar ideas are expressed in Eppstein (ed.), *Code*, 42–43.
[118] Eppstein (ed.), *Code*, 43.
[119] Messner, *Social Ethics*, 643.

The maxim of "double morality" belongs to the fundamentals of individualist liberalism, willingly adopted by modern collectivism . . . . "double morality" means that the ends of certain areas of human activity are made absolutes, the laws of those areas being derived exclusively from these absolutes. Thus the spheres of political, economic, and cultural life are relatively autonomous. Human activity in political and economic life has indeed to follow the laws prescribed by the particular ends involved.[120]

St. Thomas specifically pointed out the intrinsic relationship between politics and ethics in the fact that politics is a work of prudence and experience.[121]

Rommen notes that nations, impelled by secularism and egoism, have adopted the utilitarian doctrine that what is useful to the individual nation is good. They have stressed their "rights" out of all proportion to their recognition of communal duties. From this egocentrism has arisen excessive sensibility concerning national prestige. From this attempted dichotomy between religious principles and affairs of state has come the impotence of international law and the rule of brute power as they have vied to fill the vacuum created by the repression of universal values.

In the final analysis any community lives by the internal will for charity, for concord, for loyalty, for honesty, for the host of social virtues. They are the direct principle of life, the order of law is the framework, absolutely necessary, but not itself the life. . . . Justice and the law guarantee the independent existence, the liberty, of the members of the international community; but charity and its issue, peace, unite the community and make it a living, cooperative unity of mutual help and cultural development.

The sin of materialism, racial, class, or national, is this, that it destroys the one potential basis of the community of nations because it has destroyed the faith, the Christian faith in God the Father and supreme Lawgiver. Peace . . . calls for the consciousness of a common brotherhood in sonship of the common divine Father.[122]

[120] *Ibid.*, 69.
[121] Thomas Aquinas, *Summa Theol.*, II^a–II^{ae}, q. 104, ad 1.
[122] Rommen, *The State*, 699–700.

The "Perfect Society" Qualified

In concluding this discussion of the state, one might return to the consideration of it as a "perfect society," and make a necessary qualification which will be explained in further detail in the next chapter. Since the purpose of the state is to unite persons in a higher unity for the attaining of the "full good of human life," it is termed a perfect society. But this goal cannot be realized without a wide sharing in the material and spiritual life of the world. This sharing could be adequately accomplished only by the establishment of an international regime in which the states, without losing their own individuality and legitimate authority, would belong to international society. The *Code* explains that through the family, the state and international society are all institutions of Natural Law, corresponding to fundamental human needs; in their actual constitution they have developed successively because of the condition of society:

The peoples of the earth, having fallen from the state of original justice into barbarity, separated from each other by more or less insuperable natural barriers, by differences in climate, language and customs, had forgotten their common origin. For a long time the fact that nations were widely scattered and consequently lived in isolation prevented any considerable and fruitful international collaboration from taking place, and philosophers and moralists alike came to consider the State as a *perfect society*, endowed with all the necessary means to help its members to attain "the full good of human life." . . . The State is still a perfect society inasmuch as it possesses full authority to maintain order, peace, and justice within its boundaries, since a universal State which could claim immediate jurisdiction over all members of the human family is almost unthinkable. But the State is no longer a perfect society inasmuch as it cannot now give to its subjects, by its own means, the "fullest good of human life," such as the progress of civilization and the fruitful resources of an harmoniously organized international cooperation have rendered possible.[123]

[123] Eppstein (ed.), *Code*, 46–47.

⋆ VI ⋆

International Society
and Its Responsibilities

THE assent of the nations is not *a priori* a requisite for the existence of international society, since it is not the product of the will of men, but an institution which corresponds to the demands of human nature in promoting the common good of the whole human family. The consent of nations merely gives the positive society of states its juridical equipment and its designated authorities. Here again the authority comes from God; in every society except the family He allows men to choose their rulers and to determine the extent of their mandate. The persons invested with the authority then have the right to command and the members have the duty to obey.[1] Were there no man made charter to give effect to man's international obligations, they would still exist because of the unity of the human race and the universality of the moral law both of which were ordained by the Creator.

All men are united by common nature and destiny. . . . The word of God reveals that all men have a single origin in one common pair of

[1] Eppstein (ed.), *Code of International Ethics*, 164–65.

parents; that all men were tainted with original sin in the fall of their first parents; that all have been redeemed by the death of Christ and all are summoned to a place in the Church, the Mystical Body.[2]

International Society a Demand of Human Nature

St. Augustine voiced this Christian ideal when he said:

The heavenly city, while it sojourns on earth, calls its citizens out of all nations, and gathers together a society of pilgrims of all languages, not scrupling about diversities in the manners, laws, and institutions whereby earthly peace is secured and maintained, but recognizing that, however various these are, they all tend to one and the same end of earthly peace.[3]

In spite of the limitations of his geographical knowledge, Suarez had a worldview:

If each State, republic, or kingdom constitutes a perfect society in itself, it is nonetheless true that since these communities cannot suffice to themselves in isolation, they must maintain one with another certain relations of mutual assistance and society, for their own good and for their own development.[4]

Aloysius Taparelli d'Azeglio, nineteenth century Jesuit philosopher and writer, gave this strong defense:

It is nature itself, that eloquent interpreter of the Divine Will, which calls all peoples to form among themselves one universal society and at the same time makes it their duty to do so. . . . Thus needs and interests soon produce, and quite rightly, the desire to form with other nations, a real, definite society . . . . and unless nature is accidentally and violently frustrated in its proper evolution, all the nations cannot fail to come to take their places in this international society.[5]

[2] Higgins, *Man as Man*, 581.

[3] Neill, *Weapons*, 163, quoting from Augustine, *De Civitate Dei* (Lipsae: G. B. Teubneri, 1929), XIX, ch. 17, 385–86.

[4] Eppstein (ed.), *Code*, 48, quoting from Suarez, *De Legibus ac de Deo Legislatore*, ch. XIX, No. 9. Suarez spoke of the need for association again in *De Caritate*, XIII, II, 4.

[5] Quoted in Charles O'Donnell (ed.), *The World Society* (Washington:

Pope Leo XIII expressed himself in favor of the establishment of a World League when he thanked Father Pinchot of Budapest in a letter of December 1, 1896, for his written and spoken words on that subject.[6] Leo XIII had favored also the movement which had eventuated in the First Hague Conference. Pope Benedict XV in his encyclical "Pacem Dei Munus Pulcherrimum," May 23, 1920, urged that all nations participate in one league to safeguard the order of human society.[7] Pope Pius XII in "Summi Pontificatus" spoke of the union "by mutual bonds, moral and juridical, in one great community." [8] In successive Christmas messages he has urged adherence to an international organization. The American Bishops' Statement on Peace, November 18, 1944, reiterated the fact that it is not a question of creating an international organization, but rather of organizing it:

To do this we must repudiate absolutely the tragic fallacies of "power politics," with its balance of power, spheres of influence in a system of puppet governments, and the resort to war as a means of settling international difficulties.[9]

They added the specific notes that it must be universal and democratic in its constitution, have machinery for revision since life is not static, and possess a world court with authority to refer its decisions to the international organization for execution.

The same law of sociability which causes individuals to seek their complement in other persons, also obliges states to collaborate with other states in serving their own subjects. The twofold object of this international common good is maintenance of order so that the nations may fulfill their social tasks, and progress of civilization by sharing of material and spiritual wealth.

Catholic Association for International Peace, 1941), 8. The Taparelli source is not given, but it might be *Essai Theorique de Droit Naturel.*

[6] Donald A. MacLean, *A Dynamic World Order* (Milwaukee: Bruce, 1945), 164.

[7] Koenig, *Principles*, 488.

[8] *Ibid.*, 604.

[9] *Catholic Mind*, XLIII (January, 1945), 2-3.

States must cease to claim that absolute independence which nature has not given them and which in fact they never possessed. . . . They can command with sovereignty within their own frontiers, but must submit their authority to the higher and necessary law which ordains all national activities to the common good of humanity. . . . For as the individual "fully becomes what he has the right to be only when he ceases to think of himself alone," the State can effectively fulfill its mission only when, looking beyond the narrow circle of its national interests, it agrees to collaborate wholeheartedly in the common tasks of international society. . . . In helping to maintain international order, it provides as much as and even more than by armaments for its own security; and in promoting the cultural and economic development of other nations, it labors for the prosperity of its own security. . . . There can be no social life without self-abnegation and sacrifice.[10]

Because strong bonds have been formed between nations with the advance of civilization, it would be a grave injustice to return to the former state of isolation. Cooperation under an international authority is now a positive duty for every nation. This universality cannot be realized immediately, however, for if a state does not admit the principle of sociability, its presence within the organization would destroy its unity. Sociability involves recognition that the common good of the whole must prevail over the interests of the parts, and loyalty to one's pledged word.[11] In the pluralism of states, the object of each is the same: justice, order, and security. This order is related to man's last aim, the salvation of his soul; and in turn this order is a way to serve the last end of all creation, the glorifying of God.[12]

Among the advocates of organized international society, there is a difference of opinion between those who favor contractualism, that is, those who regard international life as based upon separate contracts entered into by the wills of the interested parties, and

[10] Eppstein (ed.), *Code*, 49–50.
[11] *Ibid.*, 169.
[12] *Ibid.*, 637.

the institutionalists who see this society as a living organism, not a product of isolated actions. The distinctions are well drawn by Gonella.[13] The agreement of the wills in a contract concerns only the contracting parties, and is revocable by them; it is destined to cease by expiration, or the like, and its terms are immutable. According to contractualism, the society of states is purely voluntary, not decreed by natural society. In contrast, an institution endures beyond the life span of the founders; it is adaptable to changing needs of social life; those who favor institutionalism recognize the will as the *efficient cause* of international order, not as the formal cause, which is to be found in the inherent order of justice.

If the international juridical order comes to be based not on an act of will but on a *fact*, that is, on an institution actually existing, organic, and natural, on the experiences of the community of States regarded as a natural institution, then a new era of relations between peoples will begin. It is a question of passing from the potentiality of nature to the reality of history. The sense of solidarity must make the bonds between the peoples closer, and then the law will have to correspond to this new reality of fact.[14]

The meeting of wills on the part of states is the efficient but not the exemplary cause, in the same sense that the matrimonial contract bears relationship to the family.

[13] Guido Gonella, *A World to Reconstruct*, trans. T. Lincoln Bouscaren, S.J. (Milwaukee: Bruce, 1945), 248–53. Dr. Gonella, an international lawyer, comments on Pius XII's principles of peace. The translation was undertaken at the behest of the Bishops' Committee on the Pope's Peace Points.

[14] *Ibid.*, 253. This kind of institutionalism was elaborated upon by the sixteenth century Catholic internationalist, Francisco de Vittoria. It is explicitly stated by Pius XII in his address to the Italian Catholic Jurists, December 6, 1953, *Catholic Mind*, LII (April, 1954), 245. Much of the inadequacy of the League of Nations resulted from the fact that it was an associational institution retaining elements of the contractual system. Instead of accepting Natural Law as the basis of international law, it looked upon the latter merely as a body of rules voluntarily agreed upon by the nations involved.

State Sovereignty and International Society

Contractualism being eliminated, there are still two different conceptions of international institutions: one, the Dantean dream of a universal kingdom which denies the multiplicity of states and relies upon subordination rather than coordination, with all men subject to a single power; the other, a coordination of powers with the nations united under a single juridical control. The latter concept is the one endorsed both by Pope Pius XII and by the American bishops, and by the main body of Catholic thinkers. Pope Pius XI made no explicit statement on the matter but his delineation of the principle of subsidiarity would certainly apply:

Just as it is gravely wrong to take from individuals what they can accomplish by their own initiative and industry and give it to the community, so also it is an injustice and at the same time a grave evil and disturbance of right order to assign to a greater and higher association what lesser and subordinate organizations can do. For every social activity ought of its very nature to furnish help to the members of the body social, and never destroy and absorb them.[15]

Pope Pius XII's position should be viewed both in light of his commendation of the World Federalists and of his description of the international community. To the Federalists he said:

Your movement dedicates itself to realizing an effective political organization of the world. Nothing is more in conformity with the traditional doctrine of the Church, nor better adapted to her teaching concerning legitimate or illegitimate war, especially in the present circumstances. . . . You are of the opinion that this world political organization, in order to be effective, must be federal in form. If by this you understand that it should not be enmeshed in an artificial uniformity, again you are in harmony with the principles of social and political life so firmly founded and sustained by the Church. Indeed no organization of the world could live if it were not harmonized

[15] Pius XI, Encyclical "Quadragesimo Anno," May 15, 1931 in Koenig, *Principles*, 422.

with the whole complex of natural relations, with that normal organic order which rules the particular relations between men and men and between different peoples. . . . In truth, it is impossible to solve the problem of a world political organization without being willing to leave the beaten path from time to time, without appealing to the witness of history, to a sane social philosophy, and even to a certain divining of the creative imagination.[16]

Later Pius XII described the goal of a community in which sovereign states, which are subordinate to no other state, "are united into a juridical community to attain definite juridical ends."

It would give a false idea of these juridical communities to compare them to world empires of the past or of the present, in which different racial stocks, peoples, and states become fused, whether they want it or not, into a single conglomeration of states.[17]

Remarking that the continuous struggles for power evidenced by history might make the establishment of a juridical community of free states seem almost utopian, he distinguished this effort from those of the past in which the motivation was subjugation of other nations. He showed the approach to be realistic:

This time, on the contrary, it is precisely the will to prevent threatening conflicts that urges men toward a supranational juridical community. Utilitarian considerations which certainly carry considerable weight, point toward the working out of peace; and finally it is perhaps this mingling of men of different nations because of technological progress that has awakened the faith, implanted in the hearts and souls of individuals, in a higher community of men, willed by the Creator, and rooted in the unity of their common origin, nature and final destiny.[18]

[16] Pius XII, Discourse to World Fourth Congress of "World Movement for World Federal Government" on April 6, 1951, *Catholic Mind*, XLIX (June, 1951), 393–95.
[17] Pius XII, Discourse to Italian Catholic Jurists, December 6, 1953, *Catholic Mind*, LII (April, 1954), 244–45. The American Bishops favored the retention of sovereignty in their statement on Peace, November 18, 1944. *Catholic Mind*, XLIII (January, 1945), 5.
[18] *Ibid.*, 244–45.

Robert M. Hutchins in his Aquinas lecture at Marquette University in 1949 acknowledged that the views of the popes, bishops, and other Catholic thinkers were somewhat at variance with the Chicago Plan for world government, of which he was a co-sponsor.[19] In his analysis of St. Thomas, he concluded that St. Thomas was prepared to admit that changing conditions might make thoroughly unsatisfactory a form of political organization which once was adequate to meet men's needs. Then in an effort to show that the discrepancy between the Hutchins Plan and current Catholic thought was more apparent than real, he stressed the fact that the popes and bishops did not intend to display any fondness for the modern state's nationalistic characteristics. The principle of subsidiarity and Maritain's defense of pluralism were indicative of the desire to reduce rather than to enlarge states' powers. Professor Carl Hensler had taken issue previously with Mortimer J. Adler's statement in *How To Think About War and Peace,* in which he asserted that Pius XII would not be proposing a program for lasting peace, but only one for a truce since he favored retention of national independence;[20] Adler's contention seemed to admit of no middle ground between absolute sovereignty and no independence.

[19] Robert M. Hutchins, *St. Thomas and the World State* (Milwaukee: Marquette University Press, 1949), 34–36. The Chicago Plan "Preliminary Draft" was printed in *Common Sense,* University of Chicago monthly, March, 1948. The sponsoring committee consisted of R. M. Hutchins, G. A. Borgese, Mortimer J. Adler, Stringfellow Barr, Albert Guerard, Harold A. Innis, Erich Kohlwe, Wilber G. Katz, Charles H. McIlwain, Robert Redfield, and Rexford G. Tugwell. In *Man and the State,* 200, Jacques Maritain recommends this as the best-balanced ideal pattern of a world constitution. Later we shall investigate Maritain's position and see the basis of his stand on sovereignty.

[20] Carl P. Hensler, "Pius XII on Sovereignty and Peace," *Catholic Mind,* XLII (November, 1944), 692. The statement of Adler is to be found in Mortimer J. Adler, *How To Think About War and Peace* (New York: Simon & Schuster, 1944), 17. Adler's other comments which are pertinent here are: that it is a contradiction to have united but independent nations, that as a proximate step he would favor a federal government which would abolish the external sovereignty of member states, but the ultimate ideal would preclude a federal structure.

The historical review of Catholic thinking on sovereignty and world society is handled by Eppstein and Rommen. John Eppstein points out that the two developments which slackened the pace of Christian thought in evolving a theory of world society were the wars with Islam and the revolts against the Holy Roman Empire. When the Christian community was under attack from without, it appeared "more as a beleagured city than as a supernational society, presupposing and making actual within itself the potential unity and fraternity of the whole human race." [21] International political unity, identified with the Holy Roman Empire, was beset by exaggerated claims to state independence which explains the influence of their times upon the neo-scholastic school which made considerable concessions to national sovereignty.

Rommen notes that Catholic political philosophy generally does not endorse the universal world monarchy of Dante's *Monarchia*.[22] St. Augustine felt that a plurality of small states living in peace would be preferable. Aquinas presupposed a plurality of states. Bellarmine, though friendly to the idea of a federation of sovereign princes under an empire, believed that its initiation would invite wars, and so concluded that because of geographic differentiation, the plurality of independent states should be recommended. Suarez reasoned that a universal legislative authority to bind all men was not necessary for the preservation of any other good of human nature, and not expedient because government of a state the size of the world would be impossible.[23]

Rommen's personal rejection of a single world state runs as follows:

[21] John Eppstein, *Catholic Tradition of Law of Nations* (Washington: Carnegie Endowment for International Peace, 1935), 248–50. Mr. Eppstein, director of the British Society for International Understanding and editor of the Malines Union's *Code of International Ethics*, is currently secretary-general of the Atlantic Treaty Association to promote support of NATO.

[22] Rommen, *The State*, 651.

[23] Messner, *Social Ethics*, 430, citing Suarez, *De Legibus*, Book III, ch. 2, No. 5; and ch. 4, No. 7.

The common good can be realized only by adaptation of political and legal institutions to the prepolitical individuality of the people who form the state and to the exigencies of that geographic and climatic part of the globe in which the people live. The greater a state becomes, the less political coherence it has and the more bureaucratic centralization may be needed to guarantee the necessary unity and the minimum of a working order.[24]

The states by their pluralism are destined to coexist as members of an international community of nations with its coordinated constitution and system of legal norms, just as the citizens of the states all have human nature in common and upon this basis form the highest and broadest community, mankind. This is why Catholic political philosophy never indulged in the unreal dream of a world-state without force and power, as did humanitarian pacifism. This, too, is why it did not content itself with the pessimistic statement that a perpetual state of war, interrupted by short truces, is unavoidable simply because there exist only nations living without a real communion among themselves. On the contrary, the pluralism of the states finds its existential perfection in the order of the community of the nations, in the teleological ordination of the individual states to the common good of mankind in which political life finds its ultimate form of perfection. The states form a community and are not isolated, absolutely independent forms, but are called to live in mutual solidarity in the order of justice and peace, realizing in interdependent action the common good of the community of nations.[25]

Rommen feels that the idea of world federation suffers from the weakness of Rousseau's theory, that in discarding particular and group-interests, and establishing liberty and equality for each member, an infallible general will would issue. It presupposes that public opinion of a majority of the states is always right. With or without world government, he states that only a concert of great powers can guarantee law enforcement—they would provide the largest contingents in an international police force. These powers must be

[24] Rommen, *The State*, 651–52.
[25] *Ibid.*, 617.

fully aware of their indivisible responsibility for peace and justice.[26] While Rommen admits that the term "sovereignty" has been tainted by philosophical positivism, he suggests that those who foster the individual nation's transfer of sovereignty to a super-state, are merely carrying over to the super-state the positivist notion that law is what the state defines it to be.[27] The concept of sovereignty is right only if it is put into proper interdependence with the principle of subsidiarity and the hierarchical order of things, and if it is subject to natural and divine law.

Messner agrees that the common good of a political community must be particularized with reference to its ethnical, geographical, historical, and spiritual conditions. Because the development of technology has brought peoples closer together, the preservation of human civilization is even more so a common concern of all nations.

This, however, is much better secured by a pluralistic international society than by the formation of one World State, because each nation will then be a guardian of liberty, whereas a one-state system can easily afford the conditions for world domination and world dictatorship by a single nation or party.

Our objections to a World State in the strict sense do not exclude World Government by a collective authority set up by the organized society of nations and charged with the fulfillment of the legislative, judicial, and executive functions for the establishment of peace and order among the nations and for the promotion of the welfare of all.[28]

The *Code of International Ethics* mentions a specious internationalism supported by Socialists and Communists, which implies the suppression of frontiers and the abolition of nationalities for the sake of class warfare.[29] Reaction against this propaganda has tended to discredit internationalism in some Catholic circles, but this is erroneous action. For true internationalism leaves intact na-

[26] *Ibid.*, 721.
[27] *Ibid.*, 408–09.
[28] Messner, *Social Ethics*, 430–31.
[29] Eppstein (ed.), *Code*, 179–80.

tional heritages while going beyond these to the identity of human nature in the reality of a supranational society. Particular societies and universal society are not mutually exclusive, but are complementary. The national societies, while remaining responsible for the common good of their subjects, must subordinate this special good to the universal good. When man tries to separate in his affections his national and international loyalties, he should remember that he belongs by nature to the greater human family, that his own country cannot prosper apart from or in conflict with the higher good of international society, and that particular ends must be subordinated to this good for their better safeguarding.

Taparelli in defining national independence, made a strong point: "In the same way as the family does not lose its domestic liberty by being united to civil society, so the nation does not lose its political liberty when it forms part of an ethnarchic society." [30]

Professor Hensler gives this interpretation of limitations upon the sovereign state,[31] in contradistinction to Adler who conceives of a unitary world state in which nations would give up external sovereignty in the sphere of international affairs, while retaining supreme authority over persons subject to their laws. Nations do not cease to be externally sovereign if their freedom of action in dealing with one another is limited by some supernational authority. All human authority is restricted by a higher law derived from God as from its first source.

The state is sovereign within the realm of its ethical ends; internal and external sovereignty are both limited "by the law of justice, by the rights of the family, and of the individual conscience, and by the claims of the whole of mankind." This parallels the concept of the genuine liberty of the individual who is not a law unto himself; in like manner "the true freedom of a nation lies not in unlimited self-determination, but in the recognition of the purpose of nations and the right of other nations." In exercising any right,

---

[30] *Ibid.*, 304, quoting Taparelli, *Essai Theorique de Droit Naturel*, Book VI, ch. V, art. II, No. 1374.
[31] Hensler, "Pius XII on Sovereignty and Peace," 695–96.

persons are not free to disregard the rights of others; the removal of all compulsions would merely provoke anarchy and insecurity. He concludes that nations can be truly independent only within a new order founded upon moral principles where a juridical institution will determine and enforce the laws limiting arbitrariness.[32]

Jacques Maritain's position could be the most easily misunderstood because of his insistence that "body politic" and "state" be kept as distinct entities. His initial point is that when neither peace nor self-sufficiency can be achieved by particular states, they are no longer perfect societies; by its capacity to achieve these requirements, the international community politically organized becomes the perfect society.

Once the perfect society required by our historical age, that is the world political society, has been brought into being, it will be bound in justice to respect to the greatest possible extent the freedoms—essential to the common good of the world—of those invaluable vessels of political, moral, and cultural life which will be its parts; but the particular states will have surrendered their full independence,—much more indeed in their external than in their internal sphere of activity, and the World State will have to enjoy, within the strict limits and the well-balanced modalities proper to such a new creation of human reason, the powers naturally required by a perfect society: legislative power, executive power, judicial power, with the coercive power necessary to enforce the law.

. . . if the idea is grounded, as we believe, on true and sound political philosophy, it cannot be impossible in itself. Therefore it is up to human intelligence and energy to make it, in the long run, not impossible with respect to the enormous yet contingent obstacles and impediments that the sociological and historical conditions which lie heavy on mankind have piled up against it. . . . Yet the greater an idea is with respect to the weakness and entanglements of the human condition, the more cautious one must be in handling it. And the more attentive one must be in not demanding its immediate realization.[33]

[32] Ibid., 697–99.
[33] Maritain, *Man and the State*, 197–200.

Then Maritain proceeds to disabuse one of the notion that he favors an absolute super-state which would be the product of a purely governmental theory; in fact, he thinks it would eventuate in the spread of the Hegelian myth with a democratic multi-national empire. To this aberration he would oppose the "political theory" based upon the world body politic, a "pluralist unity taking place only through the lasting diversity of the particular bodies politic." He does not think it would be impossible to develop a world-wide civic friendship.

We see, therefore, that the birth of a world political society would result from a growing, vital process, in which the work of all official and private institutions interested in any form of international rapprochement and cooperation would participate, but in which the essential part would be played by the will of the people, in every nation, to live together, in the world, I mean a will growing so powerful as to sweep away the obstacles caused by the myth of the States as sovereign persons or by the bias of governments, and the obstacles, still greater, caused in the people themselves by misfortune and fatigue, slowness of reason, and natural self-interest. . . .

In a world political society the nations would become by right and with the guarantees of a superior juridical order what they already are in fact, but anarchically, namely non-self-sufficient or imperfect bodies politic; and the World State, considered separately from them, and only in its supra-national institutions and life, would also be an imperfect political society. Only the world society taken as a whole both with the supranational State and the multiplicity of nations, would be a perfect political society. . . .

The States would have to surrender their privilege of being sovereign persons, that is, a privilege which they have never possessed. . . . Yet in their mutual interdependence the nations would achieve a degree of real, though imperfect, independence higher than that they possess now, from the fact that their inner political life, being freed from the threat of war and from the interference of rival nations, could become more autonomous in actual fact than it is at present.[34]

[34] *Ibid.*, 209-11.

The organization of this world political society could occur only after a long time; yet he feels that the creative process of the will to live together is at work constantly and the dangers of universal destruction give reason for man to work with greater energy at awakening the common consciousness of its necessity. He foresees that the task might be carried out through education and discussion, and through the various cooperative agencies of the United Nations. He suggests the setting up of a superior agency without power but with real moral authority, whose only function, independent of any government commitment, would be to make ethical decisions.[35] In proportion as this advisory council was really wise and independent, it would influence public opinion and disarm the fears of nations.

Maritain denies that there is such a thing as sovereignty in the sense of a natural and inalienable right to transcendent or separate supreme power in political authority either for the people or the state.[36] He would define the essence of a democratic regime to be, not sovereignty of the people, but "government of the people, by the people, for the people."

Dr. Neill, commenting on the pagan use of the term sovereignty, says that the concept can be justified morally only if it means "ultimate legal and physical power limited to promoting the welfare of all citizens and protecting them from aggression."[37]

Messner approaches sovereignty in this way. Because political authority guarantees the foundation of social order in which the integration of human existence and the fulfillment of man's material and cultural tasks takes place, the authority of the state ranks highest in the natural sphere. The end of political authority entitles it to security from external interference so that it may establish the legal order. Political authority "is indivisible inasmuch as the complete discharge of the fundamental functions of society admits of only a single sovereign authority. But it is not indivisible in the

[35] *Ibid.*, 213–14.
[36] *Ibid.*, 24–25.
[37] Neill, *Weapons*, 162.

sense that its exercise cannot be shared among a number of organs." [38]

Rommen defines the sovereign state as independent of its equal, but not free in an absolute sense:

. . . the moral and spiritual values and purposes that form the moral world are superior to each and all of the states. Precisely in the recognition of these values and in its help in realizing these ends, lies the reason for sovereignty. Thus sovereignty becomes supreme responsibility for these purposes and values and service to them. . . . Any abuse of sovereignty, that is non-recognition of these moral and spiritual values, destroys the moral foundation of civil obedience and thus the state as a moral being. . . . Its self-sufficiency is not absolute, but is imbedded in a thousand interdependencies with neighboring states on the same continent, and likewise with the world through an identical interest as well as through the recognition of the identical basic ideas of a common civilization. . . . Thus external sovereignty means that beyond the state is no secular authority but the international order. [39]

The international common good, the order of justice, peace and security for the individual man's sake, is the purpose of international cooperation. All nations are, intentionally from their subjective existence and teleologically from their objective nature, as parts ordered to the whole, to mankind, and they form a genuine community of objective character. . . . There is, therefore, no place for unlimited absolute sovereignty in the international order. Liberty and independence, yes. Liberty to rule internally as the individuality of the nation, born out of history, tradition, culture, and climate, wills it, in the ever-valid framework of natural law that refers to man and not to national individuality. . . . This order is objective and, in its essence and end, is not created either by the will of the sovereign states or by a self-limitation of the absolute sovereignty of the states. [40]

Pope Pius XII explained that sovereignty is "not a divinization of the state, or omnipotence of the state in the Hegelian sense, or after the manner of absolute juridical positivism."

[38] Messner, *Social Ethics*, 514–15.
[39] Rommen, *The State*, 404–05.
[40] *Ibid.*, 638.

"Sovereignty" in the true sense of the word means self-rule and exclusive competence concerning what has to be done in regard to the affairs of a definite territory, always within the framework of international law, without however becoming dependent on the juridical system of any other state. Every state is immediately subject to international law . . . . no state could complain about a limitation of its sovereignty if it were denied the power of acting arbitrarily and without regard for other states.[41]

J. T. Delos, O.P., shows that in assigning the relative rank to national and international society, there is no question of sacrificing one to the other, but of correlating the two in the order of their primacy:

If we consider the element in human nature that makes the nations, on the one hand, and universal human society on the other, we see that the latter derives from an essential trait of human nature: its identity in the whole race, and the duty of mutual aid and support which flows from it. The nation, on the other hand, owes its function to particular qualities of land, race, or history, contingent and variable, which add to, and are secondary to, the essential in human nature. Hence the order of relation between the two societies; the national groups are subordinate to universal society.[42]

Gonella suggests that the community of states must strive within the sphere of justice "to bring about the coincidence of the maximum particular interests of the respective States."

It is a moral obligation not to sacrifice the legitimate interests of others for the sole end of satisfying one's own particular interest. . . . A State may, and at times should, sacrifice its own interest for the good of the Community of States. . . . Whereas one state may freely sacrifice its own interests for the welfare of the Community of States, the

[41] Pius XII, Discourse to Italian Catholic Jurists, December 6, 1953, *Catholic Mind*, LII (April, 1954), 245. In "Summi Pontificatus," he also noted that absolute autonomy for the state stands in contradiction to Natural Law and destroys collaboration directed to the common good.

[42] Eppstein, *Catholic Tradition of the Law of Nations*, 370–371, quoting from J. T. Delos, O.P., *La Societé Internationale*.

interest of the Community of States cannot justify the violation of the particular rights of the individual States.[43]

The Rights of States

After placing the states in their proper perspective as sovereignties, the rights of the states in international society should be considered. Any state possesses a right to existence, regardless of its recognition by the society of nations "if without violence to the standards of civilization, it has shown itself capable of fulfilling the functions of a political community." [44] The inviolable right of the state to existence is not affected by other states' inciting members to revolution in order to cast doubt on its just title. The state possesses the right to freedom in determining its own political institutions, limited of course by the legitimate rights of others—of individuals, minorities, states, and the community of nations. If it should violate these limits, there exists a right of intervention, however, on the part of the society of nations, or in the absence of its organized condition, on the part of the states concerned with the aid of others.[45]

The state has a right to self-defense by means of armament and defensive alliances. However, if the international institution is functioning effectively the right to arm may be restricted by international authority to whatever that nation's contribution should be to international order. The state has a right to extend protection to its nationals and their property abroad; but since this right might conflict with another state's sovereignty, this right should be exercised by international treaty. Since the nation has a right to insist upon proper treatment of its nationals abroad, states are bound to enter into such agreements.[46]

The state has a right to give to social cooperation in the economic

---

[43] Gonella, *A World To Reconstruct*, 55–56.
[44] Messner, *Social Ethics*, 404.
[45] *Ibid.*, 404–05.
[46] *Ibid.*, 405.

sphere the form which it desires, so long as that is consonant with the moral consciousness of mankind. The state has a right to a proportionate share in the material well-being of the earth, so that it may assimilate its standard of living to the average within the society of nations. "Although the natural treasures of a country must first serve its people, no people has the right to exclude others from sharing in its surplus. The monopolizing of markets is as inconsistent with equality of rights for all states as is the monopolizing of sources of raw materials." [47]

Regarding equality of treatment, there are qualifications. Just as the individual's equality of right to property does not require a leveling of fortunes, so a state cannot use "equality of rights" to claim its share in the territories of which other states have secured just possession in the course of their development. In the claim of "right to living space," often freedom of access to foreign markets can make up for the lack within the state's own territory. Emigration is another solution though this involves denationalization of those who leave their native land. "Its former subjects will not forget, in their new homeland, the links which bind them to their country of origin; and that country will find in the expansion of its economic and spiritual powers ample compensation for the loss." [48] But in no case may a state use the argument of "right to life and living space" in order to attack another state. A state's restriction upon emigration may be justified only by "reasonable concern for its own self-preservation."

The *Code of International Ethics* notes that the opinions of theorists of international law differ as to whether self-preservation for a state takes precedence over every other consideration. Some say, "Let the safety of the people be the supreme law." Others insist that there is contradiction involved in the recognition of right against right when favoring the state. Taparelli, approaching the problem of "apparent equality of rights" here involved, stated that

[47] *Ibid.*, 405.
[48] Eppstein (ed.), *Code*, 74.

arbitration by impartial judges could be the only solution for the quarrel. The decision of the *Code's* authors is that if the validity of one right be admitted, the other cannot claim a hearing. The claim that a state's right to existence is threatened may be admitted only under two conditions:

First of all, the necessity invoked must be real, extreme, and threatening the very existence of the State—to be or not to be. The danger of defeat followed by an amputation of territory does not constitute a necessity in the sense of which we are speaking. Secondly, the State invoking necessity must not have brought about by its own fault the dangerous situation in which it finds itself. Thus an unjust aggressor could not plead necessity in order to make others bear the consequences of his crime.[49]

There are few cases in history where both of these conditions were present. One state's right to existence cannot prevail against another state's right to existence when the latter has been a stranger to the circumstances creating the so-called necessity.[50] The numerical importance of the population and the extent of the state's territory does not constitute the justice of the claim here. But a state's right to existence may correctly take precedence over another state's lesser right within the order of justice.

All of this should not be construed to mean that the present political firmament is immutable. Many modern states have been created in disregard of the rights of pre-existing states. There might be just defense of the *status quo ante* with other states assisting one who is not an unjust aggressor. But the *Code* qualifies the foregoing:

However well-founded their grievances may be, the needs of the common good will not allow states which have been the victims of an injustice to question perpetually the concessions they have been forced to yield. . . . This necessary sacrifice will not prevent those States from seeking by peaceful means the redress of the wrongs they have

49 *Ibid.*, 63.
50 This was treated by Pius XII in his Five Point Peace Plan, Christmas Message, 1939. Quoted in Koenig, *Principles*, 36–37.

suffered. It follows that "historic rights" are quite groundless and cannot justify the aims of bellicose nationalism.[51]

When it is not clear, however, on which side justice is to be found, or when the injured State, being incapable of defending the rights, has given up the struggle, a legitimate prescription may condone the irregular origin of the new State. From that time onwards, it definitely acquires the right to recognition by the other members of international society.[52]

The role of the small states is expressly defended in Catholic political philosophy. Messner notes that in the community of nations the small states contribute to the general good by being the "goalkeepers of humanity and civilization." [53] Their lack of strength preserves them from the idolatry of power politics" and induces them to seek respect among the nations by their cultural achievements, spiritual and material. The *Code of International Ethics* notes that because they are devoid of territorial ambitions and are eager for order and justice, they seem to take the side of right almost instinctively.[54] Frequently their unanimity has "sufficed to contain within the limits of justice certain imperialistic appetites about to be unloosed."

Whereas a nation cannot be asked to give up its existence for the benefit of another nation "or even the majority of nations," it may voluntarily relinquish its independent political existence to federate with another state. "But then it does so in its own interest, not exclusively in the interest of world peace." [55]

Dr. Neill criticizes defense of a state's "right to live" in the sense meant by Heinrich von Treitschke:

Since the state is an association of men created to accomplish a certain work—the good life for all its members—if the State fails of its purpose it can be altered, or it can be done away with and another put in

[51] Eppstein (ed.), *Code*, 84.
[52] *Ibid.*, 56.
[53] Messner, *Social Ethics*, 437.
[54] Eppstein (ed.), *Code*, 57.
[55] Rommen, *The State*, 717.

its place. Since Hegel made the state divine one hundred years ago, historians and political scientists have tended to give states a life, a will, and a destiny of their own, independent of the people who are in them. . . .

And just as no state of itself has the right to life, so no state has an unalterable right to certain boundaries or to a fixed size or to rule over a certain population. Boundaries can be changed if no injustice is done to individual persons, living now or in the future, in either of the countries concerned or in other countries that might somehow be affected. So, too, a state can cease to exist so long as no injustice is done to its members or to individual human beings in other states. . . . If the people living there wish to establish a new state, or several of them, by justifiable means no injustice would be done.[56]

After considering the state's right to existence, it seems apropos to review the citizens' right to resistance. Apart from exceptional circumstances, Messner maintains that passive resistance is the only proper means of protecting the liberties of citizens when a government abuses its power. He makes this judgment in the light of the experience which reveals that graver harm to the common good generally results from violence in civil war than from the violation of rights by the government.[57] Active resistance is justified when the essential freedoms of citizens are in grave danger and there is no other possibility of defending them. Then the defensive action is to be organized and undertaken in the name of the community and backed by a substantial portion of the people. Only such a procedure has a well-founded probability of attaining its end and of preventing "further injury to the commonweal by anarchy." To show how current circumstances affect the above, he continues:

Recent experience readily provides examples of political developments showing that passive resistance alone may be ineffective and may simply lead to the elimination of all who in this way show opposition to the regime, and give the government a chance to establish its abuse of power indefinitely by transforming the minds of the young. . . .

[56] Neill, *Weapons*, 156–57.
[57] Messner, *Social Ethics*, 534–35.

The whole traditional natural law doctrine emphasizes that the justification of the rights of active resistance depends on the certainty that there will not arise from it an equal or a greater ill for the common weal than the tyranny which is to be overthrown. They point out that as the result of political disturbances it is often small, violent, and radical groups which eventually attain to power, or again groups which are less concerned with the common good than with their own interest and ideologies.[58]

Abuse of a right cancels the right if the abuse frustrates its end. In the light of this fact, Bellarmine and Suarez justified active resistance by appeal to the right of the people to transfer political authority to another person or body.[59] Revolution against legitimate authority, lawfully exercising its rights, differs from active resistance, for since the government is not abusing the common good, it does not forfeit its rights. Such a revolution is a crime against the community.[60]

Messner demonstrates that the mere taking over of power in a state does not establish the right to legitimate authority even when such acts of force have been camouflaged by plebiscite, or by appeal to a former territorial connection, or by invention of a nation's "natural right" to political unity.[61] The legal title is based upon constitutional transfer of power. He explains the circumstances under which a *de facto* government may become *de jure*, however, if its authority has itself become a constituent element of the common good under the concrete circumstances over a period of time.

The condition of this is that the existing government is in assured possession of power, and that the common good indubitably depends

[58] *Ibid.,* 535–37.
[59] *Ibid.,* 536.
[60] Eppstein, in his introductory commentary accompanying *Code of International Ethics,* 32–33, points out the harm done to the principle of legitimate authority and to national unity, when in the course of the Second World War reckless encouragement was given to resistance movements. The known policy of the Soviet was to exploit liberation movements for the sake of promoting Communism.
[61] Messner, *Social Ethics,* 532.

upon its peacetime continuance. The validity of this legal principle, that the de facto government becomes legal in time finds confirmation in the legal consciousness of peoples as it has often been manifested in the course of history after revolutionary change.[62]

In this historical reconstruction of the common good in its actual form, he includes the consent of the people, either tacit or expressed. This interpretation by the natural law school avoids working out principles in a vacuum, but it also "rejects historicism by refusing to base moral principles merely on historical processes." When this common good has been reconstituted, this government acquires moral power to command, citizens have a moral duty to obey, and the claim of a former legitimate ruler becomes obsolete.

Professor Higgins explains the transition from an illegitimate *de facto* government to a *de jure* government in this way: there must be "peaceful possession and efficient use of authority"; there must be "absence of all probable hope of restoring the old government without convulsing the realm."

A people must have some government; and when there is actually only one, though it be illegitimate, they are bound to cooperate with it at least in what pertains to public order and ordinary administration. When this rule has become firmly established and is actually attaining the ends of the State so that the only way to restore the old government is by public upheaval and civil war, then the rights of the old government cede to the right of the community to a peaceable existence. The public welfare is of more importance than the right of an individual, family, or party to rule.[63]

But on the other hand, "where the victor disregards the good of the subjugated so that consent is unreasonable, his government must go. . . ."[64]

States are bound both by certain duties of international justice and by certain duties of charity. In working for the common good of the community of nations, they have the negative obligation

[62] *Ibid.*, 531–32.
[63] Higgins, *Man as Man*, 471.
[64] *Ibid.*, 473.

of cooperation in the struggle against common dangers and evils: war, crime, slavery, traffic in drugs, etc. They have the positive obligation to cooperate in raising the

. . . standard of intellectual and material welfare among all peoples by the exchange of raw materials, manufactured goods, ideas and ideals, the organization of the international community and the establishment of institutions to enable it to carry out its tasks. . . . To cooperate with other nations in forming an international law for the good of the international community is for every nation an obligation of international justice.[65]

Since the law of charity is universal, it is as binding upon nations as upon individuals.[66] Benevolence will be evidenced by signs of mutual respect and friendship, cordial exchange of information and services, openhanded welcome to strangers, assistance to victims of disaster. In time of conflict it will lead rulers and peoples to try to understand the mind of the enemy and recognize how far his grievances are well-founded, to seek honestly the means of satisfying these claims, and to try to mitigate the harshness of the letter of the law.

The Functions of a World Organization

Turning now to consideration of the operations of a world institution, we allude to Pope Pius XII's recommendation of three essentials: a method for the just alteration of treaties, renunciation of the use of force with changes made by juridical means, and the substructure of mutual trust upon which the machinery of international government might function.[67] While maintaining that the success of any plan for world peace depends upon the moral reconstruction of mankind, he did not commit himself on technical questions, though he counseled man to learn from the deficiencies and gaps in previous organizations.

[65] Messner, *Social Ethics*, 217.
[66] Eppstein (ed.), *Code*, 85.
[67] Neill, *Weapons*, 185–86.

Dr. Neill envisages that the international government should take on only those things "which the existing national states have clearly proved themselves incapable of doing." [68] Among the latter, he would propose the settlement of international disputes, the guarantee of independence to all states, the protection of minority rights, the regulation of international trade, the limitation of armaments, and the promotion of international cooperation. This would avoid international anarchy on the one hand, and global totalitarianism on the other.

Both the *Code of International Ethics* and Messner's analysis would view regional organizations, agreements, and alliances as compatible with the international common good if they were not directed against any other state.[69] With reference to the current United Nations Charter, the *Code* states:

. . . the fact that certain powers were accorded permanent seats on the Council can be justified as a provisional measure, on the ground that power must be in proportion to responsibilities. But it is quite incompatible with the ideal conception of international authority, that each of the great powers should have the right to veto every decision of the Council concerning the maintenance of peace, the admission of new members and amendments to the Charter of the society. The equality of all the members is an essential requirement of the reign of justice within that society.

The best way to harmonize the action of the Assembly, as the legislative organ, and that of the Council, as the executive, would be to entrust the former with the choice of those who are to be members of the latter. . . . As long as the members of this executive organ are no more than representatives of their governments, answerable to the national authorities who have appointed them, they will always be unable to exercise effectively the supreme power with which they have been invested; their agreement will be precarious, their hold upon the consciences of men uncertain. The state of affairs may be justified at the beginning of the endeavor to organize a world now imbued with

[68] *Ibid.*, 166.
[69] Eppstein (ed.), *Code*, 53; Messner, *Social Ethics*, 433–34.

an exaggerated notion of national sovereignty; it is indefensible on ideal and logical grounds.[70]

Messner outlines rather thoroughly the political, economic, and judicial functions which he would attribute to the international organization. In addition to political duties mentioned previously in this study by other authorities, he would add control over colonies and mandates, preservation of freedom of conscience and religion with a bill of human rights as an integral part of the constitution. There would be a systematic compilation of rules created by interstate conventions and international usages, and the choice of immigration territories suited climatically and ethnically to the newcomers, with assistance to collective movement of settlers.[71] The economic functions would include enlarging the volume of world trade, preventing restrictive policies by states and cartels, providing price and exchange stability, providing loans for reconstruction of debilitated countries, giving assistance in currency and credit operations, counteracting speculative movements of capital, initiating anti-depression policies among nations, and requiring observance of labor conventions which would be sufficiently elastic.[72] Submission to the international court of justice would be obligatory, with more emphasis placed upon arbitration and conciliation which would be more compatible with the nation's prestige and sovereignty. In addition to interpretation of treaties and international law, the judicature would give advisory opinions, pursue unbiased examination of charges against an aggressor, and cooperate in the development of new law relative to such matters as relieving population pressure or facilitating the importation of raw materials.[73]

After drawing the distinction between political and juridical conflicts, the *Code* notes that there is a growing tendency to consider conciliation and arbitral-judicial settlements as two successive

---

[70] *Ibid.*, 167.
[71] Messner, *Social Ethics*, 439–40.
[72] *Ibid.*, 449–50.
[73] *Ibid.*, 445.

steps of the same peace-making process.[74] To the objection that in the absence of organized international society with real jurisdiction, a nation cannot give over to others the care of its honor or vital interests, the authors reply that it is quite possible to constitute courts which give every guarantee of impartiality. Since the alternative would be recourse to war, which does not ensure the triumph of right, it seems that the judgment of disinterested arbitrators and judges would be preferable. The *Code* would make obligatory recourse to the court and acceptance of its verdict; enforcement measures could be lawfully employed by the executive authority of society. Obligatory arbitration was also part of Pope Benedict XV's peace proposal to the belligerents August 1, 1917.[75]

Catholic Realism

Lest any of these proposals make the Catholic approach to international problems seem utopian, we shall note how much confidence Catholic thinkers place in legal institutions alone, and how they would reinforce moral authority. Pope Pius XII spoke with the evident experience of a diplomat in meeting the problems consequent upon instincts for self-aggrandizement:

. . . within the limits of the possible and lawful, to promote everything that facilitates union and makes it more effective; to remove everything that disturbs it; to tolerate at times that which it is impossible to correct, but which on the other hand must not be permitted to make shipwreck of the community, from which a higher good is hoped for. The difficulty rests in the application of this principle.[76]

Rommen warns that many proposals which pretend to establish collective security without perpetuating the existing international *status quo* contain utopian elements and are based partly on an illusory concept of law and society.

[74] Eppstein (ed.), *Code*, 168.
[75] Koenig, *Principles*, 230.
[76] Pius XII, Discourse to Italian Catholic Jurists, December 6, 1953 in *Catholic Mind*, LII (April, 1954), 246.

They arouse people in times of war to great hopes in their intrinsic yet abstract perfection and lead to an optimistic belief that, once such legal machinery is instituted, it will work automatically, without the catalyst of personal or communal authority and moral responsibility, so that each nation can then return to its internal policy without bothering about a foreign policy, i.e., power politics, and individual responsibility for peace.

The underlying illusion is that legal institutions are a full substitute for power. Or what means the same thing, the thesis that power itself is evil, and the Rousseauist assertion that if there exist perfect institutions then all will be well since the people are good and any form of evil must spring simply from imperfect or corrupt institutions. . . . Forgotten is the fact that legal institutions themselves can be made the object of the nonlegal power struggle. . . .

What gives these institutions power is the moral confidence of the people, the vivid moral responsibility, the common moral convictions, and the specific impartial service for the common good; in other words, that strong moral homogeneity which is more the presupposition of the success of these institutions than their product.[77]

Thus the problem of preserving peace amounts to this: to change peacefully the positive order of treaties, the *status quo*. And it is here that the acceptance of the moral ideas of justice, liberality, and charity must prevail and that the legal institutions like a court of arbitration or a world court or a council of the League of Nations with strictly formulated competencies are of minor importance, because they cannot work if the real presupposition of their efficiency (the unity in moral ideas and the consciousness of a common good) is actually questioned.[78]

Rommen presents a lucid defense of power as a constructive element in society, but as a preliminary he gives assurance that he does not accept Hobbes' or Machiavelli's definition of the state as a power organization beyond law and morality. Nor does he agree with the opposite extreme of the liberals who tried to divest the state of power. He stresses the fact that power and wealth are the

[77] Rommen, *The State*, 718–19.
[78] *Ibid.*, 727.

measure of public responsibility for the commonweal,[79] and that the great powers have the moral duty of changing an unjust *status quo* even at the cost of sacrifice to themselves. Legal machinery in international institutions would facilitate the exercise of these responsibilities, but it does not replace it. He proposes the Catholic synthesis to be:

. . . power controlled by law, by natural and divine law, determined in positive law, the order of law enforced against the lawbreaker by power. . . . The use of force must be controlled by the moral end and the adequate licit means to the end. . . . Catholic political philosophy knows that the actual *ordo*, the framework of individual and common happiness, cannot be realized without sacrifices. It knows that the order is incessantly endangered by selfish lust for power, by uncontrolled self-interest, by the temptation of rulers to abuse the authority for selfish ends, by political corruption. . . . Therefore the estate, as St. Paul says, carries the sword; not for glory's sake or for superhuman pride and lust, but for the sake of the order of the common good.

He must distinguish between power and violence. . . . Violence is uncontrolled, unlimited, aimless. Power on the contrary, means service, responsibility to the moral end.[80] . . . Power (the ability to compel others to at least external obedience or conformity to one's demands by being able to inflict major disadvantages for nonconformity) is not in itself evil. What is wrong is the arbitrary and unreasonable, the unjust and immoral use of power for objectively wrong ends or for purposes contradictory to the self-interest and the dignity of those subject to the use of power.[81]

The American Bishops in their 1945 Statement on World Peace deny that a sound world organization is a utopian dream. To conquer the fact of human weakness, one must face it, not accept it "in a spirit of paralyzing fatalism." [82] Isolationism is no answer to

[79] *Ibid.*, 723–25.
[80] *Ibid.*, 291–93.
[81] *Ibid.*, 719.
[82] American Bishops' Statement on World Peace, April 14, 1945, in *Catholic Mind*, XLIII (June, 1945), 321–22.

the problem. They criticize here the attempt in the name of Realism to substitute an alliance of the great powers, however, for a juridical world institution: they refer especially to giving to a powerful nation in perpetuity a veto on parity of treatment for all.

Pius XII admitted that peace requires the employment of force and the support of power. But he defined the function of this force to be that of "protecting and defending," not of "lessening or suppressing rights." [83] The *Code of International Ethics* explains that the best way to ensure the triumph of right over might is to reinforce purely moral authority with the equipment of material force, with the amount and choice of weapons proportioned to the violence done or immediately threatened by the enemies of order.[84]

Yves Simon voices strong sentiments about the proper use of coercion:

Proud thinkers enjoy emphasizing the "from withinness" of virtuous action and the radical inability of coercion which proceeds from without, to cause virtue. Such rhetoric thrives on shallow psychology and incompetent analysis of causal notions. In the sense in which a bulldozer cannot build a house, coercion cannot cause virtuous action; but, just as a bulldozer can remove an obstacle which, if not removed, would make the building of a house impossible or very difficult, so coercion can remove dispositions and habits incompatible with virtue and substitute for them habits which make the acquisition of virtue and its steady practice relatively easy. When coercion has succeeded in destroying such inclinations as extreme laziness, intemperance, and violent anger, no element of virtue has been brought into existence, but virtuous acts are much less difficult to elicit.[85]

The balance of power concept is discussed at some length in the *Code* and by Messner. Whereas the theory of equilibrium would serve a valid purpose in opposing an expansionist power, it would "be wrong to give it an actual juridical basis and to consider equili-

[83] Pius XII, Christmas Message, 1943, *Catholic Mind*, XLII (February, 1944), 75–76.
[84] Eppstein (ed.), *Code*, 28, 60.
[85] Simon, *Philosophy of Democratic Government*, 111.

brium as a natural need of international life." [86] For in a well-ordered society of states, each member should be able to earn the respect of others by moral force. But so long as there is no collective organization functioning, the states may compensate for this deficiency by forming alliances—though such a maze of alliances and counter-alliances can be dangerous to world peace as an armaments race. This temporary arrangement does not lessen their obligation of striving for "a more perfect juridical organization of international relations, which will secure for the right of even the smallest State the collective guarantee of all the powers."

Commenting upon history, Messner notes that so long as states measured their rights by the opportunity force presented, there seemed to be no other method of peace than equilibrium of power groupings. Today the possibility of wars of aggression still persists since there is no agreement on disarmament. Therefore, to meet the situation he suggests that a step be taken to raise the balance of power principle "to an ethical plane" and thus transcend "the principle of mere power politics." [87] This could be accomplished if the principle of equilibrium were applied by the community of states in the general interest with obligations undertaken by all the members. To implement this, states with strategic, political, and economic interests in common might form federal units under a single joint authority to organize their defense. This offers practically the only remedy for small states, for if each had to stand alone militarily, the tendency would be as in 1939 to take refuge in neutrality, with the consequence that they would be overrun individually.

International Law

The Catholic position considers objective universal justice to be something real and attainable in international life. The best expression of this is found in an address of Pope Pius XII:

[86] Eppstein (ed.), *Code*, 59, 61.
[87] Messner, *Social Ethics*, 420–21.

Justice is not merely an absolute concept, an external ideal to which institutions must seek to conform as far as possible in a given historical moment. It is above all something inherent in man, in society, in its fundamental institutions, because of that sum total of practical principles which it dictates and imposes, of those more universal norms of conduct which form part of the objective human and civil order established by the perfect mind of the First Maker. The science of the just and the unjust supposes, therefore, a more elevated wisdom which consists in knowing the basic arrangement of the thing created and consequently of its Arranger.[88]

Through international law this order of objective justice may be established. Again it is Pius XII who identified international law to be that "which recognizes its foundations in that natural law written by God in the very conscience of every man, and from it derives ultimately its binding force." [89] Similar sentiments about international law were expressed by Vittoria in the sixteenth century:

The law of nations does not derive its binding force simply from a human convention; it really has the force of law. . . . No kingdom has the right to refuse its allegiance, for it has been established by the authority of the whole universe.[90]

Rommen says of certain categories of international law:

Thus we have a sphere of rules that are valid not because states recognized them, but because they arise immediately from man's social nature and personal dignity; a sphere of rights that are human and therefore international, and thus beyond the sovereignty and the arbitrary will of the state. . . . Consequently they are ordinances of the natural law to the states and thus part of the order of international law in-

[88] Pius XII, Address to Union of Italian Catholic Jurists, November 6, 1949, quoted in Francis J. Powers, C.S.V., *Papal Pronouncements on the Political Order* (Westminster, Md.: Newman Bookshop, 1952), 161. Hereafter referred to as *Papal Pronouncements*.

[89] Pius XII, Discourse to members of U.S. Senate Military Affairs Committee, November 2, 1945, quoted in Powers, *Papal Pronouncements*, 192.

[90] Eppstein (ed.), *Code*, 52, quoting from Francisco de Vittoria, *De Potestate Civili*.

asmuch as they produce obligations of the states. . . . Even if the respective state's own national laws are below this international standard, this is not an excuse for the violation of these international human rights and the necessary conclusions therefrom. They represent a genuine objective limitation of sovereignty. . . . An appeal against them to the national common good is impossible because this common good itself is essentially a concrete order to preserve and to protect the fundamental rights of the citizens of the particular state, not as citizens, but as human persons.[91]

The above concept of international law is not to be confused with the *Jus Gentium* or Law of Nations, whose tenets were objects of positive law incorporated in practically all state codes. The *Jus Gentium*, which arose about 243 B.C. among the peoples living in the vicinity of the Romans and which was applied in Roman courts, was based on the theory "that the adoption of a common legal concept, insofar as its moral qualities were concerned, by a number of peoples, independently of each other raised the presumption that it was the tentative concretization of the *Jus Naturale*, for no other adequate reason could explain the phenomenon." [92] From this background there evolved a quasi-positive law of the international community formed upon custom and treaty agreements. As an illustration of the connection between this positive law and Natural Law internationally, the doctrines of war, truce, peace, and international trade belong to positive international law; but the requirement that a law be just and that peoples cooperate in friendly commerce belongs to the Natural Law.[93]

The doctors of late Scholasticism, Suarez and Vittoria, built upon the Thomistic basis their concept of the order of law in the community of nations. Before the time of Hugo Grotius they developed a complete scientific system of international law as the constitution for mankind. They did not invent this law, for the

[91] Rommen, *The State*, 624.
[92] Brendan F. Brown, "Crimes Against the Law of Peace, War, and Humanity," *Catholic University of America Bulletin*, XVII (May, 1950), 8.
[93] Rommen, *The Natural Law*, 68–69.

"ever-present idea of Natural Law and common legal reason, however clouded and overshadowed by national prejudices and tribal exclusiveness," is evident as soon as regular intercourse is established between nations. These Scholastics studied the customs scientifically, and found their fundamental principles, nature, and meaning, thus arriving at the rational order in the community of nations. "They initiated the philosophy and the juridical theory of international law." [94] One source of impetus for their work was the attempt of the Iberian colonial powers to justify their conquests as a means of spreading the gospel. Hugo Grotius (1583–1645) marked the transition from the metaphysical to the rational Natural Law, although he did not imply the autonomy of human reason as any more than the proximate source of Natural Law, with God as the ultimate source. [95]

Catholic philosophy denies that only power and selfish national interests control conduct between states. It also rejects the theory that international law originates in a temporary limitation of the sovereign states for opportunist reasons or out of a suitable utilitarianism. On the contrary, there is an organic unity of common interests, of justice, and of security. The monistic or self-limitation theory met the practical need of voiding treaties which had turned against national interest. It considers all human relations to have an exclusive basis in subjective interests regulated by contractual consent; peace and justice are subjective propaganda slogans. The monistic approach is founded upon the antagonistic theory that "the mind cannot penetrate into the essences of things, that what we experience are only the external phenomena which give us no knowledge of the thing in itself, of the idea of man and of state and of mankind." [96] The major objections to this concept of international law are: 1) It attempts to avoid Natural Law by recognizing only positivism in which the will of the state is the source of obligation. 2) It denies that the metaphysical basis of norms is to be

[94] *Id., The State*, 619–20.
[95] *Id., The Natural Law*, 70.
[96] *Id., The State*, 630.

found in the essence of man and of the state. 3) The autonomous will, ignoring objective being, is guided by utility, opportunism, lust for power, and fear for self-preservation.

Messner suggests that the following differences would be evident in international law if the organized society of nations were to become its guarantor.[97] The new law would be the outcome of deliberation by an international legislative body, rather than of interstate treaties. It would be binding upon all states directly and without exception, with the sovereignty of the individual state subordinated to the constitutional law of the community of states. Interstate treaties would continue to function, but they would not be the major factor in international relations.

The Validity of Treaties

Because political utilitarianism has wrought such havoc under the name of political Realism, which dictates the putting aside of treaty obligations which turn out disadvantageously, we shall investigate the requirements of the contract, the role of *rebus sic stantibus* (things remaining as they are), and the proposed method for meeting unforeseen circumstances. The binding force terminates at the end of the period agreed upon, or with the fulfillment of terms, or by mutual consent. For validity, the treaty must be entered into by an independent state which has international legal capacity, the object must be morally and legally admissible, and the contracting states must exercise free consent.

In consideration of the object of the treaty, an offensive pact cannot have any legal existence, nor can an agreement in which a third state is recognized as a sphere of influence of one of the parties if this would threaten the right to freedom enjoyed by the third state.[98] "No treaty of alliance or friendship can force a State to cooperate in an unjust venture of its associate." [99]

[97] Messner, *Social Ethics*, 435.
[98] *Ibid.*, 415–16.
[99] Eppstein (ed.), *Code*, 89.

The question is raised whether a state which has entered into a defensive alliance, is required to fulfill the obligation if that would cost its very existence. Messner replies that "far-reaching and unforeseeable changes in circumstances relieve the partners of their obligations."

Since all the binding force of a contract originates in the real will of the partners by natural law, every treaty contains the clause: *Rebus sic stantibus*. Relatively slight changes in circumstances, however, such as could have been foreseen, do not relieve partners of their obligations; such changes are inevitable in international affairs. . . . Yet the interpretation of treaties is not a matter of utility, but of justice. It is therefore a breach of law to allege a changed situation merely as an excuse for evasion.[100]

He feels that foreknowledge of circumstances threatening the very existence of the state would have prevented the treaty's being concluded, so the obligation is not binding "unless the acceptance of such a risk is expressly included in the treaty." [101]

The *Code* in treating of the above-mentioned circumstances, states that permanent treaties can reasonably be accepted only under reservation of the tacit clause *rebus sic stantibus*.[102] It too specifies that a treaty does not cease to bind simply because the nation no longer derives any advantage from it. Pope Pius XII, speaking of unforeseen situations which make fulfillment of a treaty impossible, counseled immediate recourse to frank discussion.[103] He distinguished this from the attitude that signed pacts are written in water and are to be broken at one's own discretion whenever self-interest demands it, without regard for the other contracting party.

The *Code of International Ethics* defines strictly the two conditions which must be present for rightful exercise of unilateral

[100] Messner, *Social Ethics*, 417.
[101] *Ibid.*, 643.
[102] Eppstein (ed.), *Code*, 91–92.
[103] Pius XII, "Summi Pontificatus," quoted in Koenig, *Principles*, 31–32. He also stressed *Pacta sunt servanda* in the Christmas Message, 1941, 758–59.

denouncement of a treaty. First, the situation must have been altered so much that the state would have refused consent had it foreseen the circumstances. Secondly, before resorting to unilateral denouncement, the state must have

. . . exhausted every means of fulfilling the letter of the treaty and of bringing about, in conformity with its spirit, the modification made necessary by the new circumstances. It is only when the defendant refuses to discuss and persists in demanding the literal fulfillment of the treaty, that the plaintiff can free himself from his obligations by a unilateral act of will.[104]

Since freedom of decision of the contracting parties is a prerequisite for a valid treaty, what of a peace treaty imposed upon a defeated state by an unjust aggressor? Grotius answered that the treaty was binding because there would be no end to wars if a state, judging itself mistreated, could unilaterally declare the treaty void. The majority of international jurists seem to agree that this sacrifice must be made in the interest of the human race, lest international order be gravely imperiled.[105] While agreeing with this interpretation of Messner, Higgins notes that terms which are palpably unjust cannot be the object of any contract. As an example of the limits to which a state must serve the fellowship of nations in this matter, he mentions that it cannot be expected "to observe terms which would lead to loss of independence, acute misery of its people, or spoliation of the fundamental means of development."[106] Pope Pius XII's remarks would appear to be addressed to such a problem when he noted that in the drafting of peace treaties it is difficult to be entirely free from passions and bitterness:

. . . the establishment of juridical institutions which would serve to guarantee the loyal and faithful carrying out of terms and, in case of recognized need, the revising and correcting of them is of decisive

---

[104] Eppstein (ed.), *Code*, 92.
[105] Messner, *Social Ethics*, 416.
[106] Higgins, *Man as Man*, 563.

importance for honorable acceptance of a peace treaty and to avoid arbitrary unilateral ruptures and interpretations of treaty terms.[107]

An Evaluation of Democracy

Because the modern world tends to evaluate the acceptability of a nation's conduct in terms of democracy, this discussion would seem to have place in a chapter on international society. According to the particular category of the spokesman, the term "democracy" today might mean mob rule, dictatorship of the proletariat, state imposed material welfare, or Christian democracy. Only the latter justifies this commendation:

[It is only] because man is a spiritual and intellectual being, created and redeemed by God and destined to eternal life with Him, that it is desirable that the largest possible number of men and women should be enabled to play a conscious and responsible part in contributing to the common good of their earthly City and, through its cooperation with other human societies to the common good of mankind.[108]

No form of government in itself has absolute validity or is to be preferred under all circumstances; its value in serving the common good must be judged relative to the situation: the national character, the stage of civilization and education, the cultural climate, etc. One should not worship the machinery of government which is a means to an end, and ignore the people who must operate the machinery; the form of government does not guarantee that human rights will not be violated.[109]

In exploring the best form of government, St. Thomas Aquinas advocated monarchy, because he felt that the safety of the multitude "lies in the preservation of its unity, which is called peace. . . . Now it is manifest that what is itself one, can more efficaciously bring about unity than several. . . . Furthermore it is evident that several persons could by no means preserve the stabil-

[107] Pius XII, Christmas Message, 1939, quoted in Koenig, *Principles*, 637.
[108] Eppstein, "Commentary," *Code*, 3.
[109] Neill, *Weapons*, 158.

ity of the community if they totally disagreed." [110] However, his recognition that the power of the king needed limitation lest it lapse into tyranny, led him to modify his position in the *Summa* where he recommended a mixed regime in which the peculiar merits of monarchy, aristocracy, and democracy could be realized, and the excesses of each be thwarted.

For this is the best form of polity, being partly kingdom, since there is one at the head of all; partly aristocracy, in so far as a number of persons are set in authority; partly democracy, i.e., government by the people, and the people have the right to choose their rulers.[111]

Robert Bellarmine arrived at essentially the same conclusions in *De Romani Pontificis* in which he avoided the name of any specific type and simply referred to it as a "more useful form." Although Bellarmine concluded that monarchy was theoretically more perfect, his reaction was somewhat like this:

Monarchy, in the hands of God, who combines in Himself absolutely all the qualifications required in an ideal ruler, is indeed a perfect system of government; in the hands of imperfect man, however, it is exposed to many defects and abuses.[112]

Bellarmine listed these elements of good government: order, peace, strength, power, stability, endurance, facility of action, and efficiency.[113]

Professor Rager analyzes the United States federal government to show that it fulfills Bellarmine's standards.[114] With the president as the unifying head and with a governor in each state, there are monarchic elements to insure order, peace, and stability. The aristocratic factor could be found among the senators, representa-

[110] Thomas Aquinas, *On Kingship*, I, ch. II, 11–12.

[111] *Id., Summa Theol.*, I^a^–II^ae^, q. 105, a. 1.

[112] John C. Rager, *Democracy and Bellarmine* (Shelbyville, Ind.: Qualityprint, 1926), 35.

[113] *Ibid.*, 43, citing Robert Bellarmine, *De Romani Pontificis Ecclesiastica Monarchia*, I, II.

[114] *Ibid.*, 40–41.

tives, and governors in their relationship to the federal government. The democratic element needs no clarification.

Yves Simon defines the heart of democracy to lie in "placing the governing personnel under the control of the governed."[115] Paul Kennedy emphasizes the elective principle as a better means of securing capacity and integrity of personnel than by the principle of heredity.[116] He would hold the other institutions associated with democracy to be matters of experience and expediency rather than of principle, such as a written constitution, separation of powers, popular assemblies, equal suffrage for both sexes.

Pope Pius XII treated of democracy in the broad sense, as it may be realized in monarchies as well as in republics.[117] He distinguished between the people organized in a state and the false concept of a shapeless mass of individuals which would be the enemy of true democracy. He reminded the faithful that Leo XIII's encyclical "Libertas Praestantissimum" in 1888 stated, "the Church does not disapprove of any of the various forms of government provided they be *per se* capable of securing the good of the citizens." It was the Rousseauvian "tyranny of the majority" which Leo XIII condemned. Professor Neill describes that same error in these words:

And so Rousseau, by making the mass of mankind the ultimate source of law and justice, and by freeing that mass from any responsibility and all restrictions, grinds each individual down into nothingness. Collectively the citizens are angelic, omniscient, infallible, and omnipotent; individually they are worthless ciphers.[118]

Because popular sovereignty is so frequently misunderstood, it would be well to note the differences pointed out by Messner, between the natural law interpretation and the modern theory of

[115] Simon, *Philosophy of Democratic Government*, 99.

[116] Kennedy, S.J., "The Principles of Democracy," *Philosophy of State*, 174–75.

[117] Pius XII, Christmas Message, 1944, *Catholic Mind*, XLIII (February, 1945), 66–67.

[118] Neill, *Weapons*, 91.

absolute popular sovereignty, which bases political authority exclusively on popular will and subjects it to the whim of the latter.

No government fundamentally exercises political authority as the mandatory of the people (even in constitutional democracy), but in virtue of the natural order of the political community and therefore in the name of God. . . . This means that we obey the orders of the government ultimately not because it is elected by the people but because such obedience is commanded by the natural moral order. If, then, political authority does not reside inalienably in the people in the sense that the government exercises its authority only as the representative of the people and there is no intrinsic dependence of the essential political authority upon its constitutional form, no conclusion can be drawn from the natural law theory of sovereignty in support of a higher right for democracy than for any other forms of government. . . .

The popular will, even under democracy, cannot lawfully give any government a mandate releasing it from the observance of natural rights. Governments which make encroachments upon natural liberties by measures of economic planning in the name of socialism have therefore as little justification to appeal to the popular will or a popular mandate as totalitarian governments which seek to base their omnipotence on a will of the people expressed through plebiscite.[119]

It is a necessary preface to say that Yves Simon actually favors democracy, because otherwise his effort to explode the "democratic faith" in the infallibility of universal suffrage might be misleading. To those who worry that "for lack of enlightenment and virtue" the mass of voters might not entrust power to the most able men, his answer is that some of the worst leaders attained high position through nondemocratic processes such as birth, appointment by "wise" men, intrigue, corruption, and civil war.[120] On the other hand, he attacks a modern positivist heresy about the assent of the multitude as a criterion of truth: "This sociological notion

[119] Messner, *Social Ethics*, 525.
[120] Simon, *Philosophy of Democratic Government*, 82.

of truth is commonly interpreted in a purely pragmatic or utilitarian sense, as meaning that the human intellect is but a biological instrument, successful when it procures adaptation to environment, unsuccessful when it does not." [121] With reference to the kind of questions which should be submitted to universal vote, he concludes that with due allowance for relativity, in the stage of deliberation the multitude is of value, but in the phase of execution the judgment of one is usually preferable.

He demonstrates that the casting of a ballot by a multitude does not necessarily produce an effect traceable to the social whole if the spiritual link supplied by real community life be lacking. As a generalization, he would say that if the elector has matured in individualistic isolation, if the society is one with little traditional life where young people remain ignorant of their country's history, if most human relations are controlled by economic self-interest, it will be by sheer luck that the electoral result happens to serve the common welfare.[122] If an election is determined by mob hysteria, it cannot produce wisdom which is the principal need for a good election. He labels as romantic the component of democratic optimism which views the larger, more primitive part of society as the one superior in wisdom. He traces this to the fact that men relegate the major part of evil to the social section which they suppose to be farthest away from themselves.[123]

Yves Simon concludes that there is an element of truth and an element of myth in each component of democratic optimism. He would advise that even if one could be assured by a magical process that certain persons were perfectly qualified for office, it would still be prudent to erect as a check and a complement the power of numbers. The temptation "to think in terms of the elite and to ignore the problems of the many" is all too human. "There was a time when it was possible to believe that the destiny of the com-

[121] *Ibid.*, 85.
[122] *Ibid.*, 88.
[123] *Ibid.*, 89.

mon man was safely entrusted to the wisdom of the upper class. That time is gone, apparently forever." [124]

Messner offers the judgment that democracy is the appropriate political form for culturally advanced peoples in whom the responsibility for the management of the commonweal is awake, so that cooperation in this is seen as part of the rights of the human person.[125] Rommen enumerates as the essentials to make democracy workable: a strong sense of unity in principles balanced by a tolerance in other matters, strong loyalty to moral ideas rather than to persons, a collective moral will to live together in mutual solidarity strong enough to overcome their dissatisfaction with apparent social injustices, and conviction to use only the legal means of reform and abstain from civil violence. "Where the antagonism of groups or classes outbalances the will to live together, democracy becomes impossible, and its institutions are directly contributing factors to its destruction." [126]

---

[124] *Ibid.*, 98–99.

[125] Messner, *Social Ethics*, 543.

[126] Rommen, *The State*, 484. Paul Crane, S.J., in speaking of the mistaken direction of anti-colonialism following World War II, makes these critical statements about the vogue of democracy in the underdeveloped countries: ". . . the economic chaos consequent on the imposition of democracy on the politically immature is the greatest obstacle today to the adequate raising of world living standards. . . . Moreover, where a territory is turned over to 'democracy' overnight, the inclination of the new native politicos is to promise their electorates not an ordered process of capital development but a Welfare State on the British model, a free-for-all which they know cannot be supported by the country's resources—but which makes a fine talking point on the hustings. Ignorant populations are promised the moon by the new politicians and, precisely because of their ignorance, the people think they will get it." Paul Crane, S.J., "Politics as Primary," *Social Order*, VIII (May, 1958), 223. The author is secretary of England's Catholic Social Guild and editor of *Christian Democrat*.

⋆ VII ⋆

Selected Applications of Catholic Social Doctrine

CATHOLIC social doctrine could be applied to such a vast array of pressing contemporary issues, that selectivity is a necessary prescription. By the frequency of their mention in the Realist-Idealist controversy, the following topics seemed to deserve special attention: colonialism, use of the world's resources, Socialism, Communism, duty of intervention, laws of war, armaments, neutrality status, and the realism of peace.

Colonialism

Since the Second World War has occasioned a violent outburst of anti-colonialism and a surging of subject peoples for self-government in the underdeveloped areas of the world, the application of Catholic principle to colonialism seems essential.

Bishop Henri Chappoulie of Angers, France, supplies a balanced statement which would be useful in the introduction of the study:

[The true Christian] will admit that different civilizations will prefer other scales of values than his own and not despise them for this reason. He will not imagine that the greatest honor to be paid men of another race and culture is to assimilate them to his own civilization. . . . The common opinion among Christian thinkers today holds that colonialism is morally justifiable only in the measure in which it constitutes a service to the people whom it has subjected, usually by way of conquest. . . . The Church, therefore, cannot range itself alongside those who hold the colonial condition as permanent, who take into account only the prestige and material well-being the colony furnishes the metropolitan country and who despise the colonial peoples as inferior to their European masters and incapable of finding their own happiness in liberty.[1]

America summarizes his other remarks to this effect:

The precise moment of liberation is, of course, a temporal matter in which the Church is incompetent to judge. Indeed, for a people to rid themselves too soon of honest tutelage could result in anarchy. . . . It is rather the task of the Christian to build a bridge between diverse forms of culture and civilization so that they can live side by side, each contributing of its richness to the other.

Pope Pius XI in 1938 referred to the fact that some races seem to be abundantly endowed by divine Providence and that as colonizers they might enrich others with the benefits of civilization.[2] Whereas his words may seem to justify the claim of certain nineteenth century imperialists, he is not posing an "excuse" to rationalize a less praiseworthy motive when he says: "What else are colonies for, if they are not meant to educate races less civilized? . . . And whoever does civilizing work, cannot disregard religion and philosophy."

The *Code of International Ethics* also recognizes that some states attain "the full good of human life" at an early stage of their existence and others seem incapable of escaping from ignorance

---

[1] Bishop Henri Chappoulie of Angers, statement about October 1, 1955, quoted in "Colonialism and the Christian Conscience," *America*, XCIV (October 29, 1955), 121.

[2] Pius XI, Address to 400 Teachers in Catholic Action, September 6, 1938, quoted in Koenig, *Principles*, 545–46.

and savagery by their own means. In view of the latter, the more advanced societies have a duty to help the more backward nations lift themselves gradually "to a level of existence more in conformity with the designs of Providence." [3] Their assistance must not be devoted exclusively to material advantages of a higher culture; blessings of the mind, the heart, and the soul are to be communicated also. This educative influence requires some subordination on the part of the assisted state; it might even become a protectorate or colony. Whereas history testifies to the fact that in the past, atrocities and pillage have marred the beginnings of colonial enterprises undertaken in the name of civilization, in spite of this deplorable fact, more benefits than evils have accrued to the subject peoples: abolition of cannibalism, slavery, human sacrifice, tyranny of barbarous potentates, relative affluence in comparison with abject misery.[4] One generation paid dearly, but a long posterity profited from the new regime.

Rommen states that Vittoria, Suarez, Soto, and Bellarmine in the sixteenth century denied the claims of the Spanish conquistadors that they had just cause for war based upon their assertion that they were principally interested in the destruction of idolatry and other crimes against natural morality.[5] Suarez refuted the right of a Christian state to make war upon a pagan state simply because it indulged in idolatry, nor would he defend the right of armed protection of missioners. Robert Bellarmine made this distinction between violations of natural morality and violations of natural justice: only the latter are subject to punishment by human authorities as violations of social duties. A serious offense against innocents would give just cause for intervention provided the means employed did not provoke still greater damage to peace and order and that it was capable of attaining its purpose.

The *Code* criticizes the alleged need of over-industrialized states

[3] Eppstein (ed.), *Code*, 94. The *Code*, p. 102, criticizes the absence in the United Nations Charter, Art. 73 of any mention of the religious and moral interests of the native peoples; instead the Charter expresses an exclusively humanitarian motive.

[4] *Ibid.*, 99.

[5] Rommen, *The State*, 661–62.

for assured sources of raw materials and easily accessible markets for goods.[6] If the nation has been lacking in moderation and prudence, it alone bears the responsibility. It should be able to supply its needs by commerce with other nations. Over-population is not a solid argument.

Rarely the situation might occur that an area is occupied by savage clans whose social relationships are anarchical and thus it presents an insuperable obstacle to civilization. In that case there would be no dispossession of pre-established sovereignty. However, if barbarous people are settled in an area "with their own self-sufficient polity, they constitute a legitimate State even though it is not reckoned among the family of nations." [7] If through colonization, not conquest, a colony is settled on land overrun by nomads and too sparsely inhabited to have a government, the right of the inhabitants to their private holdings in land and the like must be respected. "Even though their titles are not recorded in a courthouse, they are as valid as those recognized among civilized men." [8]

The *Code* suggests theoretical validity for the right of conquest when a civilized state dismisses from office a native sovereign who has attacked the lives and goods of other nations' subjects, broken off promises, and infringed upon common frontiers.[9] But it promptly adds that this does not justify the many conquests which have been acts of brigandage. Obtaining from native rulers their voluntary renunciation of rights as sovereigns by treaties of friendship, alliance, or protection might be right in principle, but often the concrete circumstances make the validity of these contracts doubtful. However, there have been systems of protectorates established in which the authority of the native princes is respected at the same time that the country is guaranteed against external aggression, with the consequent flow of moral and material advantages.[10]

[6] Eppstein, (ed.), *Code*, 95.
[7] Higgins, *Man as Man*, 561.
[8] *Ibid.*, 561.
[9] Eppstein (ed.), *Code*, 96.
[10] *Ibid.*, 96.

It is often argued that so long as a true society of nations has not been organized, no society has any right to exercise jurisdiction of any sort over other independent societies. The *Code* declares that this objection is groundless because the function which the duly organized international society would exercise in developing "the common patrimony of humanity for the good of all men" and in exercising "a beneficent tutelage over the still backward nations" is necessary to good order and progress of human society. In the absence of an organization capable of fulfilling these functions, any nation which is willing and capable has the right of leading these groups to civilization.[11]

Any rights which a colonial authority can justly claim come only from their duties in regard to the well-being of the population under their care. A nation which has devoted its wealth and man-power to humanitarian colonization is entitled to a *rational* exploitation of the territories controlled, and perhaps some help in defense of the parent-state, but use of natives on the territory of the mother country should be rare.[12] The interests of the natives must never be sacrificed to those of the colonizing state as in the case of dispossessing them of their land for the sake of settlers or permitting "a disguised serfdom to replace officially abolished slavery under the pretence of educative work." There should neither be complete assimilation to the foreign culture nor absolute conservation of ancestral customs. All that is good should be retained, and a wise temporization should preside over the elimina-ation of abuses.

Messner defines the political rights of native peoples to be first, autonomy within the limits of their capacity to maintain peace and order, to protect the life and property of foreigners, and to provide for "the intellectual, hygienic, economic, and social welfare of the community." [13] Then secondly, they have a natural right to pro-

[11] *Ibid.*, 98.
[12] *Ibid.*, 100.
[13] Messner, *Social Ethics*, 455–56. Leon W. Janssen, S.J., explains the implications of the fact that growth is a law of life: "As long as Asia and

gress toward complete home rule, though not necessarily to full sovereignty.

The *Code* states the case in these terms, "Colonization means civilization, and civilization means emancipation." [14] The parent-state must make way for a cordial and lasting collaboration between two free and equal nations. But since a very real association has arisen between the two nations, upon emancipation the former colony must not break all bonds which united it to the parent-state. The faithful practice of a certain partnership would benefit the interests of both: the parent-state would have preserved the legitimate advantages to which it is entitled from a land it dedeveloped, and the former colony would have the permanent beneficent influences to which its progress is due.

Trade and the Use of the World's Resources

Man is a steward of the goods of the earth and this property must be used socially, either by distribution of superfluous goods or by

---

Africa lived in their traditional isolation, this minimum standard was a stationary and perhaps even an endurable one. Contact with other nations through the media of contemporary communications has produced an impassioned refusal to be content any longer with any such meagre standards. Generalized illiteracy becomes as unacceptable (and as impossible) within the narrowing limits of the international community as individual illiteracy is in a civilized national community. . . .

"The static societies of the past are impossible to prolong even were one prompted to make the attempt. . . . Let him stay where he is, it was said; not knowing any better, he is content; by giving him more, you will create new wants and leave him unhappier than before. Such an attitude can be maintained only by closing one's eyes to the massive poverty, disease, ignorance and even starvation rampant in the underdeveloped countries. . . . Economic progress is not, to be sure, a guarantee of personal happiness but the misery that is identified with economic stagnation clearly brings unhappiness." Leon W. Janssen, S.J., "Duties to Underdeveloped Countries," *Social Order*, VIII (May, 1958), 200. The author is a specialist in economics of underdeveloped areas; he resides at Katholiek Sociaal Centrum, Schiedam, Netherlands.

[14] Eppstein (ed.), *Code*, 104–05.

the more provident creating of profitable employment.[15] Ownership is not absolute, but it is more than a utilitarian arrangement, since it is bound up with the exigencies of human existence. Just as individual private property serves both particular interests and the common good, so must national riches and resources of the soil.[16] The scientific, artistic, and religious values of a nation radiate beyond its boundaries in a peaceful manner with no loss to the state, but since material things are more limited, competition and covetousness develop.

A state would be acting contrary to the order of Providence if it claimed the right to leave its natural resources undeveloped or refused to make them available to others in dire need.[17] Pursuit of a policy of self-sufficiency in isolation is detrimental to the progress of humanity, and it deprives that nation of the advantages which flow from division of labor and exchange of services. Divine providence seemed to contemplate this system of exchange, since there is an unequal distribution of capacities and resources.

Stress upon access by all to the world's resources as stated in the Atlantic Charter was indirectly approved by Pope Pius XII when he said, "We are very greatly consoled to find that the necessity of a common sharing in the goods of the earth is affirmed even by those nations which, in the implementing of this principle, would belong to the category of givers and not receivers."[18] Right Reverend Donald A. MacLean would include in this sharing, the

[15] Charles P. Bruehl, *The Pope's Plan for Social Reconstruction:* a Commentary on the Social Encyclicals of Pius XI (New York: Devin-Adair, 1939), 50–52. Professor Bruehl teaches sociology at St. Charles Seminary, Overbrook, Pennsylvania.

[16] Eppstein (ed.), *Code,* 81. Pius XII in an address to a World Petroleum Congress in 1955, said: "The more and more apparent world character of economics and of the duties that fall upon privileged nations toward less favored ones will have their effect on the division of the goods produced." *Catholic Mind,* LVI (January–February, 1958), 18.

[17] *Ibid.,* 81.

[18] Pius XII, Christmas Message, 1941, quoted in Koenig, *Principles,* 758. The Catholic Association for International Peace has frequently expressed this national obligation to the international common good.

use of territory on the American continents by "surplus" population from other parts of the world where they are unable to earn a decent living; this would involve a progressive removal of present immigration barriers.[19]

Although a state may protect itself against over-zealous foreign competition of industries, the weapons of protectionism must be used only in real necessity and then moderately. Charity may oblige certain states to assist a struggling country to dispose of excess products which seriously threaten its economy.[20] Legitimate efforts must be made to find international markets so as to produce a just equilibrium. Messner suggests that the international organization seek a balancing of agricultural and industrial production, compile statistics on production and consumption, give advice to individual states on agricultural policies, and secure credit and loans in time of crisis.[21] Planning by means of restriction seems absurd when people still go hungry; perhaps the planning could be applied to transportation of surpluses to areas of scarcity. Measures should be taken to insure that a creditor country be prepared to accept a proportionate quantity of goods. Unforeseen developments might make it an obligation of international justice to write off debts in whole or in part after these loans have been running for a considerable time and the greater part has been paid.[22]

In the discussion of access to the world's resources, attention should be turned to the observations of William A. Kaschmitter, M.M., who in trying to determine a practical solution to Japan's population problem and to remedy the fact that half the world's people are seriously undernourished, concluded that we have no really adequate science of international social justice. Where do the rights of a country end and the rights of hungry humanity begin? Because of a lack of organized principles for determining

[19] Donald A. MacLean, *A Dynamic World Order* (Milwaukee: Bruce, 1945), 112.
[20] Eppstein (ed.), *Code*, 82.
[21] Messner, *Social Ethics*, 966.
[22] *Ibid.*, 975.

rights and obligations, it is possible to point out injustices, but difficult to determine who is responsible for them and whose duty it is to change the situation. Therefore, he is attempting to organize world-wide intellectual and financial cooperation to support an arduous scholarly endeavor at the University of Louvain, dealing with the facts of international relationship and the pertinent theological and ethical principles.

Kaschmitter's mission is founded upon two principles and two facts:

1) God has given every human being a real right to a human existence —simply because he is a human being.
2) The correlative of a right is not charity, but justice. To give our neighbor in charity what is due to him in justice is sordid mockery.
1) In much of the world, the people don't have what is needed for a human existence—enough food, enough clothing, adequate shelter— even though the earth can supply all that is required to make such a standard universal.
2) Nobody knows just what should be done about this—or rather who must do what obviously needs to be done.[23]

He points to the Department of Agriculture's estimate that there are 16,000,000,000 acres of land in the world which could produce food, but according to the statistics of a United Nations agency only 3,400,000,000 acres are actually in use. He notes that if the standard of living of 1,500,000,000 people throughout the world were to be raised only enough to allow the purchase of needed food, the American farmer would have no problem of overproduction, and the nation would not have "to levy taxes to pay for immobilizing the land." Socially backward peoples are conscious today of their rights; the West is on the defensive because it cannot

[23] Robert G. Hoyt, "A 'Science of International Social Justice' Needed Now," *The Catholic Messenger*, Davenport, Iowa, LXXV (March 27, 1958), 14. Father Kaschmitter is a Maryknoll missionary who worked in Japan until 1956, and who in the past two years has traveled 80,000 miles throughout the world to organize the extension of Catholic social teaching in the international sphere.

place before them a satisfying set of ideas about international social justice. Only the Communists go to them with a system of ideas.

Leon W. Janssen, S.J., uses the principles of "ordered charity" to explain how serious is the moral obligation to help under-developed countries. The principles of specification are the same for social justice as for social charity.

The first principle of specification declares: The greater the need, the greater the obligation. The less a man can help himself in his distress, the greater is my obligation to aid him. . . . 'Extreme necessity' is a technical term in moral philosophy for a situation importing in another a grave obligation, even at the cost of substantial sacrifices, to aid the person in need. . . . Their poverty is both absolute and relative.

The principle of relationship declares that people who are nearer to us have a greater claim on our help than others. . . . A nation has, of course, the gravest obligations toward itself . . . . it is justified in ex-tending larger assistance to those nations which have shown a willing-ness to oppose the expansion of Communism. It further follows that the obligation to help is reduced in proportion to the sacrifice required; that the obligation of richer countries is relatively greater; and finally, that if the presumed obligation can be fulfilled by either a loan or a grant, a loan is to be preferred. . . . To the extent that the underde-veloped countries fail to apply themselves to their proper task of rais-ing standards of living—if the rich continue to live luxuriously, if order and justice are absent even for foreign investors—to that extent the obligation of other countries to aid them is reduced. We must not forget, however, that the lack of sound judgment in economic matters and even the presence of corruption and a self-conscious nationalism with overtones of xenophobia are part of the growing pains of develop-ing countries. . . .

The third principle of specification in determining obligations of social justice declares: Help is to be proportioned to its usefulness. . . . Thus when a country lacks the fundamental conditions for economic growth there is no use pumping in dollars. What is needed first is education, technical assistance and perhaps even political reform. . . . The prin-ciple of need may suggest prompt action. The principle of possibility, on the other hand, may in certain cases warn us to go slowly.

It is not unethical, then, to promise greater help on the condition that certain economic and political forms be introduced which will increase the effectiveness of that aid. . . . The moral principle in question merely declares that, given serious need, we must do what we can, taking into account the expected results and legitimate self-interest. . . . The international community, imperfectly organized though it be, is not an abstraction. . . . Within the nations responsibilities are proportioned to position: the President has more responsibility than a Member of Congress, a Congressman more than a simple voter, the director of a bank more than the ordinary investor, the editor of an influential newspaper more than the average reader. In the final analysis, however, we are all responsible . . . we are all called upon to pay the taxes to finance economic aid to underdeveloped countries, sums which in the future may mount to levels requiring substantial sacrifices. . . . International social justice requires the establishing of institutions, the creation of a stable social order in which justice is independent of the whims of individual nations.[24]

The most telling statements of informed Catholic opinion on use of the world's resources have been the separate testimonies by two outstanding spokesmen before the Foreign Affairs Committee of the House of Representatives when foreign aid bills were being considered in May and June of 1957. James L. Vizzard, S.J., sketched the contrast between the hundreds of millions who have hunger, poverty, disease and death as their daily bread, and the almost intolerably superior living standard of the United States with its enormously productive economy and disproportionate share of the world's wealth.

I'm sure that we would not subscribe to the proposition that God created the resources of this world for the exclusive benefit of those who might have had the power to seize them, or the luck to stumble upon

[24] Janssen, S.J., "Duties to Underdeveloped Countries," 201–05. Philip S. Land, S.J., writing for the same symposium, insists that "the obligation of the richer nations to the poorer will be better fulfilled by the *indirect* method of working to establish international economic order rather than by the *direct* method of giving aid." Philip S. Land, S.J., "Call for World Economic Community," *Social Order*, VIII (May, 1958), 217–20.

them, or the good fortune to be born into them. . . . We are not members of some kind of exclusive club, the sole residents of a high-walled garden of paradise, somehow specially chosen of God to enjoy the best of His creation while the great bulk of mankind struggles out-side for a meager and precarious subsistence. One of Christ's parables comes to mind: Dives and Lazarus. We have no reason to expect that the fate of a nation which might scorn the obligations which go with wealth will be any different than that of a man whose very name im-plies wealth, selfishly and exclusively enjoyed. It is also a fact, and it should be a disturbing one, that in the only portrayal of the final judgment which we have from Christ's own lips, the decision of the judge is based on the very simple and direct criterion: Did you feed the hungry, clothe the naked, heal the sick? We have no reason to believe that nations will be judged on any other basis.[25]

Christ has admonished "Thou shalt love thy neighbor as thyself," and the parable of the Good Samaritan illustrates that the neighbor is even a stranger in a faraway land, "anyone who needs help wherever he may be found and reached."

To those who hold that charity is the responsibility of the in-dividual and not of states, Vizzard replies that states were formed "to fulfill for us collectively what we cannot do individually." [26] In a world so vast and complicated the state must act as the individual's agent in reaching those who have a claim on our charity. To those who complain that charity begins at home, he rejoins, "It doesn't end there." The basis of charity is possession of a common nature and destiny, so the duty applies to all men. Of those who bewail the fact that the recipients of our help are still "uncommitted" and unappreciative, he asks how gratitude and friendship can be ex-pected when in the past we have justified aid exclusively on the basis of our self-interest. To those who plead that we need tax cuts more than foreign handouts, he answers that we have not

[25] James L. Vizzard, S.J., "Who Is My Neighbor?" *Catholic Mind*, LV (November–December, 1957), 506. Vizzard, who is vice-president of Na-tional Catholic Rural Life Conference and treasurer of the Catholic Associa-tion for International Peace, gave this testimony, May 28, 1957.
[26] *Ibid.*, 507.

begun to make the kind of sacrifices, personal and national, which we are able to sustain.

Vizzard points out that the world needs desperately a shining example of pure and disinterested service. If Communism were to disappear tomorrow, the aid program should have the same importance. "If we dedicate ourselves to a program for shared abundance, we may never again be called upon to dedicate our lives and our wealth to a program of shared disaster." [27]

The second previously mentioned testimony in behalf of foreign aid, that of Dr. C. Joseph Nuesse, states that our obligations to an international common good are "proportionate to the needs of the international community." [28] Although work of voluntary agencies in international relief is commendable, the prevention of suffering can be achieved only by technological and educational developments. Dr. Nuesse called attention to the fact that at their twenty-eighth convention in November, 1956, the National Council of Catholic Women recommended "that the United States, along with and through international organizations, continue its participation in programs of economic and technical aid aimed at helping underprivileged peoples obtain a more just share of the world's wealth." [29] Citing Barbara Ward's statement that "the lack of any political or ideological framework is the greatest single source of weakness in the aid program undertaken by the West," he relates this to recommendations made with frequency enough to be considered representative of Catholic opinion that "policies of the United States ought to rest on conviction and principle, not upon expediency and competitive bidding in the cold war." [30] He also

[27] *Ibid.*, 508.

[28] C. Joseph Nuesse, "International Social Justice," *Catholic Mind*, LVI (January–February, 1958), 19. Dr. Nuesse, who is dean of the School of Social Science at Catholic University, past-president of the Catholic Association for International Peace, and formerly of the U.S. National Commission for UNESCO, delivered this testimony June 5, 1957, before the Foreign Affairs Committee, House of Representatives.

[29] *Ibid.*, 20. This resolution has been printed in a handbook for study and discussion by the NCCW.

[30] *Ibid.*, 21.

cites statements of the National Catholic Rural Life Conference in 1955 and of the National Council of Catholic Women in 1956, indicating that technical assistance and military aid programs should be separate. The Catholic Association for International Peace, he notes, has stressed the need for long-term programs for capital expansion in underdeveloped countries.

Maritain suggests that the very existence of world society must imply a certain relative yet appreciable equalization of the standards of life of various peoples.[31] The price of peace is renunciation; if the issue were made sufficiently clear, he would hope that people in the West would accept a serious lowering of their living standard in order to provide the equivalent raising of the standard for those in Communist infiltrated areas. He grants that this would presuppose a kind of moral heroism for which we are badly prepared.

When speaking of aid to the underdeveloped countries, the question of nationalization to which they are often prone, seems to suggest itself for discussion. Pope Pius XII has made two forceful pronouncements on the subject:

Christian associations agree with nationalization only when it is seen to be required by the common good, that is, when it is seen to be the only really effective means by which to remedy an abuse, or to avoid wasting the country's productive resources and insure their being systematically organized in the economic interests of the nation.[32]

But to make nationalization the normal rule for the public organization of the economy would be to reverse the order of things. The function of the public right is to defend the private right, not to absorb it. Economy is not by its nature an institution of the State any more

[31] Maritain, *Man and the State*, 208. Pius XII said that it was an obstacle to peace if individual people of one group engaged in ceaseless increase of production and standard of living without regard to others; resentment would be inevitable. Christmas Message, 1954, *Catholic Mind*, LIII (March, 1955), 183.

[32] Pius XII, Discourse to Italian Catholic Workers' Association, March 11, 1945, quoted in Powers, *Papal Pronouncements*, 85–86.

than any other branches of human activity; it is, on the contrary, the living product of the free initiative of individuals and of their freely formed associations.[33]

Messner in his discussion of circumstances which might justify some nationalization, uses the term "socialization" which he defines as "transfer of the means of production of an industry to the ownership of the state with the object of exercising a monopoly of business in the industry." [34] He finds that socialization might be necessary in certain indispensable industries if owing to social conflicts or backwardness in technology, their inefficiency becomes a serious threat to the country's economic development, and the satisfactory reorganization cannot be expected from private initiative. State production of essential goods might be justified if the necessary capital and private enterprise were lacking. He would see no grounds for socializing industries which produce other than basic consumer goods, or for nationalizing chain stores, cooperative societies, etc.

Never would he admit grounds for real socialization of land for cultivation by the state. "Political, economic, and social reasons make the task of the state rather to promote such a distribution of property in land that as many families as possible can obtain their livelihood by their own work on their own soil." [35] Socialization of minerals such as coal and ores might be legitimate if better utilization of deposits required improvement of costly equipment, which work the owners were unable to effect, or it might be justified as a means of preventing exploitation which would thwart future development of the national economy. A case would also exist for socialization of ores necessary for production of atomic energy. Enterprises for cultural aims he would say should be completely exempted from socialization: the press, publishing, education, charitable organizations. The government might main-

[33] Pius XII, Address to International Association of Catholic Employers, May 8, 1949, quoted in Powers, *Papal Pronouncements*, 86.
[34] Messner, *Social Ethics*, 924.
[35] *Ibid.*, 925–26.

tain its own publishing house provided it did not use unfair methods of competition.

Socialism

To be distinguished from the above-mentioned departures in limited nationalization, is the system of Socialism. In "Quadragesimo Anno," Pius XI noted that Socialism had split into two sections: the one, Communism, which is inhumane in seeking its objectives of class warfare and extermination of private ownership; the other, which has retained the name Socialism, has rejected violence, and either modified or abandoned class struggle and abolition of private property. The latter he describes in this way:

One might say that terrified by its own principles and by the conclusions drawn therefrom by Communism, Socialism inclines toward, and in a certain measure approaches, the truths which Christian tradition has always held sacred; for it cannot be denied that its demands at times come very near those that Christian reformers of society justly insist upon.[36]

In reply to his rhetorical question whether this form of Socialism cannot be "baptized" and accepted by Christians, he points out the fundamental errors which cause it to remain in permanent antagonism:

Socialism, if it remains truly Socialism, even after it has yielded to truth and justice on the points which we have mentioned, cannot be reconciled with the teachings of the Catholic Church because its concept of society itself is utterly foreign to Christian truth. . . . Socialism . . . wholly ignoring and indifferent to this sublime end of both man and society, affirms that human association has been instituted for the sake of material advantages alone.

Because of the fact that goods are produced more efficiently by a suitable division of labor than by the scattered efforts of individuals, So-

[36] Pius XI, "Quadragesimo Anno," May 15, 1931, quoted in Koenig, *Principles*, 432.

cialists infer that economic activity, only the material ends of which enter into their thinking, ought of necessity to be carried on socially. Because of this necessity they hold that men are obliged, with respect to the producing of goods, to surrender and subject themselves entirely to society. Indeed, possession of the greatest possible supply of things that serve the advantages of this life is considered of such great importance that the higher goods of man, liberty not excepted, must take a secondary place and even be sacrificed to the demands of the most efficient production of goods. This damage to human dignity, undergone in the "socialized" process of production, will be easily offset, they say, by the abundance of socially produced goods which will pour out in profusion to individuals to be used freely at their pleasure for comfort and cultural development. Society, therefore, as Socialism conceives it, can on the one hand neither exist nor be thought of without an obviously excessive use of force; on the other hand, it fosters a liberty no less false since there is no place in it for social authority, which rests not on temporal and material advantages but descends from God alone, the Creator and last end of all things.[37]

Other objections to Socialism are that it makes everyone the employee of the state, in which case a worker would not have the right to strike; it restricts the freedom to choose one's occupation; and it would make inevitable forced labor if some jobs were to remain unfilled.[38] Messner points out the fallacy that state control is coextensive with social progress. "This error arises from the assumption that the machinery of formal democracy must automatically operate in the direction of social progress if once the underprivileged classes, by gaining a majority in parliament, can obtain control of this machinery."[39] While indicating the dangers of materialism, naturalism, and secularism in Socialist thought, he makes allowance for the fact that individuals with the highest moral and religious impulsions may join Socialist parties to counteract these trends, so long as the "declared programs and actual

[37] *Ibid.*, 433–34.
[38] Higgins, *Man as Man*, 281–82.
[39] Messner, *Social Ethics*, 942.

policies are not in conflict with the principles of natural law."
There seems to be no apparent contradiction between the above
statement and Pius XI's conclusion, "No one can be at the same
time a good Catholic and a true Socialist." [40]

How To Deal With Communism

John Eppstein illustrates how Communism, like other heresies,
exaggerates "one fragment of the truth to the detriment of the
whole":

Certainly man needs material goods; certainly he is a producer or a
consumer, a member of one class or another, a member of one nation
or another. . . . But no one of these facts or functions explains, nor
do all of them together explain, the phenomenon of free will, reason
and conscience, or of love, loyalty, faith, the bonds of family and
friendship, the aspiration for ideals, the searching for a happiness
never fully attained in mortal life . . . . we are forced to conclude
that any system which denies or disregards the moral and intellectual
characteristics of man, or bases itself upon the material coefficient of
his nature while ignoring the spiritual, is a lie. A social structure built
upon a lie cannot endure.[41]

In consequence of the fact that one is assured nature created by
God will prevail and Marxism be doomed to frustration, the subject can be approached with a degree of optimism. However,
Pius XII would rouse one from complacency: "We again warn
Christians of the industrial age . . . against being satisfied with
an anti-Communism founded on the slogan and defense of a liberty
which is devoid of content." [42]

The encyclical, "Divini Redemptoris," of Pius XI points out the
fundamental errors in Communism. According to its dialectical

---

[40] Pius XI, "Quadragesimo Anno," in Koenig, *Principles*, 434.
[41] John Eppstein, "Commentary," *Code*, 7.
[42] Pius XII, Christmas Message, 1955, *Catholic Mind*, LIV (March, 1956),
166.

materialism all the world is "one reality, matter, the blind forces of which evolve into plant, animal and man." [43] This leaves no place for God or the immortal soul, no place for human dignity or moral restraints. The true origin and purpose of the state are ignored; a pseudo-ideal of justice, equality, and fraternity is introduced. Its atrocities are not the usual accompaniment of great revolutions; "they are the natural fruit of a system which lacks all inner restraint." His unequivocal conclusion reads: "Communism is intrinsically wrong, and no one who would save Christian civilization may collaborate with it in any undertaking whatsoever." [44]

According to Communism, the essential evil is private property and its two props, the state and religion. Marxists trace the origin of the state to crafty men who set aside property for their own exclusive use, and then sought to confirm it with laws and armed force. From this they judge that the state keeps the masses in subjection to the masters. They trace the origin of religion to man's fear of the elements, and interpret its present function as that of an opiate to make reasonable the suffering by the masses who hope for a future reward. These evils are to be swept away by violent revolution, for the Communist commonwealth is in peril until the change is accomplished throughout the world. By means of class warfare the masses are to destroy bourgeois society and root out religion in preparation for the dictatorship of the proletariat which will level all classes. Their morality reduces itself to this: "Any act is good which furthers the revolution; any act is bad which hinders it." In action, it results in a policy of ambiguity. "The expediency of the moment and the sacredness of the cause may dictate the immediate abandonment of one policy and one set of friends for the acceptance of an opposite policy

[43] Pius XI, "Divini Redemptoris," March 19, 1937, quoted in Koenig, *Principles*, 513–18.
[44] *Ibid.*, 530. Previous papal denunciations include: Pius IX, Encyclical, "Qui Pluribus," November 9, 1846, and confirmed in *Syllabus of Errors*, IV; Leo XIII, Encyclical, "Quod Apostolici Muneris," December 28, 1878.

and the throwing overboard of principles hitherto deemed essential." [45]

In the Communist conviction, human existence is coterminous with this life, so the predominant goal is a "realm of plenty." The doctrine is basically atheistic even though the party for opportunist reasons may profess tolerance toward religion in some areas, or put church organization to the service of their aims. According to the Communist conception of law, rights are dependent upon man's aptitude for a function in the social process.[46] Hence there is no criterion for judging when regimentation has violated man's human rights. In the name of extending human freedom, power is concentrated in the hands of a totalitarian state which knows no principle of subsidiarity. In the material paradise it presumes to create as a society of the future, Communism conceives that man will be so accustomed to place the common good first, that government will be unnecessary. With the disappearance of poverty, crime will evaporate.

Because this anti-social aggression which is Communism operates through internal penetration of the social structure of the intended victim by means of propaganda, class hatred and strikes, as well as by the menace of a powerful war machine, the total aggression must be met with a total answer spiritual as well as material in the fields of economics, industrial relations, education, diplomacy, and military strategy.[47] Since false ideas and perverted motives have gone into the making of Communism, and the world has not been exorcised of these elements, there must be caution that the same root causes of selfishness, materialism, secularism, and idolatry of popular sovereignty not be applied for the purpose of healing the world schism.

The question arises whether the free world should continue to deal with Russia through the United Nations. According to Catholic principles all states are inevitably part of the natural

[45] Higgins, *Man as Man*, 272–74.
[46] Messner, *Social Ethics*, 933–34.
[47] Eppstein, "Commentary," *Code*, 28.

society of nations, and the presumption is in favor of universality in the positive organization. Eppstein, however, views the present posture of Russia as a deliberate and formidable frustration of nature, since it holds a doctrine whch repudiates the principle of sociability and objective moral law. "The power which flouts these two fundamental principles can have no claim to membership in the international society of which it is the potential enemy. Its admission would mean (and in the actual history of the United Nations has meant) the weakening and frustration of the international institution." [48]

The *Code of International Ethics* seems to endorse the same attitude on Russia though it does not refer to the country by name:

To give such a government a privileged position in the community of nations and to allow it, by the use of the veto, to block any collective action of the society, is to condemn the latter to incurable paralysis. Thus neither reason nor practical experience allows us to envisage the possibility of making the society of nations, at the start, absolutely universal . . . . as long as powerful anti-social forces are at their baneful work, the surest way to prevent aggression and war is to establish a system of effective solidarity among the greatest possible number of States who do respect the essential obligations of international society.[49]

It adds that every effort should be made to achieve the Christian ideal of universality as soon as possible, however. The proposal above does not mean an offensive against the transgressing government whose principles make it unfit for international collaboration, "for war will always remain the last and least desirable means of fighting ideas. Nor need it prevent economic and social relations with such a state and its subjects."

To those who argue that coercive police action which is of a defensive nature should have no application in lands already controlled by the antisocial power, Eppstein replies that the position

[48] *Ibid.*, 25.
[49] Eppstein (ed.), *Code*, 171.

is unmoral since justice is the same the world over.[50] If force is applied to put an end to the violation of fundamental rights and liberties, it is not a preventive war; it is a defensive police action. But at this point the virtue of prudence must prevail because neither rebellion nor armed intervention is justified if there is not reasonable prospect of success and if the good to be accomplished will not outweigh the harm accompanying it. If a resistance movement is to be initiated or encouraged, there must be reasonable assurance that it can achieve its purpose without causing great reprisals. ". . . unless it is judged to be an essential contribution to the campaign of the international society against the oppressor, and unless society can furnish prompt and powerful aid to the rising, it would be contrary both to charity and to justice to initiate or stimulate it." [51]

The case of Hungary comes to mind in relationship to intervention behind the Iron Curtain. While not giving an absolute affirmative to bold action, Pope Pius XII made this statement:

Can the world possibly lose interest in these their brothers, and abandon them to a degrading servitude? Surely the conscience of Christendom cannot shake off the moral obligation of trying every lawful means of reasserting their human dignity and of restoring their freedom . . . . one must listen to the voice of conscience, of civilization, of brotherhood; one must listen to the voice of God Himself, . . . postponing, even at the cost of great sacrifice, the solution of every other problem and every particular interest in order to solve the elementary and fundamental problem of millions of human lives reduced to slavery.

Perhaps it will come to pass—and this We desire with all Our heart —that the solid ranks of the nations that sincerely love peace and liberty will suffice to bring to a more merciful frame of mind those who withdraw themselves from the most elementary laws of human intercourse and for this reason deprive themselves of all right to speak in the name of humanity, of justice, and of peace. Their own peoples will be the first to find it impossible to remain oblivious of the need for returning

[50] Eppstein, "Commentary," *Code*, 31.
[51] *Ibid.*, 32.

to form a part of the human family, in order to enjoy its honor and its privileges.[52]

Perhaps in the area of negotiation with Russia, the words of Pius XII about toleration of objective error in the international community may have some application. Whereas in conscience one has an obligation to what is objectively true and good, the practical solution may not lie in positive repression. He cited God's own way of choosing *non impedire* when it would be possible and easy for Him to repress moral deviation. The parable of the cockle supports the contention.

Reality shows that error and sin are in the world in great measure. God reprobates them, but He permits them to exist. Hence the affirmation: religious and moral error must always be impeded, when it is possible, because toleration of them is in itself immoral, is not valid absolutely and unconditionally. . . . The duty of repressing moral and religious error cannot therefore be an ultimate norm of action. It must be subordinate to higher and more general norms, which in some circumstances permit, and even perhaps seem to indicate as the better policy, toleration of error in order to promote a greater good. . . . In his decision he will permit himself to be guided by weighing the dangerous consequences which stem from toleration, against those from which the community of nations will be spared if the formula of toleration be accepted; moreover, he will be guided by the good which according to a wise prognosis can be derived from toleration for the international community as such, and indirectly for the member state.[53]

The Pontiff in speaking of coexistence, characterized the two parties as dreading war yet putting all their "trust in war as if it were the only expedient for subsistence and the only means of regulating international relations."[54] The present coexistence in

[52] Pius XII, Radio Address to the World, November 10, 1956, printed in *The Pope Speaks*, III (Spring, 1957), 357.

[53] Pius XII, Discourse to Fifth Convention of Italian Jurists, December 6, 1953, printed in *Catholic Mind*, LII (April, 1954), 248.

[54] Pius XII, Christmas Message, 1954 (delayed by his illness, released to press January 3, 1955), printed in *Catholic Mind*, LIII (March, 1955), 180, 182.

fear "will either raise itself to a coexistence in fear of God, and thence to a truly peaceful living-together, inspired and protected by the Divine moral order; or else it will shrivel more and more into a frozen paralysis of international life." He suggested that there is well-founded hope that a bridge of peace may yet be built and the common bond re-established, but because the bridge must be of a spiritual nature, he declared unfit for the task skeptics and cynics who in their disguised materialism reduce the highest truths to physical reactions, and dismiss them as mere ideologies. Pius XII's optimism runs thus:

Now a bridge cannot be built in truth between these two separate worlds unless it be founded on the human beings living in one and the other of these worlds, and not on their governments and social systems. This is so because, while one of the two parties still strives in large measure whether consciously or unconsciously, to preserve the natural law, the system prevailing in the other has completely abandoned this basis. . . .

In both camps, there are millions in whom the imprint of Christ is preserved in a more or less active degree: they, too, no less than faithful and fervent believers, should be called upon to collaborate toward a renewed basis of unity for the human race.[55]

He rallied those in the free world who stand for truth and love to recover from excess timidity, and especially their statesmen to assume greater confidence.

The Duty of Intervention

According to Catholic thought, there is no place in the philosophy of international law for the principle of strict nonintervention.[56] The attainment of true international order requires the

[55] *Ibid.*, 186–87.
[56] Rommen, *The State*, 639. Pope Pius IX condemned the principle of nonintervention in the *Syllabus of Errors*, Section VII, No. 62. St. Ambrose in *De Officiis* said, "He who does not ward off an injury done to his fellow,

co-operative effort of individual states; the preservation of a state's existence and the defense of its rights are matters of solidary responsibility in guaranteeing that order. The right of intervention is derived from Natural Law, rather than from positive law.

The richer a nation is in population and in natural resources, the less it can retire from the duty of upholding the international order even by intervention, provided that the ways and means of actual intervention are sound policy under given circumstances. Strict adherence to the principle of nonintervention puts the principle of might makes right first in international life. . . . If by intervention the common good of the intervening state is gravely imperiled, this state has no duty to intervene. For the restoration of peace and restitution for the injury are the purpose of war. If the material means are insufficient, even a just cause does not afford either right or duty of intervention. . . . Wealth and its social effect, power, bring with them in any kind of human community a higher responsibility for the preservation of the just order in this community. In fact, the inequality in wealth and the consequent increase in power of the richer nations is justifiable only by assuming higher and more comprehensive responsibilities.[57]

Messner enumerates the following as occasions for intervention: another state's backing of a party in order to overthrow the constitutional government, preparation for aggressive action on the part of a state which threatens the external security of another, interference by a state with international regulations as in drug traffic or white slave trade, interference with the general interests of humanity as with suppression of religious or other human freedoms, or grave injustice toward minorities.[58] When the *Code of International Ethics* gives as just motives of intervention the securing of respect for the laws of nations and the defending of the rights of God, of the human personality, and of humanity against barbarism, it notes that this category of action should be

if he has the power to do so, is as much at fault as he who has perpetrated the injury." Quoted in Eppstein (ed.), *Code*, 20.

[57] *Ibid.*, 639, 662.

[58] Messner, *Social Ethics*, 404–05. Similar points are given in Eppstein (ed.), *Code*, 65–66.

effected on the authority of the organized community of nations.[59]
Because international peace is affected, other states than those
directly suffering from another's conduct, are entitled to intervene
for the sake of violated rights. Intervention does not always mean
war; it can be accomplished by diplomatic action, by insistence
upon political conditions in loan and trade agreements, by economic blockade, etc. War may be resorted to only when other
methods have failed, and only for a very grave motive.

The *Code* centers attention upon attempts to destroy social
cohesion in a state and thus reduce it to servitude without the
use of force, as with a fifth column, disruptive propaganda, and
class warfare. In this case, the other states have a right to aid
the victim nation; diplomatic and economic support might be
sufficient to bolster their resistance. Active resistance would be
a strict duty only when it is clear that that is the "only sure way
to fend off the danger which the success of the aggressor State
would bring to the international community as a whole." [60] If
the subversion causes imminent danger for neighboring peoples,
then it is for them a question of public safety. In the present unorganized international society, except in a case of positive duty,
a nation may proclaim neutrality. When no treaty of assistance
exists and when the intervention springs from charity, the state
must first protect the rights of its own members which is its
essential purpose. "Without doubt, the principle of solidarity can
make it a duty for a nation to make sacrifices on behalf of the
general welfare; but it does not require it to immolate its own
interests." [61]

All that has been said of the duty of intervention does not
preclude a nonintervention agreement between the other states,
"which may be too much divided among themselves in order to
judge the conflict properly, so that the internal troubles of a
nation may not become the cause of a general war." [62]

[59] Eppstein (ed.), *Code*, 66.
[60] *Ibid.*, 68–69.
[61] *Ibid.*, 67.
[62] *Ibid.*, 67–68.

The Morality of War and Its Practices

From the standpoint of Natural Law and Christian ethics, war is not intrinsically unjust; however, a practical instrument of international arbitration and conciliation could make war superfluous. In Christian tradition there was no blanket condemnation of military service by St. Ambrose, St. Augustine, St. Bernard, etc.[63] Since the aim of war is peace with justice, action may be directed against an unjust *status quo*. But a spirit of vengeance is not justified; a just belligerent must still consider his enemies as creatures made to the image of God, and entitled because of this fact, to respect and love.

The *Code* qualifies the above statements still more. Christian morality does not regard war as a normal institution of international life; it is evil but not absolutely so, for there are rare circumstances which justify it. By the evils it inflicts on the territory where it is waged, by the confusion and setbacks to morality and civilization, it is always a terrible calamity and cannot be a normal means of settling disputes.[64] But even in a well organized international society, recourse to arms might be the only means to overcome a recalcitrant state. The deadliness of modern war should be a factor in determining the lawfulness of recourse to arms since the expected advantage must outweigh the inevitable evil results. A certain form of war might be proscribed, but war as such might not be denied as by certain intransigent pacifists. "Appeasement" as defined in the late 1930's could hardly be called wise, since it did not protect the order, but rather safeguarded the individual interests of the appeasing nations while placing a premium on aggression outside that area.

It is not possible that a cause of war be just and at the same

---

[63] Rommen, *The State*, 654, citing Ambrose, *De Officiis*, I, 1, ch. 40; Augustine, *Epistolae ad Bonifacium*, 205 & 207; Bernard, *Sermo ad Milites*, ch. 3.

[64] Eppstein (ed.), *Code*, 113–14.

time be opposed to the common good.[65] The *Code* enumerates these conditions for a just war: 1) It must be declared by legitimate authority, in behalf of the general interest of the community, not for private ends or a class interest. 2) There must be grave and just cause proportioned to the evils it brings about. 3) It must be undertaken after all peaceful solutions have been exhausted. 4) There must be serious chance of success. 5) It must be carried out with right intention.[66] Since contradictory claims of two belligerents cannot be equally right, both cannot at the same time have just cause for war objectively speaking, though subjectively each may believe it possesses just cause. In doubtful cases of right, the settlement should be made by arbitration and conciliation. If the side with just cause refuses sincere and reasonable reparation, its cause becomes unjust. Sometimes the price which the whole of humanity must pay, makes it a duty in charity to forego just reparation rather than expose the whole world to catastrophe. It may happen that a war is objectively unjust on both sides.

In spite of the fact that one of the above conditions is reasonable hope of success in war, the *Code* states:

. . . a higher obligation—that of respecting one's plighted word, of defending the higher values of religion and civilization, and so forth —may sometimes lead to choosing an heroic defeat instead of an inglorious capitulation. The nations which have been martyrs to their duty render a supreme testimony to right which echoes throughout the centuries and keeps humanity faithful to the cult of honour and justice.[67]

Because the doctrine of preventive war against a possible aggressor gives occasion of pretext to ambitious nations, its use must be closely restricted:

Only a very real and imminent menace—such as a systematically aggressive policy, an unusual concentration of troops, and the like, can

[65] Rommen, *The State*, 659.
[66] Eppstein (ed.), *Code*, 117–18.
[67] *Ibid.*, 123.

authorize a State which considers it is menaced thereby, to demand the cessation of these suspicious activities, and, in case of refusal, to impose it by force.[68]

Whereas a war of legitimate self-defense is allowable, no state has a right to punish another state, "because punishment is the prerogative of a superior." [69]

Eppstein condemns the notion that states possess the right of war, *per se*, as a sovereign attribute, for this would deny to the international authority the curtailing of violence. "No State could survive if its individual subjects or families or local communities retained, in law, the right to use armed force, a right which they agreed to limit or delegate only by a revocable contract." [70]

As to the obligation of individuals with regard to the justice of a war, Higgins summarizes it thus:

Statesmen, legislators, volunteers for a foreign army must be *morally certain* of the justice of their acts. When the country declares war, the ordinary man may give it the benefit of any doubt, because full information is not available to him, and because his country is most seriously endangered by the mere fact of war.[71]

The legal order is not suspended in time of war nor does man cease to be a rational being; hence the demands of natural justice place limitations upon warring nations. The fundamental principle is that no act is justified except as a defense against aggression. Messner epitomizes the demands of justice quite well:

The opening of hostilities should be preceded by a declaration of war, whether by the recalling of envoys or by the delivery of an ultimatum, and the time should be stated from which a state of war exists. The reason is not only that the population must be given an opportunity to forestall the serious legal consequences entailed in war, but also that provision must be made for the protection of the population in the prospective theaters of war. The lives of the non-combatant popula-

---

[68] *Ibid.*, 121–22.
[69] Higgins, *Man as Man*, 565–66.
[70] Eppstein (ed.), *Code*, 13.
[71] Higgins, *Man as Man*, 567–68.

tion remains inviolable. . . . Compulsory transfer and deportation of workers from enemy territory and their forced employment in war production are unlawful because they are thereby compelled to support the war effort against their own country.

Since war is a conflict between states, the military authorities may, on entering enemy territory, possess themselves of enemy property, but over the private property of citizens in the occupied territory they have only so much right as the citizens' own state possesses, namely, such as derived from its defensive function in war, as, for instance, that of requisitioning billets or food not otherwise obtainable . . . . enemy wounded must receive the same care as one's own wounded; prisoners must be given the same scale of rations as one's own soldiers, and they may be employed on civilian work for pay, but never military operations. . . . Since intrinsically immoral acts are never justified, they are not justified in war. . . . Falsehood remains falsehood even in war, and nothing can justify the orgies of lies in which propaganda indulges in modern war.[72]

Messner opposes the opinion that total war alters the principles regarding noncombatants; those who provide means of subsistence in war are not to be numbered among the combatants. To those who would contend that since war involves such intolerable evil, any method of ending it is justified, he replies that methods such as a hunger blockade, the bombing of towns, the employment of poison gas, bacterial warfare, and atomic bombs can be justified only if the aggressor uses them and "it is certain no other means exist of repelling the aggressor who thus threatens a state's existence." [73]

Eppstein, commenting on the use of armed force, says:

Evidently the wholesale massacre of the very human beings whom the world society intends to liberate defeats the whole moral purpose of its coercive action. No lesson of the Second World War is more disturbing than the progressive sacrifice of the end of war to the means of war which, under the impulsion of demagogy, characterized the

[72] Messner, *Social Ethics*, 425–27.
[73] *Ibid.*, 426.

policies and military methods of the victors in its latter stages. . . . They must never cease to remember that "war is waged that peace may be attained; therefore, even while warring you must be a peacemaker, that by defeating those against whom you are fighting you may bring them back to the values of peace." . . . so much violence and such weapons may be used as are really necessary to victory; the decision largely depends upon the actual military strength of the antisocial adversary and the implements of destruction which he employs.[74]

The *Code* admits that there is disagreement on the subject of atomic warfare, but concludes that the atom bomb may never be used against elements of the population who have only a remote connection with the war, directly willing that this be a means of breaking the resistance of the enemy. As a secondary effect, inevitably bound up with a legitimate end, their lives might be lost. "There must be a reasonable proportion between the lawful end sought by the belligerent and the harm to innocent people which results from it against his direct will." [75]

Regarding the conditions which a just victor has a right to dictate to an enemy who has surrendered unconditionally, the *Code* uses Suarez's analysis: restitution of goods, reimbursement for expenses incurred owing to the injustice, some sanction for the fault committed, and guarantee for the conservation of peace.[76] But since the sums involved in modern wars are so astronomic, and because removals of such sums would cause an economic upheaval, the reparation point must be modified for "charity does not allow one to require from a State, however culpable, more than it can normally pay." And with reference to sanctions, "Considerations relating to the common good will sometimes make it wiser for the just victor to mitigate his exercise of the right of vindictive justice, or even to forego it altogether." [77]

[74] Eppstein, "Commentary," *Code,* 29. Inner quote is from Augustine, *Epistola ad Bonifacium,* 189, VI.

[75] Eppstein (ed.), *Code,* 133–34.

[76] *Ibid.,* 142–43, citing Suarez, *De tripl. virt. Theol.,* T.III, disp. XIII, sect. VII, No. 5.

[77] *Ibid.,* 143, 145. Pius XI spoke of this in "Quando del Principio," June 24, 1923; in Koenig, *Principles,* 360.

Messner attacks reparations in the form of labor service in the victor's country, since technology makes possible the production of building material in the areas of destruction with the use of volunteer labor. Deportations with the splitting up of families could lead to relapse into the practice of enslaving portions of the defeated population.[78]

Since aggressive war as a means of politics is to be condemned, the trial of war criminals has justification. Messner lists these requirements: 1) The court should consist of members of strictly neutral nations, and not of any nations which were a party to the conflict. 2) The court should pass judgment on any aggressive action of any state within the same period. 3) Anyone who abetted these actions should be tried for complicity.[79] Different is the category of those who commit crimes against existing international or municipal laws by cruelties, violations of property rights, murder, or looting. These war criminals should be tried according to the laws of the countries in which the deeds were committed, but crimes on both sides must be brought equally.

While admitting that there is a strong opinion to the contrary, Higgins says of the trials at Nurenberg and elsewhere after World War II:

First, the Natural Law does not grant an equal authority over another equal without the latter's consent. Second, no one, individual or nation, is a good judge in his own case. As both accuser and judge, the victor lacks the disinterested calm necessary to hold impartially the scales of justice between himself and a fellow disputant. . . . Third, the victor is too prone to exceed the due measure of natural vindictive justice: the vanquished will consider themselves outraged and when opportunity serves, will strike back for revenge. . . . The order of daily life forbids the individual to punish his assailants and compels him to seek redress from visible constituted authority. The nations should follow a similar procedure.[80]

[78] Messner, *Social Ethics*, 652.
[79] *Ibid.*, 447.
[80] Higgins, *Man as Man*, 577–78.

Disarmament

As Pope Pius XII stated in 1939, any peace settlement which does not provide for "mutually agreed, organic and progressive disarmament, spiritual as well as material," and which does not ensure effective implementation, will be lacking in coherence.[81] In 1941 when he spoke against excessive armament, he recommended the wisdom of "reducing the manufacture and storing of offensive weapons to a limit of sufficiency and proportion."[82] But in 1943, he gave assurance that the achievement of such a peace "would not imply in any way the abandonment of necessary guarantees and sanctions in the event of any attempt to use force against right."[83] He recognizes that the request for mutual disarmament "without moral reconstruction and some kind of institution to inforce international law" would be disastrous.

The type of reciprocal limitation of armaments and acceptance of arbitration as a substitute for armies, which Pope Benedict XV had suggested in his message of August 1, 1917, requires on the part of nations sincere adherence to fundamental principles of international sociability and morality. All states claim that they cherish no aggressive aims, that their armament is purely defensive, but the only ones which may legitimately justify their increased armaments "are those which are prepared to collaborate, without hesitation or reservation in the organization of arbitration, collective security, and disarmament."[84] In his Christmas Message when Pius XII urged that the United Nations assume effective control of armaments, he favored inspection by means of aerial observation, since equipment had been perfected to such an extent as to make camouflage difficult.[85]

[81] Pius XII, Christmas Message, 1939, in Koenig, *Principles*, 637.
[82] *Id.*, Christmas Message, 1941, in Koenig, *Principles*, 758.
[83] *Id.*, Christmas Message, 1943, *Catholic Mind*, XLII (February, 1944), 75–76.
[84] Eppstein (ed.), *Code*, 61.
[85] Pius XII, Christmas Message, 1956, *The Pope Speaks*, III (Spring, 1957), 345.

Until the hoped-for outlawing of the atomic bomb by international convention, and until there is sufficient assurance the requirements will be observed, a state is not denied the right to stock atomic weapons for purely defensive purposes. Fear of immediate reprisal would probably deter states from using them. Higgins notes that there can be no moral obligation for man to cease delving into the secrets of nature lest the discoveries be misused. "Because more and more stupendous forms of violence may be discovered, the moral obligation of being master of that violence grows apace." [86] Whereas Pius XII indicated that an obligation in conscience devolves upon nations and leaders to adopt the sum total of these three measures—renunciation of experiment with and use of atomic weapons, as well as general control of armaments—he made clear that if only the renunciation of experimentation were put into effect, there would be sufficient reason to doubt the sincere desire of those parties to effect the other two conventions. [87]

Neutrality

The *Code of International Ethics* shows the remarkable evolution of the doctrine of neutrality. A brief sketch of the reasoning seems apropos so that one may understand how variously it could be applied in particular eras and circumstances. Prior to the eighteenth century, harmless transit could be claimed by all members of the community of nations so long as they pursued honest ends. But since this led to reprisals upon the neutral, the interpretation which influenced moralists following Augustine, had to be abandoned. The idea of war as a defensive action in the service of right has been changed by some theorists of the law of nations to imply merely a trial of strength. In such circumstances "innocent transit" has no application, so the modern theory of absolute immunity for neutral territory has become the corollary.

[86] Higgins, *Man as Man*, 572.
[87] Pius XII, Christmas Message, 1955, *Catholic Mind*, LIII (March, 1955), 172.

However, the legitimacy of neutrality is dependent upon the condition of international society. When the latter is still unorganized a neutral may refuse passage even to a just belligerent, but in an organized society of nations, the repressive action of all the members is to be mobilized against the one who offends justice.[88] In these circumstances, there might still be a country which is formally accorded permanent neutrality by the society of states. The United Nations Charter is logical in requiring that all contribute to collective action including the right of passage (Art. 43, I). Eppstein, applying the principles to the current circumstances, says that until the organized society of nations becomes as effective reality demonstrating its capacity in this regard, it is possible for a state to assert neutrality should two states equally in the wrong and equally intemperate go to war.[89]

The Realism of Peace

To say that war is bound up with the nature of the state itself is to say that the forces making for war operate independently of the human will. Actually they operate through man's will in the agency of the state, so the will is ultimately called upon to govern the irrational elements.[90] Rommen attacks the theories of inevitable struggle between races, between classes, between the "souls of nations," all of which reduce life to an uncontrollable force and condemn history to a funeral procession of states, thus rendering the whole incomprehensible and enigmatic.[91] These theories do not trace war to human imperfection or to a low degree of international morality; they attribute war to life force under which arrangement states live as wolf to one another.

[88] Eppstein (ed.), *Code*, 161–62.
[89] Eppstein, "Commentary," *Code*, 16–17.
[90] Messner, *Social Ethics*, 651. Pius XII declared absurd the doctrine that war is the natural outcome of irreconcilable disputes between two countries. Christmas Message, 1954, *Catholic Mind*, LIII (March, 1955), 181.
[91] Rommen, *The State*, 643.

Gonella reflects that because there are systematic violations of moral laws, one should not consider this to be a denial of their intrinsic validity; the latter is independent of their being respected or not.[92] The infractions should provide incentive for effort that good intentions manifested by nations in time of peace, not become a dead letter when the challenge arises. Pius XII traced the prevailing pessimism to the "deep spiritual crisis which has overthrown the sound principles of private and public morality."

. . . one must not forget the essential insufficiency and weakness of every principle of social life which rests upon a purely human foundation, is inspired by merely earthly motives, and relies for its force on the sanction of a purely external authority. Where the dependence of human right upon the Divine is denied, where appeal is made only to some insecure idea of a merely human authority, and an autonomy is claimed which rests only upon a utilitarian morality, there human law itself justly forfeits in its more weighty application the essential condition for its acknowledgment and also for its demand of sacrifices.[93]

In contrast to the proposition that war is inevitable, the *Code* maintains that peace is the normal state of humanity since it "corresponds at once to the most pressing demands of human nature and to the law of Christ our Savior, Who Himself became our peace." [94] The definition of peace derived from St. Augustine and St. Thomas states that it is "the tranquility, which tranquility consists in all the appetitive movements in one man being set at rest together." [95] Perhaps some explanation for the lack of this harmony in the world is to be found in Pope Benedict XV's words, 1914:

It generally happens to States as it happened to our first parent after his failure in his duty to God. As in him, scarcely had the will been rebel to God when the passions broke loose and rebelled against the will;

[92] Gonella, *A World to Reconstruct*, 167.
[93] Pius XII, "Summi Pontificatus," October 20, 1939 (Washington: National Catholic Welfare Conference, 1939), 23.
[94] Eppstein (ed.), *Code*, 106.
[95] Thomas Aquinas, *Summa Theol.*, II^a–II^{ae}, q. 29, a. 1, ad. 1.

so too whenever those who have the rule over peoples disdain the authority of God, the peoples in their turn are prompt to hold lightly the authority of man.[96]

He finds it not surprising that men seize what belongs to others so long as it is falsely propounded that true happiness is to be found in the riches, honors, and pleasures of this life. The chief cure would be to make faith in the supernatural prevail again—with the increase of desire and hope of what is eternal, the feverish pursuit of earthly vanities would cease.

Pius XI pointed to the above same error which prevents lasting peace. Material things, being limited, cannot satisfy all, even were no one to be greedy; the greater the number, the smaller the share. But with spiritual treasures, "the more widely they are shared, the more they abound and give fruit to the advantage of each and all."[97] In "Caritate Christi Compulsi," Pius XI showed prayer and penance to be practical and realistic methods of effecting peace.[98] Prayer counteracts greed because the man who prays, meditates upon and desires the goods of heaven. "Men who in every nation pray to the same God for peace on earth cannot be at the same time bearers of discord among peoples." Penance strikes at the root of all evil, attachment to material wealth and to wanton pleasures. By means of voluntary sacrifice, the Christian subdues the passions which tend to make him violate the moral order.

Pius XII explained that peace for this generation is not a man made dream:

. . . the commandment of peace is a matter of Divine Law. Its purpose is the protection of the goods of humanity, inasmuch as they are gifts of the Creator. . . . The Christian will for peace comes from God. . . . He created the world to be an abode of peace. . . . The genuine

[96] Benedict XV, Encyclical, "Ad Beatissimi," November 1, 1914, in Koenig, *Principles,* 135.

[97] Pius XI, "Benedetto il Natale," December 24, 1930, in Koenig, *Principles,* 395.

[98] *Id.*, Encyclical, "Caritate Christi Compulsi," May 3, 1932, in Koenig, *Principles,* 462–65.

Christian will for peace means strength, not weakness or weary resignation.[99]

Pius XII based the realism of peace upon the very nature of Christ's mission:

Prince and founder of peace, such is the character of the Saviour and Redeemer of the whole human race. His sublime divine mission is to establish peace between each man and God, between men themselves and between peoples. Poor short-sighted men, whose little field of vision does not go beyond the possibilities of the present hour, beyond statistics of military and economic potential. How can they form the slightest idea of the worth and importance of religion's authority for the solution of the peace problem? Superficial minds, unable to see in all their reality and fullness the value and the creative power of Christianity, how can they help being skeptical and disdainful of the power of the Church for peace? [100]

Pius XI, who set as the goal of his pontifical work the realization of the peace of Christ, spoke of the latter as that which penetrates the souls of men, uniting, healing, and reopening their hearts.[101] Peace is not a hard, inflexible justice, but rather it is compounded almost equally of charity. Thomas Aquinas discovered in Christ's work of redemption the essence of this belief that lasting peace is more a matter of love, for justice merely does away with the injury or the obstacles. Like Pius XII, Pius XI has said:

Such a peace was acquired for us and the whole world by Jesus Christ. . . . He is our Peace, for it was He who satisfied completely divine justice by His death on the Cross, destroying thus in His own flesh all enmities toward others and making peace and reconciliation with God possible for mankind. . . . This Peace of Christ, however, surpasses all human understanding . . . and for this very reason, dominates our sinful passions and renders such evils as division, strife, and

[99] Pius XII, Christmas Message, 1948, *Catholic Mind*, XLVII (March, 1949), 183–85.

[100] *Id.*, Christmas Message, 1951, *Catholic Mind*, L (April, 1952), 250–51.

[101] Pius XI, Encyclical, "Ubi Arcano Dei," December 23, 1922, in Koenig, *Principles*, 342–44.

discord, which result solely from the unrestrained desire for earthly possessions, impossible. If the desire for worldly possessions were kept within bounds and the place of honor in our affections given to the things of the spirit, which place undoubtedly they deserve, the Peace of Christ would follow immediately, to which would be joined in a natural and happy union, as it were, a higher regard for the value and dignity of human life.[102]

To those who would reduce the winning of peace solely to a technological and economic operation, Pius XII replied that no materialism was ever an apt means to establish peace, because peace is above all "a question of spiritual unity and of moral disposi- tions." [103] Commenting upon the current emphasis on technology, he approved its proper use, since the search for the forces of nature should be at the same time the discovery of the greatness, the wisdom, and the harmony of God. Its misuse he termed as the "technological spirit" which places such absolute confidence in its possibilities as to be confounded with the infinite itself. He pointed out the fundamental falsehood in this distorted vision of the world:

The seemingly boundless panorama unfolded before the eyes of modern man, however extensive it may be, remains but a partial projection of life on reality, only expressing its relations with matter. . . . The mind which has let itself be led astray by a concept of life outlined by the "technological spirit" . . . only recognizes and reckons real what can be expressed in mathematical formulas and utilitarian calculations. . . . It is evident that whoever adopts the method of technology as the sole way of seeking truth must give up any idea of penetrating the profound realities of organic life, and even more so those of the spiritual life, the living realities of the individual person and of human society, because they cannot be analyzed into quantitative relationships. . . . The materialistic idea of life threatens to become the rule of conduct of certain busy peace agents, and the mainspring of their pacifist policy. They think that the solution lies in bringing material prosperity to all

[102] *Ibid.*, 343–44.
[103] Pius XII, Christmas Message, 1953, *Catholic Mind*, LII (March, 1954), 180–81.

nations through constant increase in productivity and in the standard of living.[104]

Certainly the Pope did not discredit efforts along the line of the latter. On the contrary, he counseled, "The present state of affairs will not improve unless all nations recognize the common spiritual and moral ends of humanity . . . unless they mutually agree to oppose the cause of division reigning among them in the discrepancy of the standard of living and of productivity." [105]

In distinguishing peace from that pacifism which is a cowardly state of mind, Dr. Neill marks that war is easier on man than peace. War is like a violent fit of temper in the individual; peace demands self-control.[106] Rommen discusses four forms of pacifism, none of which represents the Catholic view.[107] Economic pacifism stresses that economic liberty and self-interest will bring social harmony, making war superfluous since it never pays. Humanitarian pacifism, supported by some scholars and artists, envisages an international fraternity of servants of the True, the Good, and the Beautiful. Socialists are often pacifists who would premise peace upon a proletarian classless society, which has eliminated states as the instruments of capitalist exploitation. Radical religious pacifism holds that war is unjust for a Christian. Rommen observes that most of these forms endorse the idea of evolutionary progress which will produce a stateless society of mankind, the source of war being traced to the plurality of states. Radical pacifism, religious and humanitarian, scarcely grasps the real problems of war, since it neglects the matter of political philosophy.

In "Summi Pontificatus," Pius XII discouraged the slogan, "Peace through Victory."

To hope for a decisive change exclusively from the shock of war and its final issue is idle, as experience shows. The hour of victory is an

[104] *Ibid.*, 176–80.
[105] *Ibid.*, 181.
[106] Neill, *Weapons*, 25.
[107] Rommen, *The State*, 643–49.

hour of external triumph for the party to whom victory falls, but it is in equal measure the hour of temptation.[108]

The governing principles of a just peace could be distilled from the Pope's four Christmas allocutions, 1939–42. E. A. Conway, S.J., has organized the points under the headings: political, economic, social, and moral. A presentation of his arrangement might prove fruitful: [109]

The six political points advanced by Pius XII are:

1) Assurance for all nations, great and small, powerful or weak, of their right to independence.
2) Respect by all governments of the rights of all racial and religious minorities within their territories.
3) Repudiation of power politics, which generates wars by arousing fears, distrust, and suspicion among nations.
4) Suppression of that cold national egoism, which, in a state's relation with its neighbors, shows itself in narrow nationalism, and, in its relations with its own citizens, in State absolutism.
5) Establishment of permanent international institutions which shall guarantee the fulfillment of the peace conditions, and which shall be empowered to revise them when and if necessary.
6) Sincere and honest, mutually agreed upon, progressive disarmament and security for the effective implementing of such an agreement.

The one economic point is "progressive international collaboration to enable every country to ensure a proper standard of living for its citizens, especially by putting an end to the hoarding of economic resources and materials destined for the use of all."

The four social points are:

1) The guarantee by every government of the fundamental rights of the human person, such as, among others, the right to work, to worship, to marry, freely to choose one's state in life.

[108] Pius XII, "Summi Pontificatus," October 20, 1939 (NCWC publication), 32–33.
[109] E. A. Conway, S.J., "Summary of Papal Program for Peace," address delivered at the Cathedral in Denver, April 11, 1943, reported in *Denver Catholic Register*, April 15, 1943, and reprinted in James W. Naughton, S.J., *Pius XII on World Problems* (New York: America Press, 1943), 56–58.

2) Achievement of social unity through the collaboration of the nations' various classes and groups in the interest of the common good.
3) Restoration of the integrity and vitality of the family as the basic unit of society.
4) Practical recognition of the dignity of work, and of the rights of labor as expounded in the social encyclicals of the recent Popes, with special reference to the right to a living wage, and to the widest possible diffusion of private property.

The three moral points are:

1) Victory over hatred now, lest it dictate in the future a vengeful peace.
2) Universal recognition of an order of rights and obligations, called the juridic order, which imposes itself upon men and nations, and which is and must remain entirely independent of human whim, expediency or pressure of any kind. Repudiation, therefore, of the pernicious principles that utility is the basis of law, and that might makes right, must be secured.
3) Development of . . . "a sense of deep responsibility, which measures all human statutes according to the law of God, a hunger and thirst after justice and universal love which is the compendium and most universal expression of the Christian ideal."

The role of the Catholic Church in the quest for peace is forceably stated by Pope Pius XI:

There exists an institution able to safeguard the sanctity of the law of nations. This institution is a part of every nation; at the same time it is above all nations. She enjoys, too, the highest authority, the fullness of the teaching power of the Apostles. . . . Because the Church is by divine institution the sole depository and interpreter of the ideals and teachings of Christ, she alone possesses in any complete and true sense the power effectively to combat the materialistic philosophy, which has already done and still threatens such tremendous harm to the home and to the State. . . . If the teachings of the Church could only penetrate, in some such manner as We have described, the inner recesses of the consciences of mankind, be they rulers or be they subjects, all eventually would be so apprised of their personal and civic duties and their mutual responsibilities that in a short time Christ would be all, and in all.[110]

That same Pontiff proposes that once men in public and private life recognize that Christ is King, the human authority of rulers will be invested with a religious significance, and men will be more conscious of the link which binds them together with all nations, under the sway of the Kingdom of Christ.[111]

The real source of unity among mankind is something infinitely more sublime than the humanitarian approach to brotherhood. The meaning of the mystical body of Christ has dawned upon man with its blinding import only in the twentieth century. Pius XII explained this doctrine in his masterful encyclical; he distinguished this body of Christ from His physical Body, and from a merely moral or physical body in the natural order:

In a natural body the principle of unity so unites the parts that each lacks its own individual subsistence; on the contrary in the Mystical Body that mutual union, though intrinsic, links the members by a bond which leaves to each intact his own personality. . . . In the moral body, the principle of union is nothing more than the common end, and the common cooperation of all under authority for the attainment of that end; whereas in the Mystical Body, of which we are speaking, this collaboration is supplemented by a distinct internal principle, which exists effectively in the whole and in each of its parts, and whose excellence is such, that of itself it is vastly superior to whatever bonds may be found in a physical or moral body. . . . Essentially it is something infinite; uncreated: the Spirit of God. . . . What lifts the society of Christians far, far above the whole natural order is the Spirit of our Redeemer who until the end of time penetrates every part of the Church's being and is active within it. . . . To this Spirit of Christ as to an invisible principle, is to be ascribed the fact that all parts of the Body are joined one with the other and with their exalted Head; for

[110] Pius XI, "Ubi Arcano Dei," December 23, 1922, in Koenig, *Principles*, 346–47.

[111] *Id.*, Encyclical, "Quas Primas," December 11, 1925, in Koenig, *Principles*, 373.

He is entire in the Head, entire in the Body, and entire in each of the members.[112]

Nourished after the manner that a vine makes fruitful the branches which are joined to it, the members are to possess the charity of Christ "which neither diversity of race or culture, neither the wasteless tracts of ocean, nor wars, be their cause just or unjust, can ever weaken or destroy." [113]

Though there will be deficiencies in Christians not living according to this inspiration, and though "the world will never be fully reconciled with Christ within the course of human history," it should not be forgotten that the world is redeemed and quickened by the blood of Christ, "and that it badly needs to have Christians— who are not of it—live and work and love and suffer in it, in order for it to advance toward its ends." [114] There is a continued work of redemption accomplished in the mystical body by the application of the merits of Christ throughout the course of time.

The fact of so many millions of men starving and living in despair, in a life unworthy of man, is an insult to Christ and to brotherly love. As a result, the temporal mission of the Christian is to strive to eradicate such evils, and to build up a Christian-inspired social and political order, where justice and brotherhood are better and better served. Yet this job is primarily the job of the Christian laity, working in the very midst of the world and civilization. . . . There can be no rest for the Christian as long as justice and love do not hold sway over the lives of men. And since their requirements will never be completely fulfilled within history, the Christian will therefore never have rest within history—and that's perfectly proper to his condition.[115]

Maritain notes that the main advances in human history, in so far as they are not merely technical, but are moral and directed to

---

[112] Pius XII, Encyclical, "Mystici Corporis Christi," June 29, 1943 (New York: Paulist Press, 1943), 18, 20–21.

[113] *Ibid.*, 33.

[114] Maritain, *On the Philosophy of History*, ed. Joseph W. Evans (New York: Scribner's Sons, 1957), 146–49.

[115] *Ibid.*, 154–55.

a state of affairs befitting human dignity, require much love and self-sacrifice. The changes wrought through the efforts of a few men become "either institutionalized or integrated in the collective consciousness—in any case absorbed in the very fabric of this world, which is thus carried to a higher level of human civilization but which still remains the world where both God and the devil have their parts." [116] Good and evil grow side by side in human history; "from fall to fall, but also from obscure gain to obscure gain, time marches toward the resurrection." [117] Because of the fact that history progresses both in the direction of good and of evil, it gives ground to both the optimist and the pessimist. However of this law of history we can be sure:

. . . justice and rectitude . . . tend in themselves to the preservation of human societies and to a real success in the long run; . . . injustice and evil tend in themselves (leaving aside what concerns physical conditions) to the destruction of societies and to a real failure in the long run.[118]

[116] *Ibid.*, 158.
[117] *Ibid.*, 45.
[118] *Ibid.*, 61.

Conclusion

POLITICAL philosophy and its application in foreign policy are shaped basically by an evaluation of man. Reviewing the Catholic approach to man as a creature with a supernatural end, bound by the Natural Law to act according to justice and charity, deprived but not depraved by original sin, we find man capable of overcoming selfish interest on a national and on an international level. Since the state exists in order to implement man's social development, and since its functions are carried on by its citizens, its activities are subject to moral law as are the actions of individuals. Service of the national interest is justifiable so long as that is not pursued to the exclusion of the greater common good which relates to the whole human family. No one can lead his nation to peace who does not understand the purpose of society.

James L. Vizzard, S.J., states the case well:

. . . our national interest is a much broader concept and reality than is embraced by military security, political stability, and economic advantage. For, unless our nation has interests and responsibilities rooted in moral principles, just how do we differ from the arbitrary 'legality' of totalitarian states? [1]

He adds that unless justice and charity are the real and expressed motives, the nation's interest actually will not be served in the

[1] Vizzard, S.J., "Who Is My Neighbor?", 505.

present crisis where the quality of America's leadership is being critically observed. He reviews the validity and urgency of other motives which do represent different aspects of national interest. It is true that the expanding economy needs sources of raw materials and markets; the United States does need to win the uncommitted peoples for the sake of its own national security; there is justifiable fear that any loss by America means a gain by the Soviet. But if the appeal is placed on a higher level, the nation will respond more readily, since its generosity will be commensurate with the nobility of the cause. Such appeal will automatically reap its rewards in the rest of the world:

It is the universal experience of mankind that gratitude and friendship cannot be bought. Neither individuals nor nations can be bribed into secure alliances. But disinterested service, genuine love, rarely fails to call forth a similar response. If we want friends and dependable allies, we will win them only if we can make it plain that we are interested in them for their own sake, and for God's.[2]

A Catholic does not underestimate the amount in which evil struggles with good in the human heart. Man who is both angel and animal is capable of rising to the heights or of sinking to the depths. Man's end is perfection, but that is not to be achieved completely on earth. A pragmatic solution to a problem may be declared a success because it works well temporarily, but unless it is philosophically true it will ultimately engender misery, for man's nature is not a thing of the passing moment. One who is earnestly endeavoring to serve the human good of his country's citizens might endorse this balance between extreme Idealism and false Realism:

A good politician can be neither an idealist nor an opportunist. He can never forsake his ideals, but neither can he wreck the world to promote them. He can never insist on the sharp choice between his ideal and oblivion. While remaining steadfastly true to his ideals, he must know that they will never be fully realized in this world of mortal men. He must therefore at all times be satisfied with the closest possible approach

[2] *Ibid.*, 505.

to the ideal. . . . He must know how and when to compromise. And he must be able to tell when compromise has degenerated into opportunism.[3]

The Catholic position corresponds more closely to the Idealist than to the Realist interpretation of international relations, although discrepancies appear on both sides of the Great Debate. The following summary gives some of the Catholic departures from "Political Realism." Thomistic philosophy opposes the nominalism of Realists who deny the knowability of essences and declare universals to be mere vocal utterances or fictions of the mind. It also contests the definition of Realism in the debate, for spirit as well as matter constitutes reality; intellectual abstraction enables one to grasp more of the nature of reality than is visible to the senses. Truth, whose standard is the intellect and will of God (not a poll of public opinion), is grounded in being which is knowable to man. Through Natural Law the rational creature participates in the Eternal Law.

Catholic thought challenges the pessimism of the Realists about the effects of original sin upon man and political society. It derogates power and force as the primary elements of the state; it criticizes the implication that the state's end is absolute, or that it is based upon individual self-interest, or that there is natural opposition between the individual and the political community. "Reason of State" as something outside morality is hostile to the Christian idea of the state's service character; man, acting for the state, is still bound by the moral law. Catholic thought rejects the notion that war is bound up with the nature of the state itself, and that sovereignty must be abolished if war is to be avoided. The fact that moral laws are systematically violated is not accepted as a denial of their intrinsic validity; the demands of morality are the demands of reality itself and these are not determined by a majority principle.

Catholic philosophy recognizes the claims of universal justice based upon the essential needs of human nature. Because states

[3] Neill, *Weapons*, 18.

were formed to fulfill for man collectively what he could not do individually, it holds that states must act for these individuals in reaching those who have a claim upon their charity. The basis of charity being possession of a common nature and destiny, the duty applies to all men; renunciation of selfish possession of the goods of the earth is the price of peace. Diverging from the Realists, Catholics champion the possibility of peace in this generation; their optimism is founded upon the very nature of Christ's mission. The creative power of Christianity for peace should not be dismissed lightly.

The Catholic interpretation differs from that of the Realists who hold international society to be an arbitrary product of the will of men, and international law to be a body of rules without foundation in Natural Law. It recognizes that enormous obstacles are present and it does not demand immediate realization of its ideals, but it contests the attitude that the human mind is impotent in the face of power politics. International social justice requires the establishing of institutions in which justice is independent of any whims of individual nations. International obligations exist without any man made charter to give them effect because of the unity of the human race and the universality of moral law.

In contrast to "Political Realism," Catholic thought would condemn expediency and opportunism as a basis of foreign policy— what is morally bad cannot be politically and economically good. Moral values have supremacy over all others because each human act has meaning only in so far as it leads man to his final end.

The Catholic interpretation does not run parallel with the tenets of some Idealists. While it accords due attention to the necessity of proper institutions to serve individuals and states, it does not presume with the Rousseauvians that these alone will bring peace to the world. It differs from the stand of the humanitarians who believe that an earthly millennium is the goal of history, and that man's reason has the unlimited ability to attain the true and the good by its own powers. Whereas it is correct to say that acts which lead to happiness are good, some authors seem to make humanity the end in itself, and thus concentrate exclusively on the "here and now."

Among some Idealists one perceives almost an idolatry of popular sovereignty, and adherence to specious theories of contractualism. Catholic scholars would not agree with those Idealists who seem to stigmatize power and force as evils even when they are used with moral responsibility. Some solutions proposed by Idealists are purely pragmatic schemes and as such by-pass the fundamental needs of society. Prescriptions of foreign policy based solely upon a worldly prudence which serves self-interest under the guise of friendship are suspect; these convert idealism into utilitarianism.

The Catholic interpretation takes exception to the Idealists who reduce peace solely to a technological and economic operation. These methods which raise the standard of living are a necessary adjunct, but peace is "a question of spiritual unity and of moral dispositions" which cannot be evolved from any form of materialism. In the mystical body of Christ, the Church experiences a source of unity among mankind which is beyond the scope of natural brotherhood and sentimentality often fostered in the debate.

In conclusion, it may be stated that Catholic thought acknowledges the validity of national interest, but it insists that this be related to the whole international fabric of which it is a part, and to which it must be made compatible. Consciousness of international social obligations, in themselves antecedent to any law or contract, is developing slowly but definitely in this mid-twentieth century. The situation can be compared to the history of nineteenth century industrial relations in which the owners were forced to change their practices, and in the process, altered their moral attitudes. If this progress continues to be realized in international affairs, the vogue of "Political Realism" may be supplanted as the result of a more informed conscience.

Bibliography

Catholic Opinion
PRIMARY SOURCES

I. CATHOLIC CLASSICS

Aquinas, Thomas. *On Kingship:* to the King of Cyprus. Translated by Gerald B. Phelan. Revision and notes by I. Th. Eschmann, O.P. Toronto: Pontifical Institute of Mediaeval Studies, 1949.

———. *Summa Contra Gentiles.* Translated by English Dominican Fathers. Vol. III. London: Burns Oates & Washbourne Ltd., 1928.

———. *Summa Theologica.* Translated by Fathers of English Dominican Province. 3 vols. New York: Benziger Bros., Inc., 1947.

Augustine. *The City of God.* Translated by John Healey. London: J. M. Dent & Sons Ltd., 1931.

———. *The Confessions of Saint Augustine.* Translated by Edward B. Pusey. New York: Random House, 1949.

Bellarmine, Robert Francis. *De Laicis:* treatise on civil government. English translation by Kathleen E. Murphy. New York: Fordham University Press, 1928.

II. STATEMENTS BY THE POPES AND THE AMERICAN BISHOPS

"Bishops' Statement on Peace," November 18, 1944, *Catholic Mind,* XLIII (January, 1945), 1–5.

"Bishops' Statement on World Peace," April 14, 1945, *Catholic Mind,* XLIII (June, 1945), 321–26.

"Bishops' Statement," November 18, 1951, *Catholic Mind*, L (February, 1952), 121–26.

Benedict XV. Encyclical: "Ad Beatissimi," November 1, 1914, in Harry C. Koenig. *Principles for Peace:* Selections from Papal Documents Leo XIII to Pius XII, 131–39.

——. Allocution: "Gratum Vehementer" to College of Cardinals, March 7, 1929, in Koenig. *Principles*, 307–09.

——. Encyclical: "Pacem Dei Munus Pulcherrimum," May 23, 1920, in Koenig. *Principles*, 236–42.

——. "Peace Proposals to Belligerents," August 1, 1917, in Koenig. *Principles*, 229–32.

Koenig, Harry C. *Principles for Peace:* Selections from Papal Documents Leo XIII to Pius XII. Washington: National Catholic Welfare Conference, 1943.

Leo XIII. Encyclical: "Immortali Dei," November 1, 1885. New York: Paulist Press, 1941.

——. Encyclical: "Libertas Praestantissimum," June 20, 1888, in Koenig. *Principles*, 40–45.

——. Letter: "Reputantibus" to Bishops of Bohemia and Moravia, August 20, 1901, in Koenig. *Principles*, 106.

Pius IX. *Syllabus of Errors*. Huntington, Indiana: Our Sunday Visitor Press, 1926.

Pius XI. Allocution: "Benedetto il Natale" to College of Cardinals, December 24, 1930, in Koenig. *Principles*, 394–96.

——. Encyclical: "Caritate Christi Compulsi," May 3, 1932, in Koenig. *Principles*, 456–65.

——. Encyclical: "Divini Redemptoris," March 19, 1937, in Koenig. *Principles*, 510–35.

——. Address: "Egli, Che all' Inizio" to 400 teachers in Catholic Action, September 6, 1938, in Koenig. *Principles*, 545–46.

——. Address: "Le Missioni e il Nazionalismo" to Students of Collegio de Propaganda Fide, August 21, 1938, in Koenig. *Principles*, 545.

——. Encyclical: "Quadragesimo Anno," May 15, 1931, in Koenig. *Principles*, 397–446.

——. Letter: "Quando nel Principio" to Cardinal Gasparri, June 24, 1923, in Koenig. *Principles*, 359–61.

Pius XI. Encyclical: "Quas Primas," December 11, 1925, in Koenig. *Principles,* 372–75.

———. Encyclical: "Studiorum Ducem," June 29, 1923, in Koenig. *Principles,* 363–64.

———. Encyclical: "Ubi Arcano Dei," December 23, 1922, in Koenig. *Principles,* 332–55.

Pius XII. "Address to Pax Romana," April 27, 1957, *Catholic Mind,* LV (September–October, 1957), 449–53.

———. "Allocution to College of Cardinals," February 20, 1946, *Catholic Mind,* XLIV (April, 1946), 193–203.

———. "Allocution to World Congress for Lay Apostolate," October 14, 1951, *Catholic Mind,* L (February, 1952), 115–21.

———. Address: "C'est avec un Vif Sentiment," to International Union of Catholic Women's Leagues, April 14, 1939, in Koenig. *Principles,* 561–62.

———. "Christmas Message, 1939," in Koenig. *Principles,* 632–40.

———. "Christmas Message, 1941," in Koenig. *Principles,* 750–62.

———. "Christmas Message, 1942," in Koenig. *Principles,* 789–806.

———. "Christmas Message, 1943," *Catholic Mind,* XLII (February, 1944), 65–76.

———. "Christmas Message, 1944," *Catholic Mind,* XLIII (February, 1945), 65–77.

———. "Christmas Message, 1947," *Catholic Mind,* XLVI (February, 1948), 68–77.

———. "Christmas Message, 1948," *Catholic Mind,* XLVII (March, 1949), 179–87.

———. "Christmas Message, 1950," *Catholic Mind,* XLIX (March, 1951), 201–08.

———. "Christmas Message, 1951," *Catholic Mind,* L (April, 1952), 248–56.

———. "Christmas Message, 1953," *Catholic Mind,* LII (March, 1954), 174–83.

———. "Christmas Message, 1954," *Catholic Mind,* LIII (March, 1955), 178–89.

———. "Christmas Message, 1955," *Catholic Mind,* LIV (March, 1956), 159–74.

———. "Christmas Message, 1956," *The Pope Speaks,* III (Spring, 1957), 331–46.

———. "Discourse to Fourth Congress of 'World Movement for World Federal Government,' " April 6, 1951, *Catholic Mind*, XLIX (June, 1951), 393–95.

———. "Discourse to Italian Catholic Jurists," December 6, 1953, *Catholic Mind*, LII (April, 1954), 244–51.

———. "Letter to Eugene Duthoit," June 28, 1932, in Koenig. *Principles*, 465–66.

———. Encyclical: "Mystici Corporis Christi," June 29, 1943. New York: Paulist Press, 1943.

———. Encyclical: "Optissima Pax," December 18, 1947, *Catholic Mind*, XLVI (February, 1948), 65–67.

———. "Radio Address to the Peoples of the Earth," November 10, 1956. *The Pope Speaks*, III (Spring, 1957), 355–58.

———. Encyclical: "Summi Pontificatus," October 20, 1939. Washington: National Catholic Welfare Conference, 1939.

Powers, Francis J., C.S.V. *Papal Pronouncements on the Political Order*. Westminster, Md.: Newman Bookshop, 1952.

SECONDARY SOURCES

I. GENERAL PHILOSOPHICAL AND POLITICAL STUDIES

Bruehl, Charles Paul. *The Pope's Plan for Social Reconstruction:* a Commentary on the Social Encyclicals of Pius XI. New York: Devin-Adair, 1939.

Cahill, E., S.J. *The Framework of a Christian State*. Dublin: M. H. Gill & Son, 1932.

Eppstein, John. *Catholic Tradition of Law of Nations*. Washington: Carnegie Endowment for International Peace, 1935.

Eppstein, John (ed. & trans.). *Code of International Ethics*, compiled by International Union of Social Studies; revised by Malines Union. Westminster, Md.: Newman Book Shop, 1953.

Gonella, Guido. *A World To Reconstruct*. Translated by Rev. T. Lincoln Bouscaren, S.J. Milwaukee: Bruce Publishing Co., 1945.

Hayes, Carlton J. H. *Patriotism, Nationalism and the Brotherhood of Man*. New York: Paulist Press, 1937.

Higgins, Thomas J., S.J. *Man as Man, the Science and Art of Ethics*. Milwaukee: Bruce Publishing Co., 1949.

Hughes, Philip. *The Pope's New Order*. New York: Macmillan Co., 1944.

MacLean, Rt. Rev. Donald A. *A Dynamic World Order*. Milwaukee: Bruce Publishing Co., 1945.

Maritain, Jacques. *Man and the State*. Chicago: University of Chicago Press, 1951.

———. *On the Philosophy of History*. Edited by Joseph W. Evans. New York: Charles Scribner's Sons, 1957.

Messner, Johannes. *Social Ethics:* natural law in the modern world. St. Louis: B. Herder Co., 1949.

Naughton, James W., S.J. *Pius XII on World Problems*. New York: America Press, 1943.

Neill, Thomas P. *Weapons for Peace*. Milwaukee: Bruce Publishing Co., 1945.

O'Connor, Daniel A., C.S.V. *Catholic Social Doctrine*. Westminster: Newman Bookshop, 1956.

O'Donnell, Charles (ed.). *The World Society*. Washington: Catholic Association for International Peace, 1941.

Rager, Rev. John C. *Democracy and Bellarmine*. Shelbyville, Ind.: Qualityprint, Inc., 1926.

Rommen, Heinrich A. *The Natural Law:* a study in legal and social history and philosophy. Translated by Thomas R. Hanly. St. Louis: B. Herder Co., 1947.

———. *The State in Catholic Thought*. St. Louis: B. Herder Co., 1945.

Ryan, John A. and Francis J. Boland. *Catholic Principles of Politics*. New York: Macmillan Co., 1940.

Simon, Yves R. *Philosophy of Democratic Government*. Chicago: University of Chicago Press, 1951.

Wilhelmsen, Frederick D. *Man's Knowledge of Reality:* an Introduction to Thomistic Epistemology. Englewood Cliffs, N.J.: Prentice-Hall, Inc., 1956.

II. ARTICLES

Bourke, Vernon. "Thomism," *American Philosophy*. Edited by Ralph B. Winn. New York: Philosophical Library, Inc., 1955.

Chapman, Emmanuel. "The Relation Between Ethics and Politics According to Aristotle and St. Thomas," *Philosophy of State*. Edited by Charles A. Hart. Baltimore: Watkins Printing Co., 1940.

"Colonialism and the Christian Conscience," *America*, XCIV (October 29, 1955), 121.

Crane, Paul, S.J. "Politics as Primary," *Social Order*, VIII (May, 1958), 220–25.

Duff, Edward, S.J. "Postscript," *Social Order*, VIII (May, 1958), 246–54.

Hensler, Rev. Carl P., S.T.D. "Pius XII on Sovereignty and Peace," *Catholic Mind*, XLII (November, 1944), 692–700. Reprint from *Pittsburgh Catholic*, September 30, October 7, 14, 1944.

Hoyt, Robert G. "A 'Science of International Social Justice' Needed Now," *The Catholic Messenger*, LXXV (March 27, 1958), 14.

Janssen, Leon W., S.J. "Duties to Underdeveloped Countries," *Social Order*, VIII (May, 1958), 197–205.

Joyce, Thomas A., O.P. "The Need and Nature of Political Action: Its Metaphysical Basis; the Common Good," *Philosophy of State*. Edited by Charles A. Hart.

Kennedy, Paul V., S.J. "The Principles of Democracy," *Philosophy of State*. Edited by Charles A. Hart.

Land, Philip S., S.J. "Call for World Economic Community," *Social Order*, VIII (May, 1958), 217–20.

Land, Philip S., S.J., and George P. Klubertanz, S.J. "Practical Reason, Social Fact, and the Vocational Order," *The Modern Schoolman*, XXVIII (May, 1951), 239–66.

Laurent, Philippe, S.J. "The Modalities of Aid," *Social Order*, VIII (May, 1958), 240–45.

Mailloux, Noel, O.P. "Morality and Contemporary Psychology," *Catholic Theological Society of America Proceedings*, Ninth Annual Convention, June 28–30, 1954, pp. 47–66.

McCormick, John F., S.J. "The Individual and the State," *Philosophy of State*. Edited by Charles A. Hart.

Murray, John Courtney, S.J. "Contemporary Orientations of Catholic Thought on Church and State in the Light of History," *Theological Studies*, X (June, 1949), 177–234.

———. "St. Robert Bellarmine on the Indirect Power," *Theological Studies*, IX (December, 1948), 491–535.

Nuesse, C. Joseph. "International Social Justice," *Catholic Mind*, LVI (January–February, 1958), 16–22.

Trunk, Joseph V., S.M. "The Philosophy of Civil Rights," *Philosophy of State*. Edited by Charles A. Hart.

Vizzard, James L., S.J. "Who Is My Neighbor?" *Catholic Mind*, LV (November–December, 1957), 503–08.

Walsh, Charles G. "Economics and the Common Good," *Thought*, XXIX (Spring, 1954), 7–31.

Ziggamia, Alba (ed.). "Catholicism and Internationalism: a Papal Anthology," *Thought*, XXVIII (Winter, 1953–54), 485–527.

Realist-Idealist Controversy

PRIMARY SOURCES

I. CORRESPONDENCE

Morgenthau, Hans J. to author, Chicago, December 6, 1957, in answer to a letter of November 28, 1957.

Osgood, Robert E. to author, Chicago, December 6, 1957, in answer to a letter of November 29, 1957.

II. DOCUMENTS, PUBLISHED PAPERS, PHILOSOPHICAL STUDIES

Baker, Ray Stannard and William E. Dodd (eds.). *Public Papers of Woodrow Wilson*. Vols. III, IV, V, VI. New York: Harper & Bros., 1926–27.

Bemis, Samuel Flagg (ed.). *American Secretaries of State and Their Diplomacy*. Vol. I. New York: Alfred A. Knopf Co., 1927.

Bentham, Jeremy. *An Introduction to the Principles of Morals and Legislation*. New York: Hafner Publishing Co., 1948.

Commager, Henry Steele (ed.). *Documents of American History*. New York: Appleton-Century-Crofts, Inc., 1949.

Dewey, John. *Human Nature and Conduct*. New York: Henry Holt & Co., 1922.

Hamilton, Alexander. "The Letters of Pacificus," *The Federalist*. Hallowell, Me.: Masters, Smith & Co., 1857.

Hobbes, Thomas. *Hobbes Selections: Leviathan*. Modern Student's Library. Edited by Frederick J. E. Woodbridge. New York: Charles Scribner's Sons, 1930.

Madison, James. "The Letters of Helvidius," *The Federalist*. Hallowell, Me.: Masters, Smith & Co., 1857.

Nietzsche, Friedrich W. *Beyond Good and Evil:* Prelude to a Philosophy of the Future, Vol. XII of *Complete Works of F. Nietzsche*, edited by Oscar Levy. Translated by Helen Zimmern. Edinburgh: T. Foulis, 1911.

Roosevelt, Theodore. *Works of Theodore Roosevelt.* Vol. XVIII. New York: Charles Scribner's Sons, 1926.

Rosenman, Samuel I. (ed.). *The Public Papers and Addresses of Franklin D. Roosevelt.* Vol. 1933 pub. by Random House, 1938. Vols. 1937–40 pub. by Macmillan Co., 1941. Vols. 1941–45 pub. by Harper & Bros., 1950.

Rousseau, Jean Jacques. *Emile.* Translated by Barbara Foxley. London: J. M. Dent & Sons, 1911.

Smith, Adam. *The Theory of Moral Sentiment.* London: W. Strahan, J. Rivington, W. Johnston, T. Longman, 1774.

Spencer, Herbert. *The Data of Ethics.* New York: A. L. Burt Co., 1879.

Taylor, Myron C. *Wartime Correspondence between President Roosevelt and Pope Pius XII.* New York: Macmillan Co., 1947.

Wolfers, Arnold and Lawrence W. Martin (ed.). *Anglo-American Tradition in Foreign Affairs:* Readings from Thomas More to Woodrow Wilson. London: Oxford University Press, 1956.

III. STUDIES DEALING WITH NATIONAL INTEREST

Adler, Mortimer J. *How To Think About War and Peace.* New York: Simon & Schuster, 1944.

Beard, Charles A. *American Foreign Policy in the Making 1932–40:* a study in responsibilities. New Haven: Yale University Press, 1946.

———. *The Idea of National Interest.* New York: Macmillan Co., 1934.

———. *The Open Door at Home.* New York: Macmillan Co., 1935.

———. *President Roosevelt and the Coming of the War 1941:* a Study in Appearances and Realities. New Haven: Yale University Press, 1948.

Bisson, T. A. *American Policy in the Far East 1931–1940.* New York: Institute of Pacific Relations, 1940.

Bowles, Chester. *Ideas, People and Peace.* New York: Harper & Bros., 1958.

———. *The New Dimensions of Peace.* New York: Harper & Bros., 1955.

Buell, Raymond Leslie. *Isolated America.* New York: Alfred A. Knopf Co., 1940.

Cook, Thomas I. and Malcolm Moos. *Power Through Purpose:* the

Realism of Idealism as a Basis for Foreign Policy. Baltimore: Johns Hopkins University Press, 1954.

Dean, Vera Micheles. *Foreign Policy Without Fear.* New York: Mc-Graw-Hill, 1953.

Dulles, John Foster. *War or Peace.* New York: Macmillan Co., 1957.

Elliott, William Yandell *et al. United States Foreign Policy:* its organization and control; report. New York: Columbia University Press, 1952.

Fenwick, Charles G. *American Neutrality:* Trial and Failure. New York: New York University Press, 1940.

Fosdick, Dorothy. *Common Sense and World Affairs.* New York: Harcourt, Brace & Co., 1955.

Halle, Louis J. *Choice for Survival.* New York: Harper & Bros., 1958.

———. *Civilization and Foreign Policy:* An Inquiry for Americans. New York: Harper & Bros., 1955.

Hornbeck, Stanley K. *The United States and the Far East:* Certain Fundamentals of Policy. Boston: World Peace Foundation, 1942.

Horowitz, Irving L. *The Idea of War and Peace in Contemporary Philosophy.* New York: Paine-Whitman Publishers, 1957.

Hutchins, Robert Maynard. *St. Thomas and the World State.* Milwaukee: Marquette University Press, 1949.

Kennan, George. *American Diplomacy, 1900–1950.* Chicago: University of Chicago Press, 1951.

———. *Realities of American Foreign Policy.* Princeton: Princeton University Press, 1954.

Kissinger, Henry A. *Nuclear Weapons and Foreign Policy.* New York: Harper & Bros., 1957.

Lefever, Ernest Warren. *Ethics and United States Foreign Policy.* Toronto: Longmans, Green & Co., 1957.

Lerche, Charles O., Jr. *Principles of International Politics.* New York: Oxford University Press, 1956.

Lippmann, Walter. *Essays in Public Philosophy.* New York: Little, Brown, & Co., 1955.

———. *Isolation and Alliances.* Boston: Little, Brown, & Co., 1952.

———. *United States Foreign Policy: Shield of the Republic.* Boston: Little, Brown, & Co., 1943.

Mahan, Alfred T. *The Interest of America in International Conditions.* London: Sampson Low, Marston & Co., Ltd., 1910.

————. *Problem of Asia and Its Effect Upon International Policies.* Boston: Little, Brown & Co., 1900.

Marshall, Charles Burton. *The Limits of Foreign Policy.* New York: Henry Holt & Co., 1954.

McCloy, John Jay. *The Challenge to American Foreign Policy.* Cambridge: Harvard University Press, 1953.

Morgenthau, Hans J. *In Defense of the National Interest.* New York: Alfred A. Knopf Co., 1952.

————. *Politics Among Nations:* the Struggle for Power and Peace. New York: Alfred A. Knopf Co., 1954.

————. *Scientific Man vs. Power Politics.* Chicago: University of Chicago Press, 1946.

Morley, Felix. *Foreign Policy of United States.* New York: Alfred A. Knopf Co., 1952.

Mowrer, Paul Scott. *Our Foreign Affairs:* A Study in National Interest and the New Diplomacy. New York: E. P. Dutton & Co., 1924.

Niebuhr, Reinhold. *Christian Realism and Political Problems.* New York: Charles Scribner's Sons, 1953.

————. *Moral Man and Immoral Society:* a Study in Ethics and Politics. New York: Charles Scribner's Sons, 1953.

Northrop, F. S. C. *European Union and United States Foreign Policy:* a Study in Sociological Jurisprudence. New York: Macmillan Co., 1954.

Osgood, Robert Endicott. *Ideals and Self-Interest in America's Foreign Relations:* the great transformation of the twentieth century. Chicago: University of Chicago Press, 1953.

Palmer, Norman D. and Howard C. Perkins. *International Relations.* Boston: Houghton Mifflin Co., 1953.

Perkins, Dexter. *The American Approach to Foreign Policy.* Cambridge: Harvard University Press, 1952.

————. *Popular Government and Foreign Policy.* Pasadena: Ford Foundation Fund for Adult Education, 1956.

Price, Harry Bayard. *The Marshall Plan and Its Meaning.* Published under auspices of Governmental Affairs Institute, Washington, D.C. Ithaca: Cornell University Press, 1955.

Puleston, William Dilworth. *Influence of Force in Foreign Relations.* New York: Van Nostrand, 1955.

Reves, Emery. *The Anatomy of Peace.* New York: Harper & Bros., 1945.

Schuman, Frederick L. *The Commonwealth of Man:* an Inquiry into Power Politics and World Government. New York: Alfred A. Knopf Co., 1952.

Schwarzenberger, Georg. *Power Politics.* New York: Frederick A. Praeger, 1951.

Spykman, Nicholas. *American Strategy in World Politics:* the United States and the Balance of Power. New York: Harcourt, Brace & Co., 1942.

Stourzh, Gerald. *Benjamin Franklin and American Foreign Policy.* Chicago: University of Chicago Press, 1954.

Streit, Clarence. *Union Now:* Proposal for Federal Union of Democracies of the North Atlantic. New York: Harper & Bros., 1939.

Tannenbaum, Frank. *The American Tradition in Foreign Policy.* Norman: University of Oklahoma Press, 1955.

Zimmern, Sir Alfred E. *The American Road to World Peace.* New York: E. P. Dutton & Co., Inc., 1953.

IV. PERIODICAL LITERATURE

Armstrong, Hamilton Fish. "Regional Pacts: Strong Points or Storm Cellars?" *Foreign Affairs*, XXVII (April, 1949), 351–68.

Bemis, Samuel Flagg. "Shifting Strategy of American Defense and Diplomacy," *Virginia Quarterly Review*, XXIV (Summer, 1948), 321–25.

Brecker, Richard. "Truth as a Weapon of the Free World," *Annals of American Academy of Political and Social Science*, CCLXXVIII (November, 1951), 1–11.

Cook, Thomas I. and Malcolm Moos. "The American Idea of International Interest," *American Political Science Review*, XLVII (March, 1953), 6.

———. "Foreign Policy: the Realism of Idealism," *American Political Science Review*, XLVI (June, 1952), 343–56.

Dean, Vera Micheles. "United States Foreign Policy in the Atomic Age," *American Scholar*, XVII (Winter, 1947–48), 81–85.

Dulles, John Foster. "The Challenge to Freedom," Address at Williamsburg, Va., May 15, 1954, *State Department Press Release* 255, Ser. S, No. 16.

———. "The Moral Foundations of the United Nations," Address at

San Francisco, June 19, 1955, *State Department Press Release* 366, Ser. S, No. 35.

Eagleton, Clyde. "Excesses of Self-Determination," *Foreign Affairs,* XXXI (July, 1953), 592–604.

Feller, A. H. "In Defense of International Law and Morality," *Annals of the American Academy of Political and Social Science,* CCLXXXII (July, 1952), 77–83.

Fetter, Frank Whitson. "The United States and World Trade," *Annals of American Academy of Political and Social Science,* CCLV (January, 1948), 166–75.

Flannery, Harry W. "Foreign Aid: a 'New Look,'" *Social Order,* VII (June, 1957), 266–75.

"Foreign Policy of the Presidents," *Current History,* VIII, (January, 1945), 39–42.

Fox, William T. R. "The Reconciliation of the Desirable and the Possible," *American Scholar,* XVIII (Spring, 1949), 207–16.

Haas, Ernst B. "Types of Collective Security: An Examination of Operational Concepts," *American Political Science Review,* XLIX (March, 1955), 40–62.

Halle, Louis J. "A Touch of Nausea," *New Republic,* CXXXVI (January 21, 1957), 15–17.

Hinton, Harold C. "Axioms of Foreign Policy," *The Commonweal,* LXVI (August 9, 1957), 463–66.

Hughes, Charles Evans. "The Centenary of the Monroe Doctrine," *Annals of the American Academy of Political and Social Science,* CXI, Supplement (January, 1924), 7–19.

Hull, Cordell. "Our Foreign Policy or the Framework of Our National Interests," Address of September 12, 1943, *Vital Speeches,* XXIV (October 1, 1943), 757–60.

Jessup, Philip C. "Bases of United States Foreign Policy," *Department of State Bulletin,* XX (March 27, 1949), 393–95.

———. "Ends and Means of American Foreign Policy," *International Stability and Progress: United States Interests and Instruments.* New York: Columbia University, June, 1957, 11–40.

Johnson, Nelson T. "Responsibilities of the United States as a World Power," *Annals of the American Academy of Political and Social Science,* CCLV (January, 1948), 176–85.

Kennan, George F. "Foreign Aid in Framework of National Policy," *Proceedings of Academy of Political Science,* XXIII (January, 1950), 104–14.

——. (signed Mr. X). "The Sources of Soviet Conduct," *Foreign Affairs,* XXV (July, 1947), 566–82.

Kirk, Grayson. "National Power and Foreign Policy," *Foreign Affairs,* XXIII (July, 1945), 620–26.

Linebarger, Paul M. "The Struggle for the Mind of Asia," *Annals of American Academy of Political and Social Science,* CCLXXVIII (November, 1951), 32–37.

Marshall, Charles Burton. "National Interest and Current World Problems," *U.S. Department of State Bulletin,* XXVI (May 5, 1952), 698–702.

——. "Nature of Foreign Policy," *U.S. Department of State Bulletin,* XXVI (March 17, 1952), 415–20.

Morgenthau, Hans J. "Another Great Debate: the National Interest," *American Political Science Review,* XLVI (December, 1952), 961–88.

——. "The Decline of American Government," *New Republic,* CXXXVII (December 16, 1957), 7–11.

——. "The Decline of American Power," *New Republic,* CXXXVII (December 9, 1957), 10–14.

——. "The Mainsprings of American Foreign Policy: The National Interest Versus Moral Abstractions," *American Political Science Review,* XLIV (December, 1950), 833–54.

——. "The Primacy of the National Interest," *American Scholar,* XVIII (Spring, 1949), 207–12.

——. "What Is the National Interest of the United States?" *Annals of American Academy of Political and Social Science,* CCLXXXII (July, 1952), 1–7.

Mowrer, Edgar A. "The Inevitable Compromise," *American Scholar,* XVIII (Summer, 1949), 376–78.

Murray, Thomas E. "Morality and Security—the Forgotten Equation," *America,* XCVI (December 1, 1956), 258–62.

Osgood, Robert E. "Collective Security and the Lessons of History," *Confluence,* V (Winter, 1957), 341–54.

Padover, Saul K. "The American Century?" *American Scholar,* XVII (Winter, 1947–48), 85–90.

Pfaff, William. "Criticisms of U.S. Policy," *Worldview,* I (March, 1958), 3–6.

Schall, James V., S.J. "The Political Theory of Reinhold Niebuhr," *Thought,* XXXIII (Spring, 1958), 62–80.

Schuman, Frederick L. "Doctrines and Self-Interest," *American Scholar,* XIX (Winter, 1949–50), 99–101.

———. "International Ideals and the National Interest," *Annals of the American Academy of Political and Social Science,* CCLXXX (March, 1952), 27–36.

Scott, Andrew M. "Challenge and Response: a Tool for the Analysis of International Affairs," *Review of Politics,* XVIII (April, 1956), 207–26.

Sears, Lawrence. "Walking Backward Into the Future," *American Scholar,* XVIII (Autumn, 1949), 470–84.

Stimson, Henry L. "The Challenge to America," *Foreign Affairs,* XXVI (October, 1947), 6–14.

Sweezy, Paul M. "Two Conceptions of the National Interest," *American Scholar,* XVIII (Summer, 1949), 378–80.

Tannenbaum, Frank. "Anvil of American Foreign Policy," *Political Science Quarterly,* LXIII (December, 1948), 501–27.

Thompson, Kenneth W. "Beyond National Interest: A Critical Evaluation of Reinhold Niebuhr's Theory of International Politics," *Review of Politics,* XVII (April, 1955), 167–88.

Truman, Harry S. "Fundamentals of U.S. Foreign Policy," Address in Central Park, October 27, 1945, *Vital Speeches,* XII (November 15, 1945), 66–68.

SECONDARY SOURCES

I. Monographs and General Works

Bemis, Samuel Flagg. *Diplomacy of the American Revolution.* New York: Appleton-Century-Crofts, Inc., 1935.

Koch, Adrienne. *The Philosophy of Thomas Jefferson.* Gloucester, Mass.: Peter Smith, 1957.

Levy-Bruhl, Lucien. *The Philosophy of Auguste Comte.* London: Swan Sonnenschein & Co. Ltd., 1903.

Thonnard, F. J., A.A. *A Short History of Philosophy.* Translated from revised edition by Edward A. Maziary, C.PP.S. Paris: Desclee & Cie, 1956.

Weinberg, Albert Katz. *Manifest Destiny:* a study of nationalist expansionism in American history. Baltimore: Johns Hopkins Press, 1935.

White, Theodore. *Fire in the Ashes:* Europe in Mid-Century. New York: William Sloane Associates, 1953.

II. PERIODICAL LITERATURE

Barrett, Patricia, R.S.C.J. "Alexander Hamilton in Perspective," *Social Order*, VII (October, 1957), 356–63.

Index

Abstraction, 172-73, 305
Adams, John Q.
  Morgenthau, 69
Adler, Mortimer
  sovereignty, 221, 225
A priori
  Land and Klubertanz, 176
Aquinas, St. Thomas
  abstraction, 173
  common good, 187-88
  Hutchins and world state, 221
  ideal state, 176, 252-53
  man's social nature, 177
  natural law, 175, 192
  peace, 187-88, 293, 295
  plurality of states, 222
  politics and ethics, 212
  political society, 182, 199
  reality, 172
  truth, 171
  will, 174
  world state, 221
Arbitration
  Benedict XV, 241
  Eppstein (ed.), 240-41
  Kennan, 60-61
  Marshall, 100
Aristotle
  nature of a thing, 177
  state, 199
Armaments regulation, 290-91
  Beard, 12
  Higgins, 291
  Murray, 126-27
  Neill, 239
  Osgood, 156

Armaments regulation (*continued*)
  Perkins, 144
  Pius XII, 290-91, 298
Armstrong, Hamilton F., 119-20
Asia, policies regarding
  Beard, 12
  Dean, 97
  Haas, 40
  Hinton, 122
  Kennan, 57-59, 62-63
  Linebarger, 124
  Morgenthau, 74-75, 77-80
  Osgood, 156-57
  Tannenbaum, 164-66
Atlantic Charter
  Beard, 55
Augustine, St.
  evil, 191
  natural law, 192
  Niebuhr, 7-8
  origin of state, 182
  plurality of states, 222
  unity of mankind, 215

Balance of power
  Bemis, 121
  Elliott, 102
  Eppstein (ed.), 244-45
  Haas, 39-41
  Kennan, 60-64
  Messner, 244-45
  Morgenthau, 23, 68, 72, 74, 76, 78
  Osgood, 158
  Perkins, 93-94
  Tannenbaum, 113

323

Beard, Charles A., 8-14, 43-56, 162
  commerce, 11, 44-54
  dollar diplomacy, 44, 48
  immigration, 11
  national interest, 8-13, 43-54
  power politics, 43-44, 49
  territorial expansion, 45-48
Bellarmine, St. Robert
  authority in government, 183
  colonialism, 260
  democracy, 252-53
  right of resistance, 236
  sovereignty, 222
Bemis, Samuel F., 121-22
Benedict XV, Pope, 216
  arbitration, 241
  causes of war, 293-94
Bentham, Jeremy, 33
Bishops, American
  international society, 216, 219
  world organization, 243-44
Bourke, Vernon, 172-73
Britain, 59, 61, 69, 71, 74, 76, 93, 157, 169
Brown, Brendan F.
  Jus Gentium, 247
Bruehl, Charles P.
  rights of man, 179
Buell, Raymond L., 119

Calvin, John
  original sin, 180
Catholic Association for
  International Peace, 264, 271
Cecil, Hugh
  nationalism, 207
Chapman, Emmanuel
  individual and common good, 185
  man's social nature, 178
Chappoulie, Henri
  colonialism, 258-59
Charity
  bond of union, 300-01
  international obligation, 267, 269,
    305-06
  national interest, 303-04
China, 43, 55, 62-63, 80, 93, 103, 140-42,
    146, 156, 166
Church-State relations
  Murray, J. C., 189
Collective security
  Haas, 39-40
  Morgenthau, 24
  Osgood, 159-62
  Rommen, 241-43

Colonialism, Catholic approach, 258-63
  Bellarmine, Suarez, and Vittoria, 260
  Chappoulie, 258-59
  Eppstein (ed.), 258-62
  Janssen, 262-63
  Messner, 262-63
  Pius XI, 258
  Rommen, 260
Commerce
  Beard, 11, 44-54
  Messner, 240
Common good, 184-88
  Land and Klubertanz, 175
Communism, 40, 273, 275-81
  Eppstein, 275
  Flannery, 125-26
  foreign aid, 267, 270
  Kennan, 64-65
  Linebarger, 124
  Morgenthau, 77-81
  Pius XI, 275-76
  Pius XII, 275
  Sears, 122-23
Comte, Auguste
  positivism, 196
Conscience
  natural law, 175
Cook, Thomas I., 117-19, 129
  national interest, 117-18
Coordinate state
  Tannenbaum, 114, 163, 167
Crane, Paul
  democracy, 257

Dante, 219, 222
Dawson, Christopher, 197
Dean, Vera Micheles, 94-97
  balance of power, 94-95
  Russia, 97
De facto-de jure
  Higgins, 237
  Messner, 236-37
Deism, 195
Delos, J. T., 230
Democracy, 76, 252-57
  Aquinas, 252-53
  Bellarmine, 252-53
  Buell, 119
  Crane, 257
  Dean, 95
  Eppstein, 252
  foreign policy, 91-92, 101-02, 108,
    136-38, 140
  Messner, 254-55, 257

Democracy (*continued*)
  Morgenthau, 76-77, 80
  Perkins, 132
  Pius XII, 254
  Rager, 253-54
  Rommen, 257
  Simon, 254-56
  Tannenbaum, 114
  Wilson, 50, 61, 71-72, 80, 137-38, 155
Dewey, John, morals, 9
Disarmament, See "Armaments"
Dollar diplomacy
  Beard, 44, 48, 51
  Perkins, 135-37

Eagleton, Clyde, 103
Economic self-interest, 43, 53-54, 93, 103,
  135-37, 203
Eisenhower, Dwight D.
  Morgenthau, 81
Empiricism, 173, 190
Eppstein, John (ed.), *Code of International Ethics*
  arbitration, 240-41
  balance of power, 244-45
  colonialism, 258-62
  international society, 213
  intervention, 282-83
  man, 178
  minority rights, 206
  neutrality, 291-92
  patriotism and nationalism, 176-78
  peace, 293
  power, 244
  rights of states, 232-34, 238
  state as moral person, 199
  validity of treaties, 249-51
  war, 284-89
Essence, 173, 190

Feasibility, defined, 176
Federalists, 44, 46, 67-69
Feller, A. H., 104-05
  national interest, 105
  United Nations, 105
Fenwick, Charles G., 120-21
Flannery, Harry W., 125-26
Foreign aid
  Flannery, 125-26
  Janssen, 267-68
  Kaschmitter, 265-67
  Land, 268
  Maritain, 271
  Morgenthau, 79

Foreign aid (*continued*)
  Nuesse, 270-71
  Vizzard, 268-70
Fosdick, Dorothy, 126
Fox, William T. R., 105-07
  national interest, 106
Freud, Sigmund
  natural law, 196

Germany, 62-63, 73, 78, 89, 94-95, 135,
  150-52, 157, 166-67
Gonella, Guido
  institutionalism vs. contractualism, 218
  international society, 230-31
Grotius, Hugo
  international law, 247-48
  natural law, 195

Haas, Ernst B., 38-41
Halle, Louis J., 108-12
  national interest, 110-11
  power, 109
  standard of living, 109, 111
  Thucydides, 111
Hamilton, Alexander, 4
  Beard, 44, 46
  Kennan, 18
  Morgenthau, 67-69
Hegel, Georg, state, 199, 210, 227, 229,
  235
Hensler, Carl, sovereignty, 221, 225-26
Higgins, Thomas J.
  colonialism, 260-61
  de jure, 237
  end of state, 184
  individual and common good, 186
  man, 177
  nation, 206
  natural law, 192-93
  norms of morality, 190-91
  state and moral law, 211
  treaties, 251
  war, 286, 289
Hinton, Harold C., 122
Historical jurisprudence, 196
Historicism, 237
Hobbes, Thomas
  justice, 25, 87
  nominalism, 174, 194
  social contract, 183
Holmes, Oliver W., 194
Hungary
  duty of intervention, 279-80
Hume, David, morality, 195

Hutchins, Robert M.
  world government, 221
Huxley, Julian, natural law, 196

Idealism, Catholic approach, 180, 306-07
Idealist
  criticism by Osgood, 145
  definition in the controversy, viii, 3,
    82-83
  role in American history, 149-52, 154
Immigration
  Beard, 11
  Kennan, 18
  MacLean, 264
Imperialism
  Beard, 47-48
  Catholics on colonialism, 258-63
  Kennan, 57
  Osgood, 145-48
  Perkins, 131-36, 144
  Tannenbaum, 164-66
Individualism, 179, 187, 195, 203
International law, 245-49
  Jus Gentium, 247
  Messner, 247
  Rommen, 246-48
  Suarez and Vittoria, 246-48
International organization, functions of
  Eppstein, 239-40
  Messner, 240
  Neill, 239
  Pius XII, 238, 298
  Rommen, 241-43
International social justice
  conclusion, 306
  Kaschmitter, 265-67
International society, 213-49
  American Bishops, 216
  Augustine, 215
  Benedict XV, 216
  Eppstein, 213-14, 217
  Hutchins, 221
  Pius XII, 216, 218-20
  Leo XIII, 216
  Suarez, 215
  Taparelli, 215
Intervention, duty of, 118
  Eppstein, 282-83
  Messner, 282
  Pius IX, 281
  Rommen, 281
Isolationism, 217
  Beard, 45, 52 ff.
  Bishops, American, 243-44

Isolationism (*continued*)
  Cook and Moos, 129
  Halle, 110
  Morgenthau, 72, 79
  Osgood, 153
  Perkins, 129, 138-39
  Tannenbaum, 113

Japan, 51, 54, 58, 61, 94-95, 135, 139, 156-
    57, 168
Jansenism, 180
Janssen, Leon W.
  colonialism, 262-63
  obligations of charity, 267-68
Jefferson, Thomas
  Beard, 44-46, 52
  Morgenthau, 67, 69
  Perkins, 93
Jessup, Philip C., 107
Joyce, Thomas A.
  peace, 188
  purpose of society, 184
Jus Gentium, 247
Justice
  conclusion, 305-06
  foreign aid, 126, 265-71
  Hobbes, 25
  Maritain, 302
  Morgenthau, 25-26
  nominalism, 174
  Pius XII, 246
  St. Thomas, 188
  Spengler, 180
  Vizzard, 303

Kant, Immanuel
  democracy, 71
  laissez-faire, 203
  natural law, 195
Kaschmitter, William A.
  international social justice, 265-67
Kellogg-Briand Pact
  Kennan, 61
  Osgood, 156
Kennan, George F., 14-19, 56-66
  arbitration, 60-61
  Asia, 57-59, 62-63
  balance of power, 60-64
  immigration, 18
  national interest, 56
  Open Door, 58
  position of Northrop, 115
  position of Perkins, 91
  Russia, 62-65

Kennan, George F. *(continued)*
  Spanish-American War, 56-57
  World War I, 59-60
  Yalta, 62-63
Kennedy, Paul V.
  democracy, 254
  origin of state, 182-83
Klubertanz, George P., 175

Land, Philip S., 175, 268
Latin America
  Perkins, 132-35, 137
  Tannenbaum, 167-68
League of Nations
  Beard, 50-51, 53
  Lippmann, 90
  Morgenthau, 71-72
  Osgood, 153-55
  Tannenbaum, 114, 166-67
  Zimmern, 99
Legalism, Morgenthau, 74-76
Legalist-Moralist, 14, 17, 83
Leo XIII, Pope
  international society, 216
  nationalism, 208
  natural law, 198
  role of the Church, 189
  social contract, 183
  state and moral law, 211
Lerche, Charles O., 32-33
Linebarger, Paul M. A., 124
Lippmann, Walter, 88-91
  position of Osgood, 150
  position of Perkins, 91
Locke, John
  natural law, 195
  social contact, 183
Luther, Martin
  original sin, 180
  origin of state, 182

Machiavelli, 3, 194
Madison, James, 45
Man
  Catholic approach, 176 81, 304
  Morgenthau, 19-20
  political and social nature, 177-78
  Reves, 37
Manchuria
  Osgood, 156
Manifest Destiny
  Beard, 44-45
  Morgenthau, 69-70, 76
Manichaeanism, 180

Maritain, Jacques
  foreign aid, 271
  philosophy of history, 301-02
  raison d'Etat, 210
  role of Christian, 301-02
  sovereignty, 221, 226-28
  state and body politic, 198-99
Marshall, C. B., 97-101
  national interest, 97-98
Marshall Plan
  Bemis, 121
  Fox, 106
  Lippmann, 90
  Morgenthau, 76, 78-79
  Northrop, 116
  Osgood, 158
  Perkins, 134
  Price, 123-24
Marx, Karl
  natural law, 196
  power, 210
  state, 200, 203
Materialism
  conclusion, 307
  Pius XI and Pius XII, 294-96, 299
  Rommen, 212
McCloy, John J., 98-99
McCormick, John F.
  Catholic philosophy of state, ix
  individual and political community, 177
Messner, Johannes
  balance of power, 244-45
  colonialism, 262-63
  common good, 187
  de jure, 236-37
  democracy, 254-55, 257
  idealism, 180
  international law, 249
  morality, 190-91
  nation, 204-05
  nationalization, 272
  natural law, 193-94, 196
  natural rights, 178-79
  power, 209-10
  realism, 180
  resources, 265
  right of resistance, 235-37
  rights of states, 231-32, 234-38
  role of state, 186-87, 199-200
  sovereignty, 222, 224, 228-29
  state and moral law, 211
  validity of treaties, 250-51
  war, 286-87, 289

Mexican War
  Tannenbaum, 163-64
Minority rights, 206, 239, 298
Monroe Doctrine
  Beard, 44
  Morgenthau, 69-70, 78
  Perkins, 130, 135, 154
  Tannenbaum, 114, 163-64
Moos, Malcolm, 117-19
  national interest, 117-18
Morality
  conscience, 192
  dualism in, 5, 212
  duties of man, 178
  Encyclopaedia of Social Sciences, 27-28
  Fox, 106
  Halle, 108
  Kennan, 15
  Morgenthau, 27, 76
  norms of, 190-91
  Osgood, 157
  Rousseau, 191
  Spykman, 31
  state, relation to, 199, 211-12, 305
  supremacy of, 177
  utilitarians, 191
Morgenthau, Hans J., 19-29, 66-81, 162
  balance of power, 23, 68, 72, 74, 76, 78
  collective security, 24
  Communism, 77-81
  Eisenhower administration, 81
  Hamilton, 67-69
  Jefferson, 67, 69
  justice, 25-26
  legalism, 74-76
  man, 19-20
  Marshall Plan, 76, 78-79
  morality, 27, 76
  national interest, 28-29, 70-71, 73, 76-77
  neo-isolationism, 79
  Perkins, position of, 91
  Point Four, 76
  power, 20-23
  Realist defined, 2-3
  Roosevelt, F. D., 69, 72, 74
  Russia, 73-81
  sentimentalism, 76-79
  sovereignty, 23
  Truman Doctrine, 76-80
  truth, 80-81
  utopianism, 73-74
  Wilson, 70-74
  Yalta, 74-76

Morley, Felix, 32
Mowrer, Edgar A., 107
Mowrer, Paul S., 29-30
Murray, John C.
  Church-state, 189
Murray, Thomas E., 126-27

Nation, defined, 204
National Catholic Rural Life Conference
  foreign aid, 271
National Council of Catholic Women
  foreign aid, 271
National interest, 2, 82-83, 248
  Beard, 8-13, 43-54
  Bemis, 121
  conclusion, 307
  Cook and Moos, 117-18
  Elliott, 102
  Feller, 105
  Fenwick, 120
  Flannery, 125-26
  Fox, 106
  Halle, 110-11
  Hinton, 122
  Kennan, 56-65
  Marshall, C. B., 97-98
  Morgenthau, 28-29, 70-71, 73, 76-77
  Mowrer, E. A., 107
  Mowrer, Paul S., 29-30
  Osgood, 84, 86-88, 152, 155, 157
  Perkins, 93
  Tannenbaum, 114
  Vizzard, 303
Nationalism, 207-09
Nationalization
  Messner, 272
  Pius XII, 271-72
NATO
  Elliott, 104
  Haas, 40
  Lippmann, 90
  Morgenthau, 78-79
  Osgood, 159
  Perkins, 144
  Tannenbaum, 168-69
Natural law, 192-98, 305
  Augustine, 192
  Catholic approach, 180
  Lippmann, 88-89
  Osgood, 84-85
  St. Thomas, 175, 192
Natural rights, 178-79

Neill, Thomas P.
  Catholic responsibility, ix
  democracy, 254
  inalienable rights, 178
  international organization, 239
  nationalism, 207
  peace, 297
  positivism, 196
  sovereignty, 228
  state's right to life, 234-35
  welfare function of state, 201
Neutrality, 120-21, 130, 283, 291-92
Niebuhr, Reinhold, 4-8
  Catholic criticism, 6-7
  Realism defined, 1
Nietzsche, Friedrich
  power, 22-23, 151, 210
Nominalism, 173-75, 194
Northrop, F. S. C., 115-16
Nuesse, C. Joseph
  foreign aid, 270-71

Occam, William of
  nominalism, 174, 194
Open Door Policy
  Kennan, 58
  Osgood, 145, 152
  Tannenbaum, 114
Optimism
  regarding Communism, 281
  regarding peace, 306
Original sin
  Catholic approach, 179-81, 304-05
Osgood, Robert E., 84-88, 144-62
  collective security, 159-62
  criticism of Realists and Idealists, 144-45
  imperialism, 145-48
  League of Nations, 153-55
  Lippmann, 150
  national interest, 84, 86-88, 152-53
  Realist defined, 2
  Roosevelt, F. D., 157-58
  Roosevelt, T., 148-49
  United Nations, 159-62
  Wilson, W., 149-55, 159-66

Pacifism, 297
Paternalism, 201-02
Peace
  conclusion, 306-07
  Eppstein, 293
  Pius XI, 294-96, 300-01
  Pius XII, 292-300

Peace (*continued*)
  St. Thomas, 187-88, 293, 295
  war for the sake of, 287-88
Pelagianism, 180
Perkins, Dexter, 91-94, 128-44
  balance of power, 93-94
  China, 141-42
  democratic ideal, 136-38, 140
  democracy, 91-92
  expansion, 131-33
  imperialism, 132-36, 144
  isolationism, 138-39
  Latin America, 132-35
  national interest, 93
  peace, 130
  power politics, 92
  Roosevelt, F. D., 140-41
  Russia, 140-42
  United Nations, 144
  war, 129-30
  Yalta, 141
Pessimism, 1, 180, 209, 223, 293, 305
Pius IX, Pope, intervention, 281
Pius, XI, Pope
  colonialism, 259
  nationalism, 208
  peace, 294-96
  socialism, 273-75
  subsidiarity, 219
Pius XII, Pope
  Church, role of, 190
  democracy, 254
  disarmament, 290-91, 298
  international society, 216, 218-20
  intervention, 279
  justice, 246
  Mystical Body, 300-01
  nationalism, 208
  nationalization, 271-72
  order, 188
  original sin, 181
  peace, 292-300
  political realism, 241
  power, 244
  resources, 264, 298
  Russia, 280-81
  sovereignty, 220
  state, role of, 201
  state's right to existence, 233
  treaties, 250-52
  World Federalists, 219-20
Pluralism, 200, 224, 227
Point Four
  Morgenthau, 76

Point Four *(continued)*
  Northrop, 116
  Perkins, 134
Positive law, 197
Positivism, 117, 174, 194, 196, 224, 229
Power, 209-10, 248, 305, 307
  Dean, V. M., 94-95
  Elliott, 101, 104
  Eppstein, 244
  Fox, 105
  Halle, 109
  Messner, 209-10
  Morgenthau, 20-22
  Nietzsche, 22-23
  Northrop, 115
  Pius XII, 244
  Rommen, 242-43
  Schuman, 34
  Simon, 244
Power politics
  Beard, 43-44, 49
  Cook and Moos, 119
  Morgenthau, 66-70, 74-75
  Osgood, 86, 147, 158, 160-61
  Perkins, 92-93
  Pius XII, 298
  Tannenbaum, 113
Pragmatism, 176, 307
Price, Harry B., 123-24
Progress, idea of, 181
Property, use of
  Bruehl, 263-64
  Communism, 276
  nationalization, 271-72
  socialism, 273-75

Rager, John C.,
  democracy, 253-54
Realism, Catholic approach, 173, 180,
  187, 241-45, 304
Realist in the controversy
  claims on St. Augustine, 7-8
  criticized by Feller, 104-05
  criticized by Fox, 105-06
  criticized by Osgood, 144
  criticized by Perkins, 91
  criticized by Tannenbaum, 3-4, 112-13
  definition in the controversy, viii, 1-5
  evaluated by author, 305
  praised by Osgood, 157
Resistance, right of
  Eppstein, 236
  Messner, 235-37
  Suarez and Bellarmine, 236

Resources, 263-73
  Janssen, 267-68
  Kaschmitter, 265-67
  Maritain, 271
  Messner, 265
  Nuesse, 270-71
  Pius XII, 264, 298
  Vizzard, 268-70
Reves, Emery, 36-38
Rommen, Heinrich
  common good, 185
  democracy, 257
  idea of progress, 181
  individualism, 203
  international law, 246-48
  materialism, 212
  nationalism, 208-09
  natural law, 194-97
  nominalism and positivism, 174-75, 194
  original sin, 180
  pacifism, 297
  power, 242-43
  realism and empiricism, 173
  self-determination, 205
  social contract, 183-84
  social reform, 202
  sovereignty, 222-24
  state, role of, 186, 200
  utopianism, 241-42
  war, 285, 292
Roosevelt, Franklin D.
  Beard, 51-56
  Kennan, 62
  Morgenthau, 69, 72, 74
  Perkins, 140-41, 157-58
Roosevelt, Theodore
  Beard, 47-48
  Morgenthau, 69
  Osgood, 148-49, 152
Rousseau, Jean Jacques, 71, 114, 181, 183,
  191, 198, 223, 254
Russia
  Beard, 54
  Dean, 96-97
  Elliott, 103
  Eppstein, 277-79
  Kennan, 62-65
  Morgenthau, 73-81
  Perkins, 140-42
  Pius XII, 279-81
  Tannenbaum, 168-69

Schuman, Frederick L., 33-36
Scotus, Duns

Scotus, Duns *(continued)*
  will over intellect, 174
Sears, Lawrence, 122-23
Self-determination, 102-03, 205
Self-interest, 2, 197-98, 248
  Beard, 43, 53-54
  conclusion, 303, 305
  Hinton, 122
  Locke and Rousseau, 183-84
  McCloy, 97-99
  Morgenthau, 66 ff.
  Niebuhr, 5
  Osgood, 84, 86, 144-47, 152, 154-55, 157
  Perkins, 97-99
Sentimentalism
  Morgenthau, 76-79
Simon, Yves
  coercion, 244
  democracy, 254-56
  government activity, 202-03
Sociability among nations, 216
Social contract theory, 183-84
  criticized, 218
Socialism, 273-75
  Pius XI, 273-75
Socialization, See nationalization
Sovereignty, 211, 219-31
  Adler, 221
  conclusion, 305
  Eppstein, 222
  Maritain, 221, 226-28
  Messner, 222, 224, 228-29
  Morgenthau, 23
  Neill, 228
  Pius XII, 220, 229-30
  Popular sovereignty, 254-55
  Rommen, 222-24, 229
Spanish-American War
  Beard, 47-48
  Kennan, 56-57
  Morgenthau, 70
  Osgood, 148
  Tannenbaum, 164-65
Spencer, Herbert
  morals, 194
  relative ethics, 2-3
Spykman, Nicholas, 31-32
Standard of living
  Elliott, 103
  Halle, 109, 111
State, origin of, 181-84
State, rights of, 231-38
  Eppstein, 232-34, 238, 286
  Messner, 231-32, 234-38

State, rights of *(continued)*
  Neill, 234-35
  Pius XII, 233
State, role of, 176, 186-87, 198-203
  bound by moral law, 199, 211-12
  nationalization, 271-72
  organic theory, 200
  regarding charity, 269
Streit, Clarence, 104
Suarez, Francisco
  colonialism, 260
  intellect and will, 175
  international law, 247-48
  international society, 215
  neutrality, 120
  right of resistance, 236
  sovereignty, 222
  war, 288
Subsidiarity, 200, 219

Tannenbaum, Frank, 112-14, 128, 162-69
  balance of power, 113
  co-ordinate state, 114, 163
  imperialism, 164-66
  Mexican War, 163-64
  Monroe Doctrine, 163-64
  Realists, attack on, 3-4, 112-13
  Russia, 168-69
  United Nations, 169
  World War II, 168
Taparelli, Aloysius d'Azeglio, 215, 225, 232-33
Territorial expansion
  Beard, 45-48
  Kennan, 56-57
  Perkins, 131-33
Thucydides, 111
Trade, 263-73
  Beard, 11, 44-54
  Messner, 240
Treaties, validity of, 249-52
Treitschke, von, 151, 210, 234-35
Truman, Harry S.
  Beard, 56
  Morgenthau, 74, 76-77
Truman Doctrine
  Bemis, 121-22
  Fox, 106
  Lippmann, 90
  Morgenthau, 76-80
  Tannenbaum, 114
Truth
  Morgenthau, 80-81
  Thomistic approach, 171-73

Underdeveloped countries
  Janssen, 263, 267-68
  Land, 268
  Maritain, 271
  Nuesse, 270-71
  Vizzard, 268-70
United Nations
  Dean, 96
  Elliott, 101, 103-04
  Eppstein, 239-40
  Feller, 105
  Haas, 38-41
  Jessup, 107
  Kennan, 66
  Lippmann, 90
  Maritain, 228
  Messner, 240
  Morgenthau, 71, 74-75
  Northrop, 116
  Osgood, 159-62
  Perkins, 144
  Russia, 277-78
  Tannenbaum, 114, 168-69
Universal ideas, 171-73
  conclusion, 305
  Hobbes, 174
Utilitarianism, 187, 191, 202, 212, 249
Utopianism
  Morgenthau, 73-74
  Rommen, 241-42

Vittoria, Francisco de
  international law, 246-48
  international society, 120, 218
  just war, 260
Vizzard, James L.
  foreign aid, 268-70
  national interest, 303

Walsh, Charles G.
  common good, 187

War—legitimacy of, 284-89
  conclusion, 305
  Eppstein, 284-89
  Higgins, 286, 289
  Messner, 286-87, 289
  Murray, T. E., 126-27
  Rommen, 285, 292
  Suarez, 288
Ward, Barbara, 270
White, Theodore H., 65
Wilhelmsen, F. D., 171
Wilson, Woodrow
  Beard, 49
  Elliott, 104
  Kennan, 59-60
  Lippmann, 89-90
  Morgenthau, 70-72, 74
  Osgood, 147-55
  Perkins, 93, 136-38
World Federalism, 104, 116, 219-20
World War I
  Kennan, 59
  Lippmann, 89-90
  Morgenthau, 72
  Osgood, 149-56
  Perkins, 137-38
  Rommen, 196
World War II
  Eppstein, 287-88
  Higgins, 289
  Kennan, 61-63
  Morgenthau, 73, 75-76
  Perkins, 140-42
  Rommen, 196
  Tannenbaum, 168

Yalta
  Kennan, 62-63
  Morgenthau, 74-76
  Perkins, 93, 141

Zimmern, Sir Alfred, 99